LANGUAGE AND LITERACY SERIES
Dorothy S. Strickland and Celia Genishi
SERIES EDITORS

SOCIAL WORLDS
OF CHILDREN LEARNING TO WRITE
IN AN URBAN PRIMARY SCHOOL

Anne Haas Dyson

Teachers College, Columbia University
New York and London

The project discussed herein was partially supported under the Educational Research and Development Center Program (grant number R117G10036 for the National Center for the Study of Writing and Literacy) as administered by the Office of Educational Research and Improvement, U.S. Department of Education. The findings and opinions expressed in this report do not reflect the position or policies of the Office of Educational Research and Improvement or the U.S. Department of Education.

Grateful acknowledgment is made for permission to reprint Figure 5.1 from Dyson, A. Haas. (1992). *Whistle for Willie,* lost puppies, and cartoon dogs: The sociocultural dimensions of young children's composing. *JRB: A Journal of Literacy, 24.* Copyright 1992 by the National Reading Conference.

Published by Teachers College Press, 1234 Amsterdam Avenue, New York, NY 10027

Library of Congress Cataloging-in-Publication Data

Dyson, Anne Haas.
    Social worlds of children learning to write in an urban primary
school / Anne Haas Dyson.
          p.   cm.
    Includes bibliographical references (p.   ) and index.
    ISBN 0-8077-3296-6 (alk. paper). — ISBN 0-8077-3295-8 (pbk. :
alk. paper)
    1. Language arts (Primary) — United States — Case studies.
    2. Education, Urban — Social aspects — United States — Case studies.
    3. Socialization.   I. Title.
    IN PROCESS
    372.6 — dc20   93-25086

ISBN 0-8077-3296-6
ISBN 0-8077-3295-8 (pbk.)

Printed on acid-free paper
Manufactured in the United States of America

99 98 97 96 95 94 93   7 6 5 4 3 2 1

For Jameel, Eugenie, Anthony,
Lamar, William, and Ayesha

CONTENTS

PREFACE

When I was a little girl, I thought the social world was divided into the Catholics and the Publics. There was the Catholics' school and the Publics' school, to go with (or so I thought) the Catholics' church and the Publics' church. When I met someone new, I wanted to know, "Are you Catholic or Public?"

My world as a 5- and 6-year-old was defined by the borders of the small farming village in which I lived. And, within that space, I tried to figure out how the social world worked and how I fit into that world, questions that occupy most of us all our lives. The research reported herein focuses on other young children living in a different time and space but grappling with these same questions. Through the window of the children's composing, I aimed to understand not only how the children were learning to write, but how they were learning to compose social places for themselves at school. Composing such places involved negotiating complex identities as students, peers, and members of their home communities.

ACKNOWLEDGMENTS

These research themes about childhood, language, and social belonging are rooted in my own experiences with family, friends, colleagues, and students, both very young and adult, who have helped me broaden and make more complex my own worldview. Here I thank just a few of the many people who have helped me in this work.

I thank first the school faculty who allowed me entrance and, most especially, Louise, a strong and caring teacher, and her young students. I have tried to capture something of the intensity of the learning, the joy of language, and the sense of social commitment evident in Louise's classrooms.

In the daily work of observing and transcribing, photocopying and filing, retrieving and organizing, I was well assisted by Paula Crivello, a graduate student at the University of California–Berkeley. Paula was unfailingly committed and careful in her work and, just as important, unfailingly appreciative and respectful of the pleasures and responsibilities of classroom research. In the closing months of the project, Urvashi Sahni, another fine graduate student at UC–B, became my research assistant. She took charge of the seemingly never-ending details of making respectable, as it were, the pages of this book; her passion for education and her enthusiasm for the book's ideas sustained my own. Ruth Cooper and Margaret Ganahl, staff of the Division of Language and Literacy, and Andrew Bouman, Robin Wilson, Pat Segrestan, and Joanne Smith, of the Center for the Study of Writing, provided valued production assistance.

Many other colleagues provided thoughtful advice and much appreciated encouragement, among them, Jerrie Cobb Scott, Marty Conrad, Elizabeth Simons, Barbara Comber, Courtney Cazden, Keith Walters, Thomas Newkirk, Gertrude and Jon Smidt, and, most especially, Celia Genishi.

SOCIAL WORLDS
OF CHILDREN LEARNING TO WRITE
IN AN URBAN PRIMARY SCHOOL

Anne Haas Dyson

INTRODUCTION

Composing a Place in the Classroom Neighborhood

Lamar* and his kindergarten peers are stretched out on the classroom rug drawing pictures for their alphabet books. Lamar is sprawled between James and Tyler, who is lying next to Anita.

"Louise," Lamar calls to his teacher. "Just like houses. Louise, this is just like houses."

"Just like houses?" asks his perplexed teacher.

"Yeah," says Lamar. "'Cause we're all next door neighbors. Tyler is my next door neighbor, and Anita is Tyler's next door neighbor."

"No," objects Anita. "Sonya is my neighbor."

"But in *school*," explains Lamar. "Not in real life."

"We're not talking about real life," adds James. "We're talking about fake life."

"Yeah, fake life," agrees Lamar.

The children's spaces, explains Lamar, are like houses, and, as they work next to each other in the classroom, they become neighbors. Moreover, as Anita makes clear, classroom neighbors are not necessarily "real life" neighbors. But through the construction of symbolic worlds—"fake lives"—relationships between people can be reconceived and transformed into new possibilities.

Perhaps precisely because the classroom is a place where people who would not ordinarily be neighbors become so, it is possible for an adult, if respectful, unobtrusive, and patient, to erect a small unassuming house near the children, and from that house try to understand the neighborhoods being built with the tools of language.

This is the process that I undertook in the fall of 1989, when I entered

---

*All children's names throughout this book are pseudonyms.

1

Louise's K/1 class in the San Francisco East Bay. Like many schools in the area, Louise's school drew on distinctive communities. The school served both a low-income and working-class African-American community to its southwest, and an ethnically diverse (although predominantly European-American) middle- and working-class community to its northeast.

Within the school walls and, more particularly, within her classroom, Louise, like all strong teachers, worked hard to structure activities and foster relationships that would create a community of children. And yet, within the social structures she set and, more broadly, within the social structures of the broader society, the children themselves engaged in much social work. They built relationships among themselves, and they did so by using familiar tools brought into the classroom from their lives on the outside. These tools were stories, jokes, songs, language plays, and other cultural art forms or genres that people create as they construct their social lives together. In the opening anecdote, Lamar, for example, brought his peers together in a symbolic world—a row of child-houses—which they could all share. This world was "fake"—existing only through the power of Lamar's imaginative use of language—but it accomplished social work in the real world.

Symbolic worlds, however, can do their social work only if the speaker or writer share, in Geertz's (1973) words, the same "imaginative universe" (p. 13). To use Ryle's famous example (cited in Geertz, 1973), the difference between a wink as twitch or as conspiratorial signal is not in the wink but in how that individual wink is socially interpreted. Symbolic worlds of words, like winks or any *individual* acts of expression, can be achieved only through *public* means, through shared ways of interpreting symbols.

The children in Louise's room were, in fact, learning to participate in varied imaginative universes. Their classroom was a complex social place, one in which a number of worlds coexisted and intersected (see Figure I.1). There was the official school world, in which they were "students"; the peer world, in which they were "co-workers" (and perhaps "friends"); and the world of their respective home communities, which re-formed in the classroom amidst networks of peers. Each world required particular kinds of social work and valued particular kinds of ways with words. To negotiate their membership vis-à-vis these groups, the children drew on diverse cultural resources. Among these resources were the oral folk traditions learned at home, the popular or common traditions that pervaded all of their lives (particularly through the media), and the written traditions they experienced at school and/or at home.

In one conversation, for example, Lamar and his friends retold exciting moments from a popular movie about Batman, a conversation that could

FIGURE I.1.   The Multiple Social Worlds of the Classroom

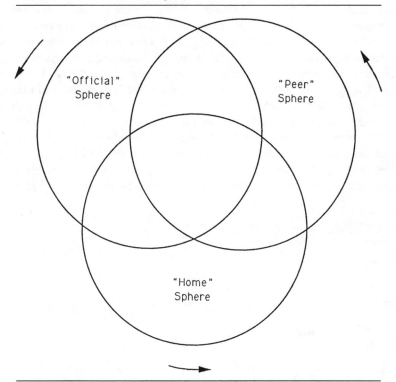

Note: In classrooms children are at once members of diverse reference spheres. The intention here is not to pull apart that essential dynamic but simply to provide a graphic metaphor of the existence of these spheres. There are no neat boundaries between "home" and "school," or between the official (teacher-controlled) sphere and that of peers.

have been carried out with many children in the room, and then they told humorous "true" stories, exaggerated tales built upon kernels of truth (Smitherman, 1986), about flying up to heaven and falling back down on their beds, stories that reflected the storytelling features of their ethnic community. Moreover, as Lamar talked, he illustrated a dictated story about finding a shell with an animal living in it and leaving it alone; this story replayed a central theme of an official class discussion that took place after Tyler had brought "live" clams to school, all quite dead. In composing each story, Lamar built an imagined world, a "fake life." To do so, he used different cultural materials—different themes, discourse structures, and styles; that is, he drew on different imaginative universes.

As I sat in my house in Louise's class, I tried to understand how these young children were differentiating and negotiating among their intersecting social worlds and especially how, with their teacher, they constructed crossroads or moments of intersection, moments that seemed to reverberate among and connect worlds. Moreover, I wondered how the children's experiences as storytellers and language players, as builders of relationships through "fake worlds," would influence the development of literacy, a new kind of social action, one in which enacted symbolic worlds are given more permanent and visual casings.

By literacy, I do not mean simply children's handwriting and spelling. I mean children's use of print to represent their ideas and to interact with other people. The "written" texts of 5- and 6-year-olds, are often multimedia affairs, interweavings of written words, spoken ones, and pictures.

FIGURE I.2.   Jameel's Singing Fish

Their graphic texts, however, just like their spoken texts, are attempts to accomplish social work. Moreover, their "written" (i.e., their multimedia) repertoires include varied genres and draw on diverse cultural materials.

For example, Lamar's peer Jameel, a first grader, combined his fledgling writing skills with his drawing and singing know-how to produce a text rich in the resources of popular culture, including pop songs, cartoons, and comics. He drew a singing fish, with "tunes" encased in air bubbles (see Figure I.2). Moreover, he wrote that song to perform for his peers, to impress them and make them laugh (which he most certainly did).

In entering school literacy, all of the focal children drew on rich language resources, and they all used those resources to engage in social work, managing relationships with peers and adults. As will be elaborated upon in the chapters to come, their resources included interrelated folk and popular cultural traditions ignored and treated as problems (not helps) in most discussions of literacy development. Moreover, their social ends included relationships with others, their audience, that rendered problematic many pedagogical suggestions for teachers. When he was performing, for example, Jameel had no use for "feedback" from an advice-giving peer audience, despite the common pedagogical suggestion that teachers structure just such feedback. He wanted their involvement, their respect. In varied ways, all the children nudged the bounds of the official imaginative universe that prevails in schools, challenging current theoretical and pedagogical thinking about writing development and pedagogy in the early years.

PURPOSE OF THE BOOK

In this book, I explore how Jameel, Lamar, and their classmates used varied kinds of language art forms and traditions, oral and written, as they constructed and participated in the complicated worlds of school. This exploration is based on a close observation of the classroom social lives of six children, kindergartners through third graders, and each child's circle of friends. All of the children had the same skilled early childhood teacher, Louise, and all came from the African-American community. I picked children with language resources that reflected the verbal traditions of the African-American community and also children with clear, distinctive personalities in the classroom community.

To help me make sense of the children's talk-filled worlds, I envisioned the complex landscape of discourse described by Bakhtin (1981, 1986), a philosopher interested in the social nature of language and literature. He described stories and other kinds of texts as situated within a complex of

human relationships. When people speak or write, they position themselves within these relationships, responding to and anticipating a response
from others; each text is "dialogic," a reaching out in a world riddled with
voices talking to, past, and over each other. In Bakhtin's view, there are
no integrated cultural or language worlds, and so it was for the children
in the classroom. They participated in different imaginative universes,
different social dialogues.

Through studying this complexity and attempting to reveal it in child
scenes and child words far different from anything found in Bakhtin's
treatises, I aim to contribute in a number of ways to the ongoing conversations about education in general and literacy in particular. First, I aim to
counteract visions of literacy learning and teaching that are grounded in
narrow imaginative universes, universes that see literacy as taking root
comfortably only for children with middle-class backgrounds who speak
Standard English and respond to school-like tasks in conventional ways.

Many researchers and teachers have emphasized literacy's beginnings in
the home. They articulate the kinds of knowledge about written language
children bring to school with them, especially the language of storybooks,
and they worry about children from nonmainstream homes (i.e., not
middle-class and/or not Anglo), who may be less likely to have experiences
with books (e.g., Anderson, Hiebert, Scott, & Wilkinson, 1985; Teale &
Sulzby, 1986). However, young children from diverse backgrounds bring
diverse experiences to symbol-producing—talking, drawing, playing,
storytelling, and, in our society, some kind of experience with print, all of
which are resources with which both teachers and children can build new
possibilities. In this book, I aim to document how children build literacy
tools from social and language resources that include those rooted in children's experiences with popular and folk traditions.

A second and interrelated goal is to illustrate the sociocultural intelligence of young child composers, an intelligence demanded by the complex
urban classroom. Given the diversity of American school children, it is
striking that there are so few systematic looks at how that diversity figures
into the teaching and learning of writing, particularly in the early years.
Equally striking is the uniformity of the images of child composers in the
pedagogical literature. Indeed, the descriptions of writing teaching and
learning seem curiously acultural to me, like the melting pot children's
books Rudine Sims Bishop (Sims, 1982) describes. Books may feature a
minority child, but that child's ways of living and talking—the child's
composing processes—in no way reflect the child's culture. The child is an
"every child," devoid of tradition and history.

In this book, I aim to allow young children's composing processes sociocultural depth and breadth by setting them clearly within the complex

worlds of urban schools. The composing of written texts, like the composing of oral ones, is a distinctly sociocultural process that involves making decisions, conscious or otherwise, about how one figures into the social world at any one point in time. Variation in the kind of oral and written language genres the children used, in the kinds of discourse traditions they drew upon, and in the kind of relationships they enacted with others will illustrate this link between composing a text and composing a place in the social world, which is the key theme of the book.

Finally, through the hard work and good fun of Louise and her children, I aim as well to allow insight into the successes and the challenges confronted by teachers and children as they work to construct a shared universe in school. Research on successful schools for diverse learners demonstrates that in such schools there is a sense of identification and connection among teachers and children, a sense of common purpose, of neighborhood (Committee on Policy for Racial Justice, 1989). Such a sense of identification and connection is fostered by school curricula, and by teachers, that work to acknowledge the social and language resources of the children they serve, resources that draw on rich and complex cultural traditions.

In sum, I take readers into the neighborhood corners and alley ways, off the beaten path of the curricular road, where the social action is. Peering into these social places reveals children intensely engaged in social work, using story and other verbal art forms to manage their social relationships with others. Lamar, Jameel, and their friends engaged in social processes that would allow them social respect and connection in the classroom neighborhoods, in or out of the official classroom world. I aim to contribute to a better understanding of the social work of childhood, the ways that social work shapes both oral and written composing, and ways of creating classroom crossroads where worlds can come together and open up to new places. To these ends, we enter the neighborhoods of Louise and her children.

PLAN OF THE BOOK

In Chapter 1, I first provide a theoretical framework for this exploration of children's social worlds, cultural traditions, and literacy development. I provide as well a methodological backdrop, explaining how I went about gaining entry into the children's neighborhoods and the tools I used to come to understand their inner workings.

While the focus of this book is on children's social and language lives, those lives were influenced by the classroom structure Louise constructed with and for them. In Chapter 2, then, I examine the official community, its key themes and social processes. I emphasize its "permeable" nature— its openness to the children and their experiences. I detail as well the writing program, which embodied the best of currently recommended practices. It was the boundaries of this program—the cultural traditions it valued, the social work between composers and audiences it espoused— that the children would negotiate with their teacher.

Then, in Chapter 3, I turn to the children's unofficial social worlds. I examine their repertoire of narratives and other genres, the cultural traditions they drew upon, and the social work—the relationship building and managing—the children accomplished through the use of those genres. This chapter provides a backdrop for Chapter 4, which introduces four of the children, kindergartners Lamar and Anthony and first graders Eugenie and Jameel. I explore how, early in the year, literacy for each child was emerging within the classroom social relationships—the classroom social places—that they had negotiated for themselves.

In Chapters 5 through 8, I focus on the literacy histories of individual children. I illustrate their successes and frustrations, as they tested, crossed, and were diverted from the social and cultural boundaries of their multiple classroom worlds.

Finally, in Chapter 9, I consider the implications of this study for literacy teaching and learning in socioculturally diverse classrooms. The stories I have to tell are not of children easily learning to write in an idyllic school setting. By no means. The children fail and succeed for reasons that do not have to do only with what happens inside the school; the racial and economic inequities of the broader society were woven into the fabric of the children's lives. I hope, therefore, that this vision of the classroom lives of Louise and her children can complement the visions provided by researchers who study communities and societal institutions in their efforts to create worlds that allow more social, intellectual, and artistic space for all children.

CHAPTER 1

FRAMING CHILD TEXTS WITH CHILD WORLDS

Ways of Studying Language, Literacy, and Diversity

Life as event presumes selves that are performers. To be successful, the relation between me and the other must be shaped into a coherent performance, and thus the architectonic activity of authorship, which is the building of a text, parallels the activity of human existence, which is the building of a self.
— Clark & Holquist, *Mikhail Bakhtin*, 1984, p. 64

In this book, I explore children's language and literacy by viewing their texts—their spoken or written words—as a way of accomplishing social work, as a way of shaping "the relation between me and the other . . . into a coherent performance." In this chapter, I explain this point of view and describe how it was shaped by and, in turn, shaped my way of coming to know Louise's children.

To begin, I turn to a dramatic performance by first grader Jameel as he stands in front of his K/1 class and reads his text, his declaration of self in the classroom.

Sat on Cat. Sat on Hat.
Hat Sat on CAT.
CAt GoN. 911 for CAt. (punctuation added)

After Jameel reads his story about Cat and Hat, one of his classmates, Edward G., says appreciatively, "It's like a poem." But another, Mollie, objects with the key line of primary-grade literacy pedagogy: "It doesn't make any sense." After a spirited attempt to explain his story about the fatally wounded cat to the exasperated Mollie, Jameel explodes, "BUT

IT'S MY DECISION," and then laments, "I don't get it. She *don't* get it. I don't got no more friends."

To try to understand Jameel's text and Mollie's response, we might frame Jameel's text with a discussion of writing "levels" or "stages," such as the evaluative tool offered by McCaig (1981). To be "competent" for early-primary-grade writing, Jameel's text must contain at least three "complete thoughts that can be readily understood and are about the same topic" (p. 77). "Sat on Cat," we would have to say, may not qualify as "a complete thought." Or, following Graves (1983), Jameel's text could be examined for "important gaps in sequences" of information, "causes without effects" or effects without causes (p. 259). From the text alone, we would also have to say, it is not clear why the cat is "gone."

These sorts of evaluative frames will not help us understand the encounter between Mollie and Jameel, nor will they allow insight into Jameel's performance; indeed they were not designed to do so. However, these common frames, reflective of current thinking in literacy pedagogy, do illustrate a key idea. A "coherent performance" is a matter of judgment, existing within an "imaginative universe" (Geertz, 1983) — a shared way of imbuing objects, including children's stories, with meaning. The school world's universe frames children's efforts and informs researchers' "explanations" of the school failure of many low-income and minority children in our society.

To make sense of performances such as Jameel's "911 for cat" story, the coming chapters will frame children's texts with children's social worlds — with what they are trying to do and to be at any one historical moment — and with the imaginative universes that guide their efforts. As Jameel made clear, what was at stake in his difficult encounter with Mollie was his social world: "I don't get it. She *don't* get it [my text]. I don't got no more friends."

Undergirding this concern with children's social worlds is Bakhtin's (1981, 1986) vision of texts as embedded in social dialogue. Each time speakers or writers compose a fictional story or any kind of text or genre — any patterned way of using language — they "temporarily crystallize a network of relations" between themselves and other people, as Morson (1986, p. 89) explains; those relations include the author's sense of (a) her or his power and status vis-à-vis others, (b) the purposes that have brought them together, (c) the topic of their discourse, and (d) the history of other conversations, other dialogues, they have had. In using language in certain ways, composers are conveying a certain attitude, positioning themselves, as it were, in a certain social place.

Thus, in the opening anecdote, Jameel was not just using unexpected (or "incompetent") text features. He had certain notions of his power and status as a composer and certain notions too of appropriate conversational responses. The use of symbolic worlds of words to engage with others has deep, developmental and sociocultural roots for all children. In the following sections, I first describe the social challenges Jameel and his peers faced in learning to construct written symbolic worlds in school. Then I turn to the diverse cultural traditions that both supported and complicated their efforts to compose places for themselves in school. Finally, I describe my own efforts to study the children's social and text worlds.

LEARNING TO WRITE AS SOCIAL WORK

From infancy on, we as human beings are remarkably social (Bruner, 1986). Indeed, a young child's developing sense of *self* is characterized by an expanding sense of how to share experiences with others (Stern, 1985). This sharing includes the first offerings of invented symbolic forms (e.g., playful actions, drawings, songs) and early social comments on forms fashioned by others (e.g., "Look at this book, this picture, this show"; see also Bruner, 1990). We work to create more intimate, more particular worlds that capture some aspect of the experiences we share with other people. This human urge is fundamental to the whole of our intellectual and emotional lives, as it helps set in play the search for mutuality, for understanding and for being understood.

Young children bring to school their experiences in establishing spheres of relatedness. That is, children bring to school a repertoire of genres or familiar ways of constructing symbolic worlds or, in James's words, "fake lives"; among these genres are stories, songs, and jokes. They have learned these routine ways of using language—these genres—from participating in situations in which people using language adopt certain roles toward each other and toward experience. For example, children come to understand how people tell jokes, to whom, and about what. They may learn, for instance, that teasing one's sister by casting her as a character in a scatological joke is more fun than teasing one's mother in a similar way (Dunn, 1988).

While children continue to use familiar genres in school, they also face increased pressure—and, for many children, their first pressure—to use the medium of written language. Learning to write in school involves figuring out the kinds of social work accomplished through that medium and, thereby, gaining entry into the range of social dialogues it furthers. In accomplishing written language activities, children draw upon their rich resources as users of other symbolic media—not only talk, but also drawing and dramatic play—as they figure out how the written medium works and what new social possibilities it allows.

In an earlier project, I observed how children's social relationships with others, especially with their peers, supported their growth as composers of written story worlds (Dyson, 1989a). Initially the observed children "wrote" primarily by drawing and talking. With those tools, they not only represented their imagined worlds but also connected with their friends, as they talked about and at times playfully dramatized each others' drawn and told stories. Their actual writing was but a small part of their multi-media productions.

In time and in the context of much critical and playful talk with their peers, the children began to confront the artistic tensions between their drawn and spoken worlds and what they had actually written. Gradually, their written stories contained more narrative action, their pictures more illustrations of key ideas. Moreover, they began to use writing to accomplish social work, that is, to maintain and manipulate their relationships with peers. Their friends became characters in their written stories, and they also began to deliberately plan to include certain words or actions to amuse or tease their friends. Thus, over time, writing became more embedded in their imagined, experienced, and ongoing social worlds—in their "multiple worlds," which was the guiding metaphor of the project.

I took this metaphor with me to Louise's classroom. Here too I observed writing taking root within children's social lives; gradually, writing assumed a place amidst children's symbolic repertoires. But my original metaphor made explicit only *one ongoing social world*. Thus, the metaphor fractured in Louise's room. Each child seemed posed amidst various ongoing social worlds. The social work to be accomplished through composing—the relationships to be managed—seemed much more complex. Undoubtedly there were various social worlds in the previous classroom as well, but the sociocultural differences were more dramatic in Louise's classroom and, thus, the complexity of the children's social worlds was foregrounded.

In that previous classroom, guided by another strong teacher, Margaret, there were children from many different social and cultural backgrounds. There were no "majorities," no "minorities." In addition, there was no clear relationship between race and class. The school was an urban magnet school, and its population was monitored to ensure diversity; further, the neighborhood surrounding the school was itself an integrated community of modest homes and small apartments. Moreover, the children were classroom peers from kindergarten through third grade in a small school of approximately 80 children. In three years of intense work at the site, I rarely heard spontaneous comments about race or class from the children, other than their questions about biracial children's parents (e.g., "Your mom is White!?") or discussions of official classroom topics that were race-related (e.g., civil rights lessons, parent presentations of ethnic customs, children's discussions of family histories).

Louise's school, on the other hand, had approximately 360 students. It drew on distinctive urban neighborhoods, and there were clear connections between race and class. Certainly play and work groups formed and re-formed across racial and gender lines, depending on the activity. And there *was* a peer social world, in which the children generally conveyed a sense of "being in this together," as they reacted — as children do — to the constraints and regulations of the official school world (Corsaro, 1985; D'Amato, 1987; Dyson, 1989a; Roberts, 1970). But Jameel, Lamar, and the other focal children were also members of a sociocultural community in which they felt a sense of "being in this together," and this was increasingly evident as the children grew older. Spontaneous child talk about race was not uncommon. Most important for this study, the children's dynamic positionings of themselves in the classroom social worlds were audible and visible in the telling and writing of stories and other texts, which drew on diverse cultural materials or "traditions."

CULTURAL TRADITIONS IN SCHOOL WORLDS

To make sense of the social and language challenges facing Jameel and the other observed children, imagine that each of their social worlds is a language world, and those worlds are suspended inside the larger language world of American English. (If the children were bilingual, their worlds would become even more complex, most certainly.) To again rely on Bakhtin (1981), any one national language, like English, is composed of "a multitude of concrete worlds" (p. 288), each world with its own social beliefs and language values.

These social spheres exist because of varied kinds of stratification, including that for particular age groups, ethnic groups, and disciplines. All of these groups have their own ways of speaking. For example, the observed children spoke a variety of English sometimes referred to as African-American Vernacular English. To varying degrees, they spoke a Standard English variety as well; their talk among themselves was sometimes strikingly different from their talk with their teacher. Interwoven with such social stratification is generic stratification, a repertoire of ways of using language in particular situations. The children, for example, told stories, engaged in intense arguments, and told (from their point of view) funny jokes.

The social spheres of interest here — the official school world, the unofficial peer world, and the sociocultural community as realized in the classroom — did not always agree on appropriate genre themes, structures, and styles; that is,they had overlapping but distinctive imaginative universes (e.g., Cazden, 1988; Heath, 1983; Miller, Potts, & Fung, 1989). In a sense, the focal children had sociocultural or "folk" genres they shared among themselves, "popular" genres they shared with the wider peer world, and the "written literary" genres they shared with teacher and peers in the official school world.

These notions of different cultural traditions — the sociocultural folk, the popular, and the written literary — are a helpful heuristic, a way of approaching and thinking about the complexity of the children's social and language lives. But societal categories for these fluid fuzzy concepts are just that — fluid and fuzzy, intertwined in complex, dialogic relationships.[1]

For example, the daily rhythms of music and talk that arise from the regional and ethnic cultures of our society — from the "folk" — have transformed both "popular" and "high" culture (Gates, 1989). In addition, popular cultural forms can express an oppositional attitude — a distancing, a playfulness, to the "high," the serious, the "towering" (Bakhtin, 1981), which may account for their appeal to the young.

As central as popular culture is to children in U.S. schools, its genres — pop songs and cartoons, for example — have seldom been taken seriously in the literacy development literature, although educators have worried about such genres diverting children from "quality" literature (Taxel, 1990) and about their sometimes racist and sexist images. (Certainly "quality" literature is not immune from these charges [Gilbert, 1989; Sims, 1982].) And yet, as Meek (1988) suggests, children's attentiveness to these genres suggests that they must learn from them something about how texts work, about the kinds of human social work — stances toward the world and other people — they may further. Indeed, cartoons, pop songs, raps, horror stories, even baseball and basketball cards figured into the social lives and text worlds of Louise's children.

Unlike the genres of popular culture, the folk or performative verbal arts have figured into theory and research on literacy development. The narratives of children from nonmainstream cultures are sometimes "respected" as evidence of "cultural differences," but they have seldom been put forth as resources for literacy learning. Rather, they have become tangled up in clumsy constructs such as "oral" and "literate" styles. It is to these unruly notions I now turn.

Perspectives on Verbal Performance and Literacy Learning

Speakers and writers are always performing, in that they must use language in ways judged by a community of speakers as socially appropriate (Hymes, 1972). One sense of *performance*, though, refers to spoken acts in which speakers are evaluated for their ability to exploit the expressive qualities of the medium, that is, for their verbal artistry (Bauman, 1977, 1986; Hymes, 1974, 1975). (For a similar differentiation of the meanings of performance, see Goffman, 1974.)

Within a particular culture, performers tend to use certain kinds of texts, like stories or jokes, but there is no automatic link between performance and genre. A story, for example, may simply be reported, or it may be performed artistically. To create a performance, narrators use varied techniques to infuse their feelings into a story (Labov, 1972). These techniques vary across different sociocultural communities and, within the African-American tradition, include such musical phenomena as the rhythmic use of language, patterns of repetition and variation (including rhyme), expressive sounds, and phenomena encouraging participative sensemaking, like dialogue, tropes, hyperbole, and call and response (Abrahams, 1972, 1976; Bauman, 1977; Foster, 1989; Heath, 1983; Kochman, 1972; Labov, 1972; Mitchell-Kernan, 1971; Smitherman, 1986; Tannen, 1989).

In performing a text, an individual makes use of cultural resources (i.e., performance conventions) to take action in her or his social world. Through a performance, the speaker aims to "elicit the participative attention and energy of his audience. . . . When this happens, the performer gains a measure of prestige and control over the audience" (Bauman, 1977, pp. 43–44). A performance, then, has the potential for allowing the performer to transform the existent social structure, to change her or his social position (Abrahams, 1972; Simons, 1990; Smitherman, 1986). In other words, it accomplishes particular kinds of social work.

In research on young children's literacy, the discourse structure and linguistic features of told stories have been highlighted, rather than the social work they may accomplish. Scholars have compared the oral performances of children considered "nonmainstream" (not middle-class and/or not European-American) with the more explicit and analytic — *expository* — language of mainstream children's stories, patterns often labeled "literate" language (e.g., Gee, 1989; Michaels & Collins, 1984).

These scholars often consider "literate" ways of using language as important, if not more important, to school success than the "literacy" skills of encoding and decoding (e.g., Olson, 1977; Snow, 1983; Wells, 1981). The seeds of school success and failure are thus viewed as sown in the home, where some children learn a "literate" style orally, as their parents read and talk to them in particular ways about their own narratives and those of books. Parents might, for example, ask their children to recount an experience in an orderly fashion, with all information made explicit.

"Literate" language, from this perspective, exists on its own, independent from any particular human relationship. All references are made explicit in the text — there are no unanchored *he's, she's,* or *it's* to be taken for granted by speaker and listener; the syntax is complex, and information is permanent — the text reads the same way time and again. Thus, authors can and should reflect on their words for their appropriateness, their aptness for advancing explicit sense, rather than for their attunement to some kind of structural rhythm that might support memory. Readers are not audience members swept into the flow of a performance but analytic consumers who compare and contrast texts, analyzing and synthesizing the meaning found in each, constructing new texts.

The argument for the importance of "literate" narratives (and, more broadly, all kinds of texts) is entirely consistent with the official "imaginative universe," the values for judging written texts earlier discussed; there should be "no gaps in information," and "coherent statements on the same topic." Moreover, the argument is also consistent with valued pedagogical relationships between speaker and/or writer and audience. In current understandings of pedagogical best practices in writing, child composers present "drafts" (often personal narratives) to an "audience," and that audience responds with appreciation and questions about missing or unclear information (Graves, 1983). The composer is never a performer, only a communicator. The audience determines the success of the "communication" by deciding whether or not the text's message is clear.

This theoretical argument might also conceivably explain Jameel's and Mollie's conflict. Indeed, as will be seen, Jameel did use many school writing events to perform, often exploiting the music — the rhythm and rhyme of language — while other class members aimed more straightforwardly to communicate. And, from Jameel's point of view, his end goal was to control his audience, to involve them in his humorous worlds. The audience had no business seeking to teach him about his own story.

But the conglomerate called "oral style," pitted as it is against a "literate" style, will fracture, just as did my peer social world, amidst the complex neighborhoods of Louise's classroom. In the chapters to come, Jameel, like all the focal children, will not be presented as a child with an "oral" style of language use. Rather, he will be presented as a child who participated in social dialogues involving *a range* of ways with words. From the perspective of this book, the kind of language, oral or written, children produce depends on the kind of social work they are doing.[2]

Within the complexity of children's own social spaces, no simple links could be assumed between written texts and a reflective or conscious attitude toward language, nor could any opposition be assumed between control of explicit, elaborate language and the use of performative, artful discourse.

Learning to control the written symbol system did indeed require a kind of reflective attitude to language. This is one aspect of the system that makes it a relatively complex one (i.e., a written symbol represents an oral symbol [a spoken word] for a referent) and that also contributes to its potential value as a tool. But there are many ways of making use of this tool—from list writing to story creation and exposition construction; the kind of social work to which the technology is put determines the kind of reflection it requires (Hymes, 1973; Scribner & Cole, 1981). What we are concerned about in early schooling is children harnessing this technology as a tool to augment the social and intellectual work and play they engage in—and broadening the social and intellectual universes to which they have access.

Moreover, the children conveyed a reflective attitude toward language and discourse quite separately from a concern with written texts. Like other young school children, they played with the double meaning of words to tease and amuse each other (Honig, 1988), argued over who had said what to whom and what they had actually or "really" meant, and disputed the exact wording of popular raps or songs and, even, the characteristics of particular popular superheroes.[3]

Further, in the children's classroom, the strategies of oral storytellers—the exploitation of the musical possibilities of language and the dialogic nature of human interaction—were present in the most highly valued texts, those found in the classroom and school libraries. All fiction writers tend to use such strategies (Tannen, 1982, 1988, 1989), but currently popular reading programs for young children do so to a marked degree. Most recommended are rhythmic picture books, full of repetition and rhyme, which children can easily learn to perform and which are the substance of many extended class discussions (see, for example, Holdaway, 1979).

In sum, learning to write involves figuring out how to manipulate the words on the page in order to accomplish particular kinds of social work; that social work, however, must meet the evaluative criteria of the "imaginative universe" one is in, and, in school, there are in fact multiple such universes potentially operating at any one moment, each with values not always made explicit. It was understanding and negotiating among all these worlds that posed the critical challenge for the observed children, and no doubt for many children in modern societies (Hymes, 1980). Like all children, the focal children had new ways of using language to develop; but the key to furthering their growth lay not in simply analyzing their language differences or similarities but in tapping their discourse flexibility and their sociocultural intelligence.

CHILDREN DISCOVERING AND CROSSING CULTURAL BOUNDARIES

Children come to school with rich histories of using words. Their growing ability to take social action through narratives and other genres helps children develop a sense of control and agency and, in addition, a sense of connection with others. However, the children also come with varying commands over diverse discourse traditions and genres.

Because there are sociocultural differences in family and community uses of written and oral language, educators use the metaphor of a cultural bridge (e.g., Heath, 1983). Teachers must be knowledgeable and accepting of children's ways of speaking; in this way, they allow their students a bridge from the culture of the home into the culture of the school. Gradually, teachers can introduce new ways of using language.

The boundaries of the cultural bridge inevitably blur inside the children's worlds, because, from their points of view, school is not *one* social sphere. The issue thus becomes not how children make a transition from the home world to "the" school world, but how they find themselves — how they compose a place for themselves — amidst the diverse, potentially contradiction-ridden worlds of the classroom.

Composing such classroom places demanded of the observed children sociocultural breadth and depth. By breadth, I mean how their language varied in different social spheres. While not necessarily consciously made, their genre choices (their choices of theme, style, and organizational structure) and the social relationships implicit in those choices illustrated children's emergent ability to situate themselves, to claim social places for themselves, as complex individuals within the social arenas of the classroom. In this sense, readers might recall Lamar's three stories from the Introduction: the "Batman" story of the peer world, the "flying up to heaven" story of his sociocultural heritage, and the clam story of his official school world.

Moreover, Louise's writing period was particularly interesting, given this complexity. Children were sitting and composing within the official school world. However, as they composed, they sat and talked with their peers. While all peers were classmates, some were neighbors from the same sociocultural community. At the end of the composing period, each child was given the opportunity to share a written text, at least potentially, with the entire class, although a child could (and sometimes did) use sharing time to connect with selected others. Within this "official" world activity, then, there was ample space for "unofficial" worlds.

By depth, I mean how children's composing worked to connect worlds. As Bakhtin (1981) explained, people learn language not from dictionaries but from other people in particular situations (p. 293). Thus, when a speaker (or writer) uses language in any one situation, contextual over-tones — the tracings of many previous uses of that language — surround it, imbuing that language with social meaning, with the values and authority structures of the social world within which it has lived. To take control of that language, speakers must give those words their own accent, infuse them in some way with their own intention. Moreover, they must find ways to "de-privilege" or "dialogize" the language, to render it an option among options, a world among worlds (Holquist, 1981, pp. 426–427).

As they gained experience in school, the observed children manipulated and connected the sometimes contradictory classroom worlds and their respective ways of using language. They brought themes, discourse struc-tures, and styles from their unofficial worlds and used them to stake claims on — to compose texts in — the official school world. Conversely, they brought official school material into their unofficial worlds, de-privileging it by playing with it. Thus, their texts could function as crossroads; the texts were supported by and allowed children to take action in diverse worlds. That is, their texts had sociocultural depth — complex overtones that reverberated within and connected varied worlds.

While the children composed varied kinds of texts, fictional stories fig-ured in particularly important ways in their social lives. Child authors, like adult ones, weave everyday voices into complex "fake worlds." They literally appropriate the utterances of others (their characters) in order to express their own attitudes, take their own stands (Bakhtin, 1981). The children's stories — especially those of the kindergartners and first grad-ers — looked quite different from the complex adult prose analyzed by Bakhtin. Their stories were composed of diverse media (drawing, talking, and writing), and they were often playfully, even collaboratively, com-posed, but they were still complex social undertakings. Through stories, the children could bring together the voices of diverse worlds for artful presentation, playful entertainment, or reflective contemplation. More-over, through such composing, their own voices entered into the ongoing classroom dialogues.

All of which brings us back to Jameel standing before the class putting forth his "911" story. That story did indeed blend the voices of everyday worlds, although in an "innocent," seemingly unconscious way. Drawn, dramatized, and written, the story was influenced by Dr. Seuss's (1957) *The Cat in the Hat*, by a morning accident after which 911 had been called, and by Jameel's own worries that his cat Panther, now "gone," had been hit by a car. The story was held together with a performative style all his own but reflective of his sociocultural heritage. And it was put out on the classroom stage to claim his place as a respected and competent child performer. And, there, he entered through his text into a dialogue with the wider world.

STUDYING CHILDREN'S SOCIAL AND TEXT WORLDS

These ideas about writing as children's social work, about the diverse social arenas in which children live, and about the challenges they face in moving among and connecting social worlds and cultural traditions arose as I sat in my "house" amidst the classroom neighborhoods in Louise's classroom. Before entering Louise's school in earnest in Chapter 2, I close this chapter by briefly describing the procedures and certain key analytic constructs with which I worked.

TABLE 1.1. Racial Composition of City, School District, Project School, and Two Sample Census Tracts in Project School Attendance Zone

	White	Black	Asian/ Pacific Islander	Hispa- nic	Native Ameri- can	Other
City	58.3%	18.2%	14.4%	8.4%	0.5%	0.3%
School District (K-12)	54.0%	40.0%	10.0%	9.0%	–	7.0%
Project School	27.0%	52.3%	5.7%	3.3%	0.3%	11.4%
NE Tract	68.0%	2.0%	17.5%	11.0%	0.6%	0.4%
SW Tract	14.8%	72.6%	4.8%	7.2%	0.3%	0.2%

Note: City data based on 1990 census. School district and project school data by school district, October 1990.

Project Site and Participants

Louise and her children worked and played in a K–3 school in the south-central area of the city school district. The school itself was founded in 1892, but the current two-story building dates from the 1950s. Like all district schools, within its walls children meet other children from diverse social and cultural backgrounds. Since the early 1970s, however, a large number of White children have moved to private schools, and the school enrollment, like district enrollment, does not reflect the racial balance of the surrounding city, as Table 1.1 indicates.[4]

Louise's school serves children from primarily two neighborhoods: During my years at the school, approximately 52% came from a low-income and working-class African-American community, and the others from an integrated but primarily European-American working- and middle-class community; about 27% of the children were Anglo and then there were small percentages of children from many different ethnic heritages, among them Chinese, Filipino, Mexican, and Native American. Approximately 35% of the children were supported by Aid to Families with Dependent Children.

Indeed, the differences among the socioeconomic circumstances of the children were striking. Table 1.2 contrasts the furthest northeast census tract within the school's attendance zone with the tract furthest southwest. Census tracts do not lie in any neat way over communities; the tracts nonetheless suggest the differences among the children. Those who were from comfortably middle-class families attended school with those from

TABLE 1.2. Nature of Households for Two Sample Census Tracts

	Married Couples with Related Children	Single Parent with Related Children	Median Value of Owner-Occupied Homes
NE Tract	74.8%	25.2%	$378,600
SW Tract	34.8%	65.2%	$145,700

Note: Percentages are based on total number of households with children related to adults of household. All data based on 1990 census.

families receiving public assistance. I stress, however — to counteract stereotypes, unintended contextual overtones — that despite the urban problems evident in the southwest side of the city, problems of poverty and of crime, the children I came to know had a positive sense of community and connection. Third grader Rashanda's essay makes the point well.

MY HOUSE

Actually I don't live in a house. I live in an apartment building. I live at 2299 Redding St. #A. I love my community. Even though there are bumps in the ground. I don't like that there's a tatoo place by my house. And I like it because there's a store and I can go to the store for my mom. And all my friends like me around there.

Louise, European-American and in her forties, is an experienced and highly skilled teacher, knowledgeable about recent pedagogical innovations (including writing pedagogy) and sensitive to the social issues important to her children. She holds a Masters Degree in Child Development from Tufts University and worked in nursery school programs for many years before she began teaching in the elementary school.

At one time, she was a project director for a children's center inside a prison and wrote a handbook for children with parents in prison. Within the book, 10 children write in honest ways about their experiences; Louise frames their ideas with her own clear prose, emphasizing the importance of supportive and straightforward relationships between adults and children, and the importance of children's sense of themselves as having some control, some decision-making power, over their lives. The themes of honest relationships, of children as decision-makers, *and* of the power of talk and writing for self-expression and social communication were woven throughout Louise's classroom, as Chapter 2 will detail.

In September 1989, I began visiting Louise's K/1 classroom.[5] I became intrigued with the classroom neighborhoods forming and re-forming, with the children's diverse ways of talking and writing. I continued visiting the class the entire year. While I came to know all of Louise's children, I focused on four: first graders Jameel and Eugenie and kindergartners Lamar and Anthony, all four from low-income backgrounds (as determined by qualification for federal school lunch program). Table 1.3 details the grade, sex, and ethnicity of Louise's class. In Appendix A, I list the grade, sex, and ethnicity of all the K/1 children who figure significantly in the chapters to come.

Throughout the year, Louise worked with an instructional assistant, Mrs. Johnson, a middle-aged African-American woman, who was considering becoming a teacher herself. Mrs. Johnson was a gentle woman,

TABLE 1.3. Grade, Sex, and Ethnicity of K/1 Children

	K	1st	Total
Sex			
Female (F)	3	8	11
Male (M)	9	7	16
Ethnicity			
Af. Am	6 (0F, 6M)	6 (4F, 2M)	12
Eur. Am.	3 (1F, 2M)	8 (4F, 4M)	11
Latino	2 (2F, 0M)	1 (0F, 1M)	3
Other	1 (0F, 1M)	0	1
Total	12	15	27

soft-spoken, and attentive to the children. She figured especially in the classroom experiences of Jameel. On mornings when he arrived without having eaten and too late for school breakfast, Mrs. Johnson found something in the classroom cupboards for him to eat. Moreover, Mrs. Johnson invariably found Jameel's written stories and jokes funny, and she became a reliable audience for him.

The next year, Jameel did not attend the school, but Eugenie, Lamar, and Anthony returned to the school, entering other classroom neighborhoods. Louise too had a change, an unexpected one. After a fall leave, when she went on a family trip, she expected to return to the 4- to 6-year-olds (as did I). However, one of the three third-grade teachers had died, and another had been transferred to a junior high; Louise found herself teaching in the latter's old classroom.

I returned to the school too, observing Eugenie, Lamar, and Anthony in their new classrooms and entering Louise's new room. I added two new focal children in Louise's third grade, William and Ayesha. I had not anticipated studying a third-grade classroom, but observing the older children (many of whom I had heard the younger children discuss) was critically important. The third graders, especially William and Ayesha, had clear visions of the boundaries between classroom neighborhoods and engaged in complex, often difficult negotiations. The social work of children, the sociocultural decision making that composing requires, and the hard

TABLE 1.4.   Data Collection Procedures

Academic Year	Month	Major procedures
Year 1: 1989–1990	Sept.	Dyson begins visiting school •
		Familiarizing self with K/1 classroom members and routines
		Selecting 2 first graders as focal children: Jameel and Eugenie
	Oct. through mid-Jan.	Dyson begins formal data collection
		Observing/audiotaping in K/1 classroom 1–2 times weekly; focus on composing period
		Photocopying K/1 children's drawn and written products
	Mid-Jan.	Selecting 2 kindergarten focal children: Lamar and Anthony
		Crivello begins visiting school
	Feb. through mid-June	Dyson and Crivello continue formal data collection
		Observing/audiotaping in K/1 classroom at least 2 times weekly by each observer; focus on composing but take running records (Clay, 1979) of focal children's reading monthly
		Photocopying K/1 children's drawn and written products, as well as samples of books read by focal children
Year 2: 1990–1991	Dec. through mid-April	Dyson does follow-up observations
		Observing/audiotaping Eugenie and Lamar (in a 1st/2nd grade classroom) and Anthony (in a 1st grade classroom); each child observed 6–8 times
		Photocopying drawn/written products
	Jan.	Dyson begins visiting 3rd grade
		Familiarizing self with classroom members and routines
		Selecting 2 focal children: William and Ayesha

Academic Year	Month	Major procedures
	Feb. through mid-June	Dyson and Crivello formally collect data
		Observing/audiotaping at least 1-2 times weekly by each observer
		Photocopying children's written and drawn products

Note: During the fall I had tentatively selected Lamar and Amanda, an African-American girl. However, Amanda moved. As Table 1.3 shows, the remaining 3 kindergarten girls were Hispanic (2) and Anglo (1). I then selected Anthony.

work of the teacher, who, like the children, must negotiate among worlds, were all accentuated, writ large. Details about classroom members and about my own work in the third-grade classroom will be presented in Chapter 8.

Data Collection Procedures

Table 1.4 details my involvement in the school over the two years of the study. In this section, I concentrate on how I studied Louise's K/1 classroom. The described procedures will be elaborated upon in the chapters to come as I enter other classrooms, introduce other children.

I gathered observational data in the classroom from September through mid-June, assisted from January on by Paula Crivello.[6] We observed primarily during the two-hour morning period, when many language arts activities occurred. Among those activities was a regular composing time, in which children had opportunities to interact in ways both informal (e.g., quiet talking among children during drawing and writing) and formal (e.g., daily sharing of compositions during whole class meetings on the rug). While we concentrated on composing, we also observed focal children in both small group and "partner" reading (i.e., two children collaboratively reading a book). In addition, we sometimes went with the children to the school library and followed them out onto the playground and, periodically, into the lunchroom.

Our stance in the room was that of friendly, minimally reactive adults (Corsaro, 1981). We did not attempt to guide or help the children with

149459

their work, because we were "busy" with our own work, as we told them. We typically sat behind and to the side of the child being observed, so that we were outside the child's line of vision; tape-recorders were in leather or canvas bags slipped over a child's chair or left dangling from our wrists. We concealed neither our interest nor our taping, but we did not in any way become intrusive. Moreover, I initially selected focal children who seemed involved with their own activity and/or with their peers and did not seek involvement with me. This passiveness was important, because I wanted to observe the children as they went about their own social work.

Perhaps because I entered the classroom when school began, the children seemed to view being observed by the quiet, smiling lady with the notepad as a normal part of school life; they showed no evident discomfort when Paula, another smiling lady with a notepad, entered the classroom in mid-January. While there were clear differences among the children's ways of speaking in varied classroom social worlds, I noted none when either I or Paula sat down by them.

This is not to say that our presence did not matter. The children seemed not only comfortable with us but quite sophisticated about our stance. One day Jameel was loudly singing "Oh my darling, Clementine" as he sat by Monique and Daisy, working on a reading activity. His singing was irritating Monique. She turned to Paula, who had begun observing in the classroom.

MONIQUE: Can you tell him to be quiet?
  JAMEEL: She's not a teacher.
MONIQUE: She's a grown-up.
  JAMEEL: She's a grown-up, but she's not a teacher.
MONIQUE: She's grown up enough to tell you to be quiet!
  JAMEEL: But will she? NO! But will she? NO! Is she working? Yes!
            Is she doing her job?

With his retort, Jameel made clear that he understood our "job" as observers.

Moreover, our work was important to the children. It is flattering to have someone interested in your doings. As the year progressed, the children sometimes checked with me as I put on my coat and readied to leave; they wanted to make sure I had taken their work to photocopy. Upon request, I made extra copies for them to take home, often for showing "mom" or playing school. Moreover, they began to explain classroom activities to me, especially Jameel, who valued my rather ignorant but exceedingly attentive stance. He gave me lectures about class study units, pointed out new books in the classroom, and informed me about the science fair, Reading-Is-Fundamental days (when all the children could select a free book), and other happenings he thought I might want to write down. This desire of Jameel to teach me, to help me "get the point," accounts for his prominent role in the project; he was a major informant on classroom life and its cultural and social boundaries.

As we observed, Paula and I made handwritten observation notes, audiorecorded the children's spontaneous talk, and photocopied any drawn or written products. Immediately after each observation session, audiotapes were transcribed and annotated, using the observation notes. The focal first graders were each closely observed from 2 to 5 times a month throughout the first year of the study, the kindergartners from 2 to 5 times a month beginning in January, by which time they had settled into school.

Data Analysis Categories

To make sense of the accumulation of transcripts and products, I grouped together all data for each observed literacy *event*. A literacy event is an activity engaged in by at least one person (the focal child) involving the use of graphic media (print, drawing) for some purpose and viewed by the child as a "reading" or "writing" activity (even if an adult might consider it "drawing" or "playing"). The focal child's event was ended when the child changed the topic or purpose of the activity.

During the daily composing period, the children engaged in official literacy events. However, as they composed, they sat and talked with their peers. Therefore, within each official event yielding an official graphic product, there were *episodes* or segments of talk about particular people, objects, and/or events. In many of these episodes, unofficial texts were deliberately fashioned (i.e., within the conversational exchange, there was oral composing of narratives, jokes, and other genres).

For each focal child, I studied all literacy events, and the episodes they contained. I selected events for careful study that seemed to capture the child's characteristic ways of participating in classroom events and that also revealed significant changes in ways of participation across the school year. By *participation*, I mean the child's guiding purposes, ways of relating to others involved in the activity, the mood of the event, topics or subjects he or she chose to focus on, ways of organizing the symbolic product, and particular discourse features of those products (Hymes, 1972). The most dramatic changes in way of participation were revealed by the child's stances or ways of relating to teacher and peers, the moods that emotionally colored those stances, and the kinds of oral or written products mediating the relationships. (*Product* refers to a deliberately shaped oral or written text; a joke, for example, could be told and/or written during a composing activity.)

I next developed a set of categories — a vocabulary of sorts — with which to describe these stances, moods, and products (see Appendix B). These categories are not mutually exclusive. For example, telling a joke suggests a playful mood and a presentational stance. However, a joke can be told seriously (in order to analyze its workings) as well as playfully. Further, the categories can be combined: A joke can be both presentational and collaborative if jointly told.

Because of the importance of the notions of "oral" and "literate" styles in the developmental literature, I paid particular attention to these aspects of the children's language products. I identified all events in which a child used a *performative style*. Performative texts are characterized by the discourse features earlier described (particularly dialogue and exploitation of the musical possibilities of language). In contrast, *communicative style* refers here to more straightforward language use; the text is relatively unmarked by the discourse features associated with oral performance.

I also identified events in which the focal child's language was characterized by the use of analytic or so-called literate discourse features (e.g., labeling objects, asking substantive questions, using previous statements as a basis for a present statement, putting forth hypothetical situations [if *x*, then *y*], requesting clarification or elaboration, linking ideas explicitly, talking about form and style [based on Chafe, 1982; Heath & Mangiola, 1991; and Michaels & Collins, 1984]).

In essence, I constructed discourse maps of each child's school life, paying attention to how each child used varied kinds of texts to enact and to negotiate social relationships with diverse others. By comparing the focal children's composing behaviors with each other and with less intensive observations of all class members, I aimed

1. To identify the kinds of social work or goals that energized children's oral or written composing of texts in official and unofficial social spheres
2. To understand the interrelationships between children's social work and their ways of participating in composing activities, including
   — their stances toward teachers and peers
   — their product themes and discourse features
   — their use of genre themes, structures, and styles rooted in written literary, popular, and folk traditions
3. To reveal changes over time in how children used the genre themes, styles, or structures of one social sphere to take action in another,

that is, to understand the social and discourse processes through
which children differentiate and connect their social worlds

In the next five chapters, then, I concentrate on Louise's K/1 classroom,
exploring how school literacy, particularly writing, emerged within the
context of children's social worlds. I pay special attention to moments in
which the children seemed caught on cultural and social boundaries and,
conversely, when they seemed strikingly successful in constructing dialogic
connections among worlds. In the later chapters of the book, when I
turn to the older children's classrooms, these boundary negotiations will
become sharper, as the children themselves were more sophisticated and
more politically and socially aware.

By studying the complex world negotiations taking place in Louise's
classrooms, I hope to offer insight into how other educators, in other
places, might take advantage of the social and discourse knowledge and
know-how children bring. With the children's assistance, we might broad-
en the imaginative universes that exist in classrooms and, at the same
time, engage children in what should be continuing, ever more complex
dialogues with the world about them.

CHAPTER 2

THE OFFICIAL CLASSROOM WORLD
A Permeable Curriculum

For it is the particular kind of shared life created by all those who work together in a school which determines how language will be used by teachers and pupils. It is the voice of this shared life which marks out the boundaries of possible discourse. . . . "What does this place say to me?" [the children] ask and look for the answer in every intonation of the institution. In finding the answer they also discover what it is possible for them to say.

— Rosen & Rosen, *The Language of Primary School Children*, 1973, p. 21

"What does this school, this classroom, this teacher say to me?" the children ask. "Who can I be here?" "Is there a place for me?" The children's daily actions are their dialogic responses to whatever messages they find. The forthcoming nature of Louise's children — their desire to have a say, as it were — suggests that the messages they found in her classroom were inviting of their words and works.

In this chapter, I take readers into Louise's school, describing the physical face with which it greeted the children each morning. I then introduce Louise's classroom and describe her curriculum. I emphasize the permeable nature of that curriculum, its openness to the children's experiences and language. Woven throughout the classroom dialogue between Louise and her students were the themes of individual and group diversity, as well as the social power and the playful fun to be found in varied ways of using oral and written language.

Finally, I allow readers a close-up view of Louise's language arts program, one highly reflective of currently recommended practices. I stress the genres that were valued and the social relationships that were enacted in both reading and writing activities. It was the boundaries of the writing

30

program—the cultural traditions it assumed, the social work between composer and audiences it espoused—that Louise and the children negotiated as those children quite literally wrote themselves into the literary life of the classroom.

A DIALOGUE OF IMAGES AND SOUNDS: THE SCHOOL CONTEXT

It's 8:30 in the morning. The children in the first- through third-grade classrooms are lining up on the playground to the west of the large two-story building; those in K and K/1 classes are entering their rooms from the smaller play area to the south. It's a gray winter day—cloudy, misty. Despite the early hour, the children are lively; in parkas and shirt sleeves, old sweats and hip jump suits, they chat and laugh, shove playfully and not-so-playfully, a few still running wildly in the midst of some invisible adventure.

The building is gray, nondescript. But it has small patches of child-scrawled initials and names and, on the lower-right side of its western face, a painted mural proclaiming, "We're all a family under one sky." The school's annual peace march is a prominent feature of the mural. "Children of Our School Hold the World in Their Hands," shouts a sign held by marching children; "Child Care Not War," "We Hate Guns," and "Peace," say others. Children are depicted jumping rope, singing, reading; they are studying whales and dinosaurs, working math problems, and examining the stars through a telescope. They shout "hello" and "hola"; they sit in wheelchairs and stand on the grass; they are girls and boys of different colors, sizes, and shapes—as are, of course, the three-dimensional children being greeted, hugged, and scolded by the teachers coming out from the building to claim their classes.

I have been running up the sidewalk beside the school grounds, having found a parking place a couple of blocks away. I am winded but relieved to arrive just as the older children, now in semi-orderly rows, wind their way into the building. I get in line behind a child and follow her through the large double doors.

Inside, the walls are friendly, alternating between child- and adult-made displays. There are commercial posters of picture books and child-made posters urging classmates to "Please write letters to friends." (A large mailbox, shaped just like the U.S. Post Office models, partially blocks the posters.) One bulletin board invites onlookers to meet school faculty and staff, whose pictures are arranged in careful rows. Another details news for parents and community members—an upcoming school program, a meeting, some special event. Still others display photos of children and teachers participating in important school activities — picking up litter in a neighborhood park, tending a garden, carrying signs in the peace march.

Many displays are of children's work. "I am happy when . . . " reads the lettering on one such display; "When I am upset I . . . " says another; "I have a dream . . . " proclaims a third. The peace march and dream speeches suggest the school's special honoring of the ideals of Martin Luther King and of the civil rights movement, which children study from kindergarten on. Some of the child work was done in special programs for children; among them, the extended-day program for low-income families, which cares for children before and after school, and the "Break-the-Cycle" tutoring program, in which university students provide children with homework help.

The posters and bulletin boards fill the walls on both floors of the school. Positioned in between the displays are the doors to 14 regular classrooms, kindergarten through third grade, each with a lettered greeting of "Welcome." There are other important school meeting places as well. There is the small room housing a school library of about 7,000 books, where periodically the children enjoy R.I.F. — Reading is Fundamental, a federally supported program allowing each school child to select a free book. And there is that most lively place, the cafeteria.

As I pass the cafeteria this morning, some children are hurriedly finishing their breakfasts. Sometime during the morning, one child or another will discuss the lunchtime menu with peers. The children's favorites are corn dogs, pizza, and tacos. Individual servings are wrapped in aluminum foil, sometimes accompanied by bags of chips. At times the children have need of plastic forks and spoons, but I have yet to see a dinner plate, a bowl that's reusable. Lunchtime always seems like a lively picnic to me — or maybe a kind of child stockmarket where food shares are distributed among loyal friends, while others make offers of fair trades.

As I near the center of the school, I hear cackling chickens, something of an oddity in an urban school. In fact, in the school's center courtyard are hens, roosters, rabbits, goats, and lambs, all carefully fenced in, separated from the neat vegetable and flower gardens. While the "Farm and Garden" was started about five years ago, it is a rekindling of a gardening tradition that stretches back to the school's founding. Rosalinda, a young woman who grew up on a farm, guides the children as they tend the animals and plants. The Farm and Garden is thoroughly enjoyed by all the children I know. In that place, I witness wild worm hunts, as earth worms are located, discussed, and even raced; I observe loving hellos to sprouting peas and beans, and friendly overtures to chickens, and free spirited romping, seemingly inspired by whatever spirits dwell in that place.

As I pass by the Farm and Garden and round the corner near Louise's K/1 classroom, I come upon an empty wheelchair. It could be Ervin's, a kindergartner with cerebral palsy and a child treated with great care by his classmates in Louise's room, especially by Lamar, Anthony, and their friends. I hear those children now, as they complete a round of "Hello, Hello, Hello and How Are You," and begin the other morning song, "This Land Is Your Land." I enter the room and see James standing in front of the children, who are seated on the classroom rug. Louise is asking him if he wants to lead the children in whistling or clapping the song. It's his choice as leader what they will do.

Some children are in rapt attention; a couple are whispering back and forth; one is nudging a too-close child. Jameel is at the back of the rug, thumb in mouth, staring, seemingly not quite awake. Eugenie is up front, between Shawnda and Monique, singing loudly. Anthony is at the side of the rug, studying his new shoes, while Lamar has just arrived. He reports a big dog in front of the school, which sets off a round of teasing about being scared of dogs. Lamar gives his peers a stern look, hangs up his parka, and sits down. I hang up my raincoat and sit down too.

So has begun the day.

THE CLASSROOM CONTEXT

Just as the displays on the school face were planned by adults but constructed through the interplay of adult and child images and voices, so too were the activities in Louise's classroom jointly shaped.

Louise began each day by leading the children in song, accompanying their voices on her guitar. After morning singing, she led the children in a variety of whole class activities on the rug. She usually had "something interesting" to discuss that she noticed the night before when "looking over your writing." Someone had tried a new spelling strategy (e.g., skipping letters they did not know), come up with a particularly funny title, drawn an "amazing" picture.

Then Louise brought out adult authors' stories and poems to share. By December the children themselves suggested poems by title; most requested were poems by Shel Silverstein.

Next Louise typically led the children in a discussion of their study unit, the talk sometimes centering on new objects to explore—feathers (not to mention two live cockatiels) for the bird unit, shells for the ocean unit, tapes and books on civil rights, charts on space. The children themselves often contributed objects—Sonya brought in shells, Mollie tadpoles from a creek, Tyler (in a well-intentioned but ill-fated move) "live clams," as earlier noted. The objects, displayed on a large shelf or hung on the wall, were enormously interesting to the children.

Early in the year, the 20- to 40-minute morning opening was followed by exercises and games on the playground: aerobic stretches and jumps, and children's games, like duck-duck-goose. The latter was a confusing experience for some kindergartners who, upon being chosen, ran around and around the circle, misguided but happy.

Next came language arts. During this period, which lasted at least an hour, a variety of reading and writing activities occurred, some completed independently by the children as Louise or Mrs. Johnson circulated among them, others done in small adult-led groups. During composing activities, the first graders typically drew and wrote, Louise encouraging them to figure out their own spellings. The kindergartners drew and wrote as well, but they also dictated stories, which prompted some class discussion on whether or not that was "fair." (The first graders, who knew they knew more, ended up with shorter stories than those of the dictating kindergartners.) Often the children chose their own topics for composing, but Louise sometimes suggested topics related to the ongoing study unit or to some other aspect of classroom life (e.g., thank you letters to classroom visitors, greeting cards for sick children).

For morning reading instruction, the first graders gathered in small groups to read storybooks or selections from the literature reader; both first graders and kindergartners did "partner reading," the collaborative reading of a familiar story. The kindergartners also talked about letter names and sounds, primarily in the context of making an alphabet book, although they sometimes played instructional games.

In addition to language arts activities, the children chose additional tasks: They read classroom library books, did puzzles, built with manipulatives, worked on art projects, and, very often, gathered around the objects on the large shelf bordering the rug to talk about the many interesting displays.

Right before or after the 10:15 break for snack and recess, the language arts period concluded with another rug meeting. This time the children shared their morning drawing and writing. During the 15-minute recess that followed, the children slid down the slide, dug in the sand, hung from the hanging bars, or chased after one another in a game of "police," "monsters," or "boys against girls." After recess, Louise often read again to the children before beginning mathematics activities, which could be followed by another whole class meeting on the rug before noon lunch and recess.

In the afternoon, after the kindergartners went home at 1:30, there was another hour of language arts activities. During this time, the first graders again read in small groups or with partners. Louise also led the class in word study activities; the children often sat with small chalkboards and tried their hands at varied spelling patterns.

While Louise had a schedule, she was also very flexible. In part this flexibility was demanded by the many activities that took the children out of the classroom or brought the outside community in. There were weekly visits to the library and, every other week, lessons in the Farm and Garden. Louise took the children on a number of trips, major and minor — to the aquarium, the symphony, the park, the store. And visitors often attended the class — to explain about particular careers, kinds of music, special ethnic customs, ways of caring for pets.

Moreover, Louise was open to unexpected child requests. When Louise walked into her classroom one morning and discovered Easter eggs in strange places, hidden by a "secret friend," she immediately planned a morning egg hunt, accompanied by much talking, drawing, and writing about who the secret friend might be. When Mollie said they should make deviled eggs, Louise agreed, and they all walked to Louise's house, which was a few blocks from the school, to get the mayonnaise. (Cooking was a common activity in Louise's class; as such, it involved writing and reading recipes, following directions, counting, and measuring, eating new foods.)

The curricular activities in Louise's room, then, were dialogic, in that there was space for child choice as well as for adult plans and a willingness to consider changing adult plans at a child's suggestion. I will take a closer look at Louise's language arts program in the closing section of this chapter. First, however, I want to pursue more deeply the dialogic nature of Louise's curriculum by looking at its enactment through teacher and child dialogue. It was within this dialogue that the children were introduced to school literacy.

THE DIALOGIC CURRICULUM

Reflection and Action

Implicit in Louise's interaction with her class was the notion that, in the enacted curriculum, children and teachers have rights and responsibilities toward each other, as Genishi (1992) discusses. Louise worked to share responsibility with her children, not only in allowing space for children's activity choices, but also in the very way she talked with them, as illustrated in the following interaction. (For the following and all other transcripts presented throughout this book, please refer to Figure 2.1, which provides a key to the typographic conventions I have used.)

Morning singing is over. Louise has an important question to bring up. Brett has asked her where space begins and ends. "How," she asks the class, "might we find out the answer to Brett's question?"

MOLLIE: Ask a scientist.

JAMEEL: Read a book or think about it.

JULIAN: Go in a space rocket.

LOUISE: Maybe we could do some empirical research.

BERTO: Yeah, but Louise doesn't know very much about going into a space rocket and going up to space either.

Louise has to agree with Berto's evaluation. What she has done, she says, is "pretty much what Jameel suggested." She has gone to the school library and gotten three space books. But she is not happy with them. The copyright dates are in the 1960s.

LOUISE: Let me tell you something, folks. In 1960, I was in high school. They've learned a lot about space since I was in high school.

BRAD: We weren't even born.

SHAWNDA: Usually people who graduated then, they be dead by now.

The notion of a copyright date is fascinating to the children, and for the remainder of the year, one child or another will remind Louise to check the date when she reads to them. Louise tells the children that all the books in their school library are very old.

MONIQUE: Go to another library.

LOUISE: Good suggestion. Monique says let's go to another library. Do you have a library by your house with space books in it? Could you look for a book this weekend and see if you can find a space book that's written after 1962?

                                    . . .
What's another solution?

HANNAH: Bookstore.

Louise says that this is something they need to do, but Jameel objects. He is homeless and stays with relatives or in shelters, and he is especially sensitive to situations that require money.

JAMEEL: I don't think going to a bookstore is a very good thing to do. I think you should go by my house, and they got a library down the street, and you can check out books for three weeks, and they got all kinds of books about space, and storybooks.

FIGURE 2.1.   Conventions Used in the Presentation of Transcripts

()   Parentheses enclosing text contain notes, usually about contextual and nonverbal information, e.g., (laughs, points at her).

Empty parentheses, on the other hand, indicate unintelligible words or phrases, e.g.,

Shawnda: And WOW! I ().

[]   Brackets contain explanatory information inserted into quotations by me, rather than by the speaker.

[A single large bracket is used to indicate overlapping speech; e.g.,

Vera: Every time I see on TV a rock star, they be having
          ⌈a mohawk.
Jameel: ⌊a mohawk.

N-O   Capitalized letters separated by hyphens indicate that letters were spoken or words were spelled aloud by the speaker.

NO   A capitalized word or phrase indicates increased volume.

<u>no</u>   An underlined word indicates a stressed word.

/n/   Parallel slashed lines indicate that the speaker made the sound of the enclosed letter or letters.

/n:/ A colon inserted into word or sentence indicates that the sound of the previous letter was elongated.

...   Ellipsis points inserted in the middle of a blank line indicate omitted material; e.g.,

Shawnda: I know. And that ain't fair and Dorine [the school secretary] say--
               ...
And Dorine say first graders and second graders too scared to be out in the woo:ds.

Conventional punctuation marks are used to indicate ends of utterances or sentences, usually indicated by slight pauses on the audiotape. Commas refer to pauses within words or word phrases. Dashes [--] indicate interrupted utterances.

The interaction between Louise and her children, as exemplified above, was quite different from stereotypical teacher/child interaction (see, for example, Mehan, 1979; Sinclair & Coulthard, 1975). In that stereotyped pattern, the teacher asks a question, the child responds, and the teacher evaluates the correctness of the response. Louise did indeed include such an interactional pattern in her repertoire, as do most school teachers in our society (Cazden, 1988). But this pattern did not dominate in class discussions. Rather, Louise shared the following three instructional roles with her children: the roles of question-asker, information-conveyer, and evaluator.

For example, in the above event, Brett had in fact raised the original question motivating the space discussion. Louise brought this question to the children. "How might we find the answer to Brett's question?" she asked, transforming the question into one the children could and did answer in different ways. As the children responded, Louise sometimes withheld evaluation or referred a response to the class for agreement or disagreement.[1] Berto himself spontaneously offered a critique, one that pointed out the limitations of Louise's own knowledge.

Moreover, both Louise and, as the year progressed, her children incorporated each others' responses into their own next speaking turns, a valuable style of interaction for both language development and disciplinary learning (Cazden, 1988; Collins, 1982; Cross, 1978; Nystrand & Gamoran, 1991). Louise often recast her children's ideas in the language of the discipline they were studying, thereby linking their words to the wider world (Lemke, 1990). "True," she said in response to Berto, "I'd have a hard time doing empirical research."

Further, Louise and her children were not only building vertically on each others' responses. They also built horizontally, by referring to other discussions, other texts in other dialogues. Listen to the continuation of the space book discussion a few days later. Louise once again refers to Brett's question and to their discussion of copyright dates.

> During morning rug time, Louise tells the class that she found some more space books from the City Public Library. In fact, Sonya also has brought in books she found at the library by her house. Louise notes that all of the books have more recent copyright dates and wonders if the children remember what that means.
>
> JAMEEL: The year it was made.
>
> MONIQUE: It wasn't like we weren't born, and you were like coming out of high school. [Note how Monique echoes and combines earlier child and teacher comments.]
>
> Louise reads the section from each book that answers Brett's original question. Each book gives a different answer. Louise asks the children why this might be.
>
> HANNAH: I think maybe space tips, and it's different in different places.
>
> LOUISE: Hannah thinks the earth is uneven, so it would be differ-

ent distances at different points. Maybe they measured it
from different places.

BERTO: They might be saying different ways of measuring. [Lou-
ise nods.]

At this point, Edward G. weaves in the concept of "copyright date."

EDWARD G: I think that book was longer [older]. That one [the more
recent one] has better information.

. . .

AUSTIN: That book was 1962 and that one was 1985 so the 1962
has more information. [Austin seems to be measuring
from the current time backward, so the "longer" or older
book has more information.]

MONIQUE: The new book is right!

And thus the conversation continues, with Louise providing the framework (highlighting questions, issues, key concepts) and the children carrying the bulk of the interactive work.

One consequence of Louise's interactional style was the enactment of
a curriculum with a thematic emphasis on individual decision making.
Louise helped her children to participate in disciplinary activities as reflective individuals—as people who could deliberately manipulate verbalized
ideas. She lent them her own awareness, her own ability to name actions
and to place them inside a disciplinary context (Bruner, 1986; Moll, 1990).
In the words of the psychologist Vygotsky (1978), the theorist who most
influenced current social views of development, she was using language to
help her students "grow into the intellectual life of those around them" (p.
88). She encouraged them to reflect on their options and then act in some
way—find a book, make a prediction, offer a critique.

However, to understand Louise's enacted curriculum, and the children's
participation in it, we must go beyond the notion of individual reflection
in culturally valued ways. We must enter the complex, sociohistorical and
political world described by Bakhtin. For Louise encouraged the children
to reflect not only on the official language of school, but on the language
of the social world within which the school existed, a world where gender,
ethnicity, race, and class all mattered. This was illustrated most clearly in
the careers unit, to which example I now turn.

Linking Individual Responsibility and Social Possibility

As in all study units, the careers unit was dialogic, constructed through
the involvement of the children and, in this case, their parents. Parents
from all walks of life, as well as varied community members, visited;

among them were a baker, a child care worker, a police officer, a mail
carrier, and, to start the unit off, Angie's mother — a career counselor.

Also as in all units, the involvement of children was evident in the
construction of dialogue itself, the interplay between and among adults
and children. Louise again shared responsibility for instructional roles —
asking questions, providing information, offering critiques — with others.
With Louise's guidance, the children wrote an interview guide; they asked
each visiting adult a set of four questions, recorded on chart paper. After
each visit, Louise led a discussion in which chart answers were compared.

By the fourth visit, excerpted below, the children clearly dominated the
interviews. Children asked questions, reflected on answers ("That's what
everybody says!"), and probed for additional information. Certainly in
these whole class discussions, not all individuals were heard unless Louise
deliberately sought them out, which she did. But a class attitude of respectful assertiveness was encouraged, as is illustrated in the following
exchange.

Berto's mother, a cabinet maker, is visiting.

SHAWNDA: (reading the first question) What's boring about your
job?

GUEST: Well, a lot of times I have to do the same things over and
over.

MONIQUE: That's what everybody says! [And indeed, it is a remark
made by other guests.]

GUEST: Oh, really! A very hard life, you know? And some of the
things I do are real interesting and some things are not so
interesting. In order to make things look really nice, I
have to do the same things over and over.

EUGENIE: (reading the next question) What's fun about your job?

GUEST: I'm the kind of person, I like to be very careful and accurate and take things one thing at a time. I'm very organized. And the thing that's the most fun is, I like to make
things.

Louise discusses the word *organized* with the children and then begins to thank Berto's mother for coming, but Berto interrupts.

BERTO: You left something out.

Jameel reads the left-out question.

JAMEEL: What do you do in your job?

And after Berto's mom explains all the cutting, nailing, and hammer-
ing she does, Jameel has a spontaneous follow-up.

JAMEEL: Do you ever get a scratch?

In the careers unit, the thematic emphasis on individual diversity — on unique individuals having their say — was complemented by an emphasis on group diversity. Louise was most concerned with issues of equity — with people acting together to make sure that all groups were treated fairly. Particularly salient, given the Bakhtinian perspective of this book, was Louise's concern with the contextual reverberations of certain words, that is, with how words bring forth images of the people to whom they belong. It was this concern that linked individual and group, responsibility and possibility. In the following episode, Louise and the class create an object lesson about the link between the constraining images engendered by words and the power of the individual to imagine possibilities for self and others.

Today Hannah's dad, a scientist, has been interviewed. Afterward, Louise asks the children what they might want to be, acknowledging that they can and do change their minds a lot. Four children declare themselves future scientists. Shawnda then says that she will be a police officer, which James objects to.

SHAWNDA: There are women police officers.

. . .

JAMES: But they suppose to be a police woman, she means.

LOUISE: You know, that's an interesting thing to say, James. Because it has to do with words. And when Shawnda said what she wanted to do, she didn't say police man. [She said] police officer. Why do you suppose they say police officer instead of police woman?

MONIQUE: Because they don't have to say man or woman. They can just call theirselves police officer. That's the best way to say it, without having to talk about whether they're a boy or a girl or a woman or a man.

. . .

Louise has previously discussed with the children words that imply only men can assume certain roles (e.g., "mailman"); she has also discussed how certain words can make people think of men or women (e.g., "nurse"; Daisy's father is a nurse). She now calls the children's attention to a related concept.

LOUISE: You know, I want to show you something interesting. Could I see the hands of the people who said they want to be scientists? Could I have those four people sit in the middle of the — the center? Here's an important problem.

. . .

	If I went into the center of that ring, I would make it different. What is it, Celia?
CELIA:	They're all um — they're all boys.
LOUISE:	They're all boys.
SHAWNDA:	There can be girl scientists. (with conviction)
LOUISE:	Wait a minute. There's something else that's the same about the four of them. Edward Johnson, could you go join them? Edward's about to make it different.
MONIQUE:	He has a pen — that pen.
BERTO:	Oh, I know. They're all White and Edward's not.
MONIQUE:	THAT'S NOT A GOOD WAY TO TALK ABOUT THE COLORS! (distressed; in peer situations, Monique has commented that she is "not supposed to talk about the colors.")
LOUISE:	Hey. You know, you're right, Monique. It's a real problem if the only people in this world who want to be a scientist are White boys. That's a problem. (Monique may be concerned that Berto is inappropriately bringing up race, not that there is a "problem" with the population of scientists. Nonetheless, she understands Louise's comment, as will be clear.)
SHAWNDA:	No, they can be Black boys being scientists. They can't just be White people. It can be Black or White.
	. . .
LOUISE:	Well it's something you might want to think about when you think about what you are going to be when you grow up. Can you be something that most people thought only White boys could do?
JAMEEL:	Like bus drivers. Only White people — used to be only White people were driving buses and now people can. (Jameel may know this from out-of-school sources, but, in school, the children have extensively discussed the civil rights movement, including the importance of Rosa Parks's action on the city bus.)
LOUISE:	That's right. Now women can, and Black people can, and Asian people can. Chicanos can.
MONIQUE:	'Cause some women and 'cause some Black people and some people want to be scientists. They don't only have to be White.
LOUISE:	And, you know, in fact there are some very important men and women and Blacks and Asians and Hispanics

who are scientists, and I think next week that's something
we should look at. Thank you future scientists of America
(to children sitting in middle of rug, who have been listening attentively). There are a few other people I need to
hear from. Tyler, what are you going to do when you
grow up?

TYLER: Uh, scientist.

Louise calls on Celia.

CELIA: A scientist.

She calls on Anthony.

ANTHONY: A scientist.

By now, everyone is laughing. Louise asks "all those people who are
going to be scientists" to get in the center of the rug. All of the children but one get in the center, and a great gleeful noise goes up
(added to by Mrs. Johnson and me; we are laughing too. "I think I'm
gonna change my mind and be a scientist," chuckles Mrs. Johnson).
Hannah's father is also in the center of the rug. Louise gets her camera and takes everyone's picture — except for Hannah who will not go
into the center. She has been quite firm in her stated desire to be a
zoo veterinarian.

As illustrated, Louise made legitimate the topics of gender, class (more
accurately, having money or not having money for varied activities), and
race. Indeed, Louise was not raising topics the children themselves did
not implicitly raise. Within the week, Berto objected to Vera's desire to be
a baseball player: "Women do not play baseball." Earlier, both Jesse and
Julian had voiced their opinions that most poor people are Black.

In encouraging individual assertiveness and sensitivity to social fairness,
in promoting talk about talk, Louise was enacting what might be termed
critical pedagogy, education that aims to support students' efforts to name
and take action in their worlds (Freire, 1985; Greene, 1988; Ramsey,
1987; Sleeter, 1991). By playing with words, children might gain some
freedom of imagination, an ability to envision new possibilities for themselves and others.

The dialogic nature of the curriculum — the encouragement of individual assertiveness and group sensitivity, the inviting in of the children and
their points of view — did not give rise to a classroom utopia. The children,
after all, were in a different time and social space from Louise, indeed
from all adults. No matter how strong the teacher — indeed, perhaps particularly with strong, sensitive teachers — the act of teaching, like living
itself, is a constant responding to the sometimes unexpected responses of

others. As Bakhtin points out, the "I" cannot see its own social place, for "I" can only look at "you"; rather, we know ourselves only through the responses of others (Bakhtin, 1990; Clark & Holquist, 1984).

Thus, the responses of Jameel, Eugenie, Lamar, and Anthony within official curricular spaces were often surprising; by saying unexpected words, authoring surprising texts, they illuminated the social expectations of not only Louise's classroom, but of current ways of thinking about children's literacy growth. In this project, the writing of stories was a key site for such illumination.

Exploring and Exploiting the Potential Power of Print

Interwoven in the preceding examples have been the tools of literacy. Like diversity, the usefulness of literacy was a consistent theme in Louise's class. In the examples presented above, books are sources of information; writing, a way of recording information for further reflection. However, there are other important purposes of print, including aesthetic purposes. The power of crafted texts to engage, entertain, and move others was most evident in Louise's literacy program. While this project focuses on children's composing, I first detail the reading aspect of Louise's language arts program, because it provided an important reference point for the children's own writing.

A Diversity of Adult-Crafted Texts. The professional texts used in the reading aspect of the language arts program incorporated our intertwined folk, popular, and literary heritages.[2] For example, Louise's repertoire included Pete Seeger's (1986) folk song *Abiyoyo*, Eloise Greenfield's (1978) warm *Honey, I Love*, written in vernacular African-American speech patterns, and traditional tales of Native American peoples; she read humorous texts, like the irreverent poetry of Shel Silverstein and the cartoon-like silliness of Dr. Seuss's rhythmic verses, as well as the more flowing prose of classics like Sendak's (1963) *Where the Wild Things Are* and Gag's (1977) *Millions of Cats*.

In the K/1, Louise did not typically name the traditions books drew upon. For example, in reading books with African-American English dialogue, Louise did not specifically call attention to the cultural context evoked by the talk. Nor did she refer to Dr. Seuss as cartoon-like or Shel Silverstein as filled with the brash humor of the peer world. Nonetheless, Louise deliberately chose to set out a diversity of books, of imaginative possibilities, for her children.

This valuing of diverse art forms was evident in fact throughout the curriculum. For example, Louise often sang folk songs with the children.

The children also attended the symphony and prepared for it by listening to symphonic music and learning the names and sounds of the instruments. They heard classics like *Peter and the Wolf* and more contemporary compositions, like those of Bay Area composer John Adams, who came to talk with the children. The children moved to the music's rhythm, responded to dramatic crescendos by holding their breath in anticipation, and gave cheers with the eventual full tones, behavior that could not, Louise noted, occur in the concert theater. (Indeed, the children's utter enthusiasm was strikingly different from the responses of Louise's third graders a year later, who generally considered symphony music "boring" and much preferred the class study of rap music.)

Although a wide variety of books were read from the beginning of the year, Louise initially made particular use of rhythmic and repetitive ("pattern") books and poems, which the children could easily remember. Among these selections were Bill Martin's (1982) *Brown Bear, Brown Bear, What Do You See?* and texts based on children's songs like "Old MacDonald Had a Farm" and "A Huntin' We Will Go." In addition, the first graders used the preprimers of the school reading program (Houghton Mifflin Literary readers [1989]), which contained many rhythmic and repetitive stories.[3] Jameel and Eugenie, like the most of the first graders, repeatedly read such books in the opening months of school, making up the parts they did not remember and gradually attending more carefully to the graphics.

Louise also used linguistic readers (textbooks that gradually introduce phonic patterns) for a short period of time; through these books, she aimed to give the first graders opportunities to apply their knowledge of letter sounds and word families. Jameel in particular enjoyed these books, which he considered "joke books" and filled with "silly" happenings (e.g., "The cat had a bat").

Louise introduced almost all stories and poems by reading them in a dramatic and artful style. She, in fact, performed them for her children, who were an attentive audience, smiling, laughing, and sometimes reading along with her. In a related manner, Louise and small groups of six or seven first graders performed stories in chorus before individuals took character parts or sprawled on the rug to reread stories with a partner. When individual children read, Louise asked them to read dialogue just like they imagined the character would have talked.[4]

As the year progressed, and particularly as the children began reading stories with more substantive plots, Louise guided the children's reading of the stories with a dialogic style similar to that used throughout the curriculum. The children made many unsolicited comments about the stories, which Louise built on, and the children responded to her own comments. The easy, back-and-forth quality of their discussions is illustrated in the following lesson excerpt.

Louise and the children have been reading a story in which a fox attempts to trick a young rabbit, whose mother runs a cafe. The fox tells the little rabbit that he is a frog. The rabbit in turn tells the "frog" that he will let his mother know that a frog wants lunch. This displeases the fox. Later in the story, the knowing mother fixes the "frog" fly soup, which sends him running.

LOUISE: Does the rabbit, does the [little] rabbit think he's talking to a fox?
CHILDREN: NO! He thinks he's talking to a frog!
EUGENIE: A frog go ribbet, ribbet. He might tell the difference from a frog. (with exasperation; Eugenie is commenting on the stupidity of the rabbit.)

LOUISE: Let's go back to where it says, "Fox was not pleased." Why wasn't he pleased that the rabbit was gonna—
EUGENIE: Because the mama knows that that's a rabbit—that he's [the fox] playing a trick.
LOUISE: Yeah, that mama's gonna know that! Let's go on.
And after reading a few more pages:
EUGENIE: They could tell the difference 'cause they grown, but the child is not grown.

LOUISE: What did her fly soup do?
EUGENIE: It made him mad.
SHAWNDA: It tasted gross! I would never be that Fox in that book again.

HANNAH: If I were that—if we were going to act out that, I would be the Little Rabbit.
LOUISE: You'd be the Little Rabbit?
SHAWNDA: Me too.

Louise also conducted more extended discussions, in which the children compared the settings, characters, and plots of different stories, encouraging reflection about verbalized experience. In one particularly engrossing discussion, the children considered whether James Marshall, the author who wrote the story about the fox pretending to be a frog, had used the same fox character in writing another story. This discussion began when

Eugenie incorrectly but quite sensibly assumed that the friendly girl fox in the new story was the same old tricky fox.

HANNAH: But that one [fox in the other book] was a boy, and this one was a girl!

LOUISE: A ha!

EUGENIE: (to Hannah) Uh uh. You don't know what's the difference. See, foxes are boys. There's not girls. There's no such thing as girl foxes. They all be boys!

HANNAH: Yes there is!

LOUISE: Well, take a look at that fox [who is wearing a dress]. (Recall that Eugenie thinks that the fox is just trying to trick the other animals.)

EUGENIE: Well, he don't have a bow on his head!

LOUISE: That's true.

MOLLIE: There is such a thing as girl foxes!

HANNAH: Yeah, there wouldn't be any — there wouldn't be any —

EUGENIE: Well, do you have to agree, Hannah? (irritated)

MOLLIE: There wouldn't be any babies. There wouldn't be any foxes if there wouldn't be any mothers!

Louise suggests that the children reread the other story, which they do with a partner. When they return to the discussion, there is still general disagreement as to whether or not the fox is the same fox. Louise says she has an idea. She asks them to listen. She reads from the new story: "The Fox came by. She —"

EUGENIE: She! It said a she.

LOUISE: Listen to this one [the old story]. "Fox was not pleased. But he said, "OK."

And everyone agrees that one is truly a girl, the other a boy, although sincere, friendly foxes are rare in their books, as are female foxes.

A Diversity of Child-Crafted Texts. From the beginning of the school year, all the children were allowed a stage for presenting their own work to an audience, just as Louise presented adult authors' work. While initially the children's efforts were brief and Louise did more talking than any individual child, each did have a turn, a moment in the spotlight. Early in the year, if objections to a child's text were raised, Louise always deferred to the author, as illustrated in the following example.

It's early in October. The children are joining Louise on the rug after a composing period. Louise focuses the children's attention on the different decisions individuals have made about how to craft their texts. Edward J. is making his writing book all about sports. Today he has drawn a boxer and written a backwards "3." The 3, he explains, is because "it's the third round."

Other children, comments Louise, have decided to "label" their pictures. For example, Monique has drawn a tepee and written, "This is me and my TP." Louise comments that hers "could be a picture book." "A picture book for a little kid," adds a child. Austin has a twist on the picture book idea. He has made a "guess-what's-happening book." Louise points out that, on the back of each of his pictures, there's a "description of what's happening."

Calvin's is a "wordless picture," featuring a tree, a man, and a hat.
"What do you think Calvin was thinking of?" she asks.
"*Caps for Sale* [Slobodkina, 1940]," sings the child chorus.
"He doesn't have a month," comments a child.
"Does he need a mouth?" Louise asks Calvin.
"No," says Calvin.
"No," says Louise.

After each work was appreciated, Louise made comments oriented to children's reflection and decision making. As is particularly evident in the above example, Louise initiated the children into writing by linking their efforts in specific ways with the books the children read. Certainly there were, as has already been suggested, many ways in which literacy was used throughout the school day. The children made lists and charts for science and social studies, wrote thank you notes and made happy birthday cards; they even wrote letters of protest to the School Board when they complained about a standardized test they had taken. But the initial and most prominent connection during language arts time was to crafted — artistic — books.

The children were themselves constructing these interesting objects called "books." In fact, the children's first writing task was to make "wordless picture books." As the year progressed, Louise not only used the genre labels of books (e.g., "picture books"), she and the children noted connections of topic, character, plot, and language style (e.g., the use of a rhyming pattern).

The following exchange, which took place in early February after another composing period, illustrates both the continuing emphasis on child decision making, with the individual author clearly in charge of the crafted text, and the consistent use of professional language (or "scientific concepts," to adopt Vygotsky's [1962] phrase), which language provided the children tools for reflection.

Louise comments first on the diversity of individual children's work during the morning composing period.

LOUISE: People did all different kinds of writing this morning. Austin continued working on the story he did about the alligator and the jack rabbit. He has a new spelling strategy for what to do when he thinks a word is spelled wrong.

Austin explains his strategy, and then Louise continues, commenting on each child's work in turn as she moves around the child-circle on the rug.

LOUISE: Hannah has the beginning of a great story. It only has a title so far, "The Magic Piece of Hair."

JAMEEL: I love to hear it.

HANNAH: It's going to have a lot of chapters.

Next Louise raises Daisy's "interesting question" about "if a sign says something, should I put it in quotation marks." Then she asks Edward J. to read his piece, noting that Edward "got to a whole new stage on his basketball story." Next she comes to Angie, who has yet to speak in whole class sessions of any kind. Louise, however, still asks her if she would like to read her story, and, when Angie declines, she secures Angie's permission, an affirmative nod, to read the piece herself. Angie has written another story about a little girl.

LOUISE: You almost have a whole bunch of chapter stories about these girls. You have the one where they wouldn't let the boys play ball, and you have the teasing one.

Monique now reads hers, or more accurately, explains hers by pointing to varied objects in her picture.

MONIQUE: The rainbow, the trees, the heart with lots of shapes.

LOUISE: And so is it describing the picture? [Monique nods] Could you read that to us again?

MONIQUE: (now reads) This is the rainbow. This is the trees. This is a big heart with lots of shapes. Sophie.

LOUISE: What are you going to do with the word *Sophie*?

MONIQUE: I'm writing a title for the chapter.

LOUISE: And it's going to be about Sophie?

MONIQUE: No. Sophie's gonna be—I didn't get to write the title, but the title is gonna be every kinda thing, like a chocolate!

LOUISE: Uh huh. It's kinda like an every-kind-of-thing page.

James has a dictated story.

JAMES: It has three parts. (James's paper is divided into three parts. He reads the first part.) There lived an old woman and an old man.

> JAMEEL: *Thousands of Cats*! [in reference to *Millions of Cats* (Gag, 1977)]
> SHAWNDA: *The Gingerbread Boy*!
> BRAD: *The Turnip*!
> LOUISE: Yes, lots of stories begin this way, and it worked very well for James.

As the preceding excerpt illustrates, by this time of the school year, Louise's children were beginning themselves to use a more elaborate language of construction, referring, for example, to "chapters," "titles," and "parts." There was a clear sense that a crafted text has some kind of organizational sense, illustrated most clearly by Monique's efforts to provide an organizational label for Louise and for herself.

At this time too, Louise began to implement a more structured writing program, a "process" pedagogy. On the surface, a writing process approach seems compatible with the curriculum Louise had initiated: In such a pedagogy there is an emphasis on children as "real" authors who make decisions about what and how they are going to write. However, as suggested in Chapter 1, process pedagogy is undergirded by an imaginative universe rooted in a dichotomous view of "oral" and "literate" texts, and more generally in a narrow conception of school literacy.[5]

From the perspective of process pedagogy, the author's social role is to communicate to an audience; the essential goal is a text with adequate information to accomplish this social work. Given that role, it is appropriate for the "audience" to let the author know whether or not the information has been "communicated," and to "respond" to a text with advice as to the additional *information* needed in order to adequately understand its "sense" (see, for example, Graves, 1983). Thus, Louise began to refer to the children's texts as "drafts" and to specifically provide for teacher and peer "response" to their efforts.

However, as will also be seen in coming chapters, as Louise worked to implement a more structured writing process program, tensions surfaced. For example, Louise placed great emphasis on the children crafting books, just as did the authors they read. But those read books included many in which it was not the referential sense of the words that was highlighted but their musical possibilities — their rhythm and rhyme — and their humorous, sometimes *nonsensical* images. Further, the generic material (the themes, structures, and styles) of these books were informed by cultural traditions — imaginative universes — much more diverse than those codified in the evaluative guides for teachers, as discussed in Chapter 1.

Moreover, Louise had invited the children to the classroom social stage and arranged herself and her students as audience to the child author.

And on that stage, the children could enact roles other than mere communicator. As already noted, Louise herself often performed books, and, as Jameel's "911" story suggested (see Chapter 1), the children would sometimes claim that role for themselves. The relationships between performer and audience is not the same as that between performer and critic, or performer and helper.

Louise had created a permeable curriculum, which invited the children in as individual decision-makers and social actors, as did, in fact, the school as a whole. But when the focal children entered, they brought unanticipated genres and unexpected social goals, all informed by the intersecting and complex traditions of their popular, folk, and literary heritages. The children's ways of participating in composing activities raised questions about the contextual reverberations adults and children may have about words like "sense" and "audience."

To view the breadth of the social and language powers the children were bringing to their school experiences, I looked outside the official school world, into unofficial arenas. In the next chapter, therefore, I introduce readers to the children's repertoire of narratives and other genres and to the social work — the relationship building and managing — they accomplished and the cultural traditions they drew upon. Before reentering the official classroom world, then, I hope to portray the complex social and language neighborhoods the children managed.

CHAPTER 3

UNOFFICIAL CLASSROOM WORLDS
Children Taking Action Through Language

> *Children are gifted at [language learning], of course. But it requires a different order of respect to take in the possibility that children make up languages, change languages, perhaps have been carrying the responsibility for evolving language from the first human communication to twentieth century speech. . . . The environment required . . . was simply enough children, enough children crowded together in circumstances where they could spend a lot of time playing together. . . . It makes an interesting scenario. The adults and wise elders of the tribe, sitting around a fire—speaking a small-talk pidgin. . . . Somewhere nearby, that critical mass of noisy young children, gabbing and shouting at each other, their voices rising in the exultation of discovery, talking, talking, and forever thereafter never stopping.*
> — Lewis Thomas, *Late Night Thoughts on Listening to Mahler's Ninth Symphony*, 1983, pp. 53–54

It is not wise, Lewis Thomas reminds us, to see children only as small apprentices to the adult world. Within the social arrangements set by adults, a "critical mass" of young children will construct their own social worlds, and they will do so with the tools of language (Cook-Gumperz, 1981; Corsaro, 1985; D'Amato, 1987; Ervin-Tripp & Mitchell-Kernan, 1977).

Classrooms provide such a mass of children. Thus, as Louise organized the official classroom world, the children organized unofficial worlds. These worlds were formed in response to adult-governed worlds, but they were collaboratively enacted within the life space of the children. In this enactment, the children appropriated the social stances and discourse acts of others, including adults (Bakhtin, 1986; Vygotsky, 1962; Wertsch, 1991), but they used them in their own social spheres. To let the children themselves introduce this point, consider the following conversation.

Kindergartners Lamar, James, and Tyler are sitting around a table drawing animals that live in shells, when Tyler makes a provocative statement.

TYLER: When we grow up we gonna be tattle tellers, we gonna be—

Tyler's statement may be a slip of the tongue that he is trying to correct ("we <u>not</u> gonna be . . . "), but Lamar reacts quickly.

LAMAR: <u>I</u>'m not gonna be a tattle teller when I grow up.

TYLER: I'm not gonna be a tattle teller either.

LAMAR: You said you were gonna be a tattle teller when you grow up.

JAMES: He <u>is</u> gonna be a tattle teller. Ain't he gonna be a tattle teller? (to Lamar)

. . .

LAMAR: 'Cause you always be telling on people. (to Tyler)

JAMES: Yep. And we tell you (adopting a scolding voice), "Don't tell on people."

LAMAR: I know.

JAMES: And you go and just do it. (sighs)

LAMAR: I know. You just go on and do it. (sighs, shakes head)

Louise, as guide of the official school world, stressed that telling a "grown-up" about a child's rule-breaking could be responsible behavior, a way of taking action to solve a potential problem. However, a tattle tale could have quite a different meaning in the imaginative universe shared by peers. Telling the teacher about a peer's rule-breaking could be a sign of disloyalty and weakness. In fact, most children would agree with Lamar and James about the tattle tale, a part of child lore found in many countries (Opie & Opie, 1959): Peers should not cast each other in the role of the accused in front of an adult audience.

In managing unofficial social worlds, Lamar and his friends, like adults, used talk to organize their social worlds, that is, to articulate who they were relative to others (Goffman, 1974). Thus, in their own talk, Lamar and James collaboratively cast Tyler himself in the role of the accused; Tyler was at once their addressee and their subject, distanced from the peer closeness their own collaborative talk displayed. Moreover, in accomplishing this social work—this relationship building and managing—Lamar and James appropriated the scolding utterances of the adult world, but they used them for their own purposes.

In this chapter, I aim to allow insight into the unofficial social dynamics that undergird the official world and, more specifically to this project, to the dynamics that undergirded the school experiences of Louise's children. To this end, I examine the interactions of Jameel, Lamar, Eugenie, Anthony, and their classmates in unofficial school worlds. I emphasize the kinds of social work the children accomplished through their talk, especially through their use of popular and folk art forms, particularly narratives.[1]

While certain of the children's performative resources were specific to their sociocultural heritage, the existence of unofficial peer social worlds — and the intensive relationship work entailed in those worlds — is not specific to any one cultural group in our society. However, the nature of peer group dynamics in any one classroom is influenced by the divisions and inequities of the larger society; those divisions are particularized in the surface characteristics (e.g., age, sex, race), social attitudes, and cultural behaviors of the children themselves (Ramsey, 1991). Thus, before examining the children's social work in detail, I first elaborate on the complexity of their worlds.

THE COMPLEXITY OF THE CHILDREN'S SOCIAL WORLDS

In exploring the social work of the peer group, I am not entering a homogeneous social world (cf. Corsaro, 1985). In urban classrooms, just as in urban society as a whole, the social work that goes on involves the management of complex social borders. Indeed, as Rosaldo (1989) argues, "contemporary ethnographers look less for homogeneous communities than for border zones . . . in motion" (p. 27). Such zones are often formed around borders of age, gender, race, ethnicity, class, and religion, among other possible differences. Moreover, as Bakhtin (1986) explains, although individuals may share particular ways of using language, rooted in common social experiences and values, no two individuals share exactly the same set of experiences or belong to exactly the same set of social worlds. Dialogue always involves negotiations between differences.

Thus, although I am emphasizing potential social borders of institutional authority (the "peer" world) and of sociocultural background (the "home" world), I am only bringing into relief certain of the complex social borders that figured into the social work — and the language use — of the children. The children used "we" to align themselves in complex and shifting ways; neither they nor their social worlds were easily labeled. For example, in the following conversation, Shawnda, Jameel, and Vera, all African-American first graders, negotiate a complex of borders.

> The three children are working on their stories for the day and, at the same time, talking about a range of issues. At this point, Shawnda brings up her career ambition.
> SHAWNDA: I wanna be a rock singer.
>   JAMEEL: A:h. She gonna have a mohawk. (A "mohawk" is a haircut

style worn especially by teen-age boys; the head is bald except for a strip of hair down the middle of the scalp.)

SHAWNDA: Uh uh.

VERA: (giggles) Uh huh. Every time I look on TV —

JAMEEL: Last time —

SHAWNDA: No. I don't wanna have a mohawk.

VERA: Every time I see on TV a rock star, they be having
    ⎡ a mohawk.

JAMEEL: ⎣ a mohawk. Ba boom.

SHAWNDA: No. I don't wanna be a rock star. I wanna be a singer.

VERA: I know and those boys I know and those boys —

SHAWNDA: You don't know what I'm gonna do to my hair.

VERA: I know and those White boys (giggles), they're having
their hair hang down like girls. (giggles)

SHAWNDA: I know but I'm gonna do it different.
I'm gonna take my brai:ds out of my hair ().
Take my brai:ds out of my hair,
'cause I wear barrettes in there.
And I'm gonna have me some lo:ng hai:r.
Brush it.
Put it in a pony tail.
And WOW! I ().

VERA: I know 'cause grown-ups, grown-ups — grown-ups don't
wear barrettes. (laughs)

SHAWNDA: And I get me a car.
I get me a car.
I get me a car that the hoo:d comes down in the summer.
And I be going down the street going BEEP BEEP.

In the above exchange, Shawnda is working hard to position herself in
social space. She is not going to be a boy rock star with a mohawk. Nor is
she going to be like the White boys, who let their long hair hang down.
She *is* going to be a grown-up, not a child who wears barrettes. Child vs.
adult, female vs. male, Black vs. White; all these social borders figure in
complex ways in her talk, which centers on social signs the children, by
virtue of their common experiences, interpret similarly: mohawks, long
hair hanging down, barrettes, not to mention a car with a hood that
comes down.

These social borders figured in all the focal children's talk; they were
part of the underlying, shared background of experiences, a part of the
texture of their conversations. Indeed, the most explicit verbal negotiations
about such borders involved gender. The boys especially were alert to the

use of "girl words" (e.g., "pretty") and to references to girls as "friends."
Listen to how Lamar's tease about James having a girl friend becomes a
straightforward statement about having friends.

LAMAR: O:: wee! James got a girl friend. (teasing)
JAMES: Not me.
LAMAR: James got a boy — a girl friend.
JAMES: No no.
LAMAR: You got a boy friend too. (said matter of factly)

                       .   .   .

JAMES: Lamar, girls can have girl friends, and boys can have boy
         friends. That's not ma — because they could be <u>friends</u>.

Another social border often discussed was grade level. Grade levels provide the basic organizational structure of elementary schools, as children
well know; and those social borders influence the child privileges that are
allowed or withheld. For example, just before the "rock star" conversation, the three first graders (Jameel, Shawnda, and Vera) had questioned
the fairness of the third-grade overnight camping trip.

SHAWNDA: Is it fair that those third graders always get to go on camp-
           ing trips?
JAMEEL: Every year they go on camping trips.
SHAWNDA: I know. And that ain't fair and Dorine [the school secre-
           tary] say —

                       .   .   .

           And Dorine say first graders and second graders too scared
           to be out in the woo:ds.
VERA: I'm not scared of no woods.
SHAWNDA: And they say they gonna be too frightened about the bears
           and ants and grass and —
VERA: What's so scary about ants?
SHAWNDA: And swimming and fishing and sharks and things.
JAMEEL: I ain't scared of no —
VERA: Sharks are not in no woods. They're in the ocean. (lowers
           voice as Louise is coming) And they're all the way in the
           deep.

Within grade levels, there were proclamations of children's own competence ("I knew it already") and praise or insults of others ("You a first
grader! You should know how to spell *dear*"). But individual children's
academic standing was rarely a matter of peer group talk. Moreover,
children who engaged in academic bragging were reprimanded by other

children ("Do you hafta open your mouth?"; an observation consistent with Dyson, 1989a).

Movement *between* grades, however, was a matter of peer group talk. For example, near the end of the year, first grader Brad, who was struggling with reading, began to meet with a small group of kindergartners for work on spelling patterns. Louise felt Brad was happy to participate with the group; from my point of view, too, he seemed quite content with the arrangement. However, the first graders had their own opinion on this matter.

Jameel, Eugenie, Daisy, Monique, Angie, Austin, Edward J., and Edward G. are sitting around a large table completing a composing activity. As they work, they ask each other about the spelling of one word and then another. Jameel calls their attention to Brad and the kindergartners, who are meeting with Louise in the hall.

JAMEEL: They doing their spelling words. I know it. I know it! I just know it. They doing, they doing their spelling words. I know it! I just know it!

EUGENIE: Easy! (All children are chuckling at the kindergartners.)

JAMEEL: Brad taking kindergarten words! Ah Ah:HA:! Brad gonna lose anyway 'cause he don't even know 'em! He used to be in the class last year and he was the goodest kid. But then this year, he outa here!

General exclamations of "I know!" and "That is so easy!"

AUSTIN: Mat, M-A-T!

EDWARD J: So? I know the easy spelling words too.

Brad by no means became a social outcast; he continued to work and play with his first-grade peers. However, Brad did "lose anyway," in Jameel's sense, since he was not promoted to second grade. Needing help could be negotiated in a face-saving way—but flunking was altogether another matter.

In this book, what matters most is not *explicit* reference to social borders, but the *use* of discourse, especially imaginative worlds of words, to take action amidst them. In the next section, then, I explore how children used narratives to participate in and construct the unofficial neighborhoods of their classroom.

COMPOSING UNOFFICIAL NEIGHBORHOODS

Within the peer group, the major social work of young children is to gain some sense of control and agency (Cook-Gumperz, 1981; Corsaro, 1985; Genishi & DiPaolo, 1982; Goodwin, 1990). While a range of genres figured in this work, for the observed children key social work was accomplished through narrative genres, detailed in Appendix B.

Any narrative allows the speaker to communicate or illustrate information about the world. When socially enacted, though, narratives not only communicate, but they also allow their authors to manipulate or regulate their own identities and those of others. Through their narratives, the observed children worked to (a) establish commonalities, or social cohesion, with others; (b) criticize others or defend themselves from others' criticisms; and (c) take the stage, the interactional spotlight, for an artistic performance. These social goals are not necessarily mutually exclusive.[2]

To accomplish particular social goals, the children adopted particular interactional stances toward others. For example, a "presentational" stance ("Let me tell you about this") accompanied a performance; a "collegial" ("I'll go along with that") or "collaborative" one ("We'll do this together") could indicate a bid for cohesion; a "protestant" one ("You've got no right") suggested a defense against an intrusion. (See Appendix B for a definition of "stances.")

A social stance, though, can only be negotiated, not assumed. That is, when language users position themselves in a certain social place, they also negotiate the positions of others (Goodwin, 1990).[3] Simply talking, for example, assigns people roles as "speakers" and "hearers." In beginning a narrative, a speaker may transform a hearer into a story "character." Speakers require cooperative others who help enact a "participant structure" (Philips, 1972), a framework in which people acknowledge their interactional rights and responsibilities.

Thus, to take social action in their worlds, the observed children required responsive relationships with others. Moreover, to achieve particular relational goals (e.g., social cohesion) with particular others (e.g., the peer group), only certain kinds of texts — only certain experiential and thematic material, discourse styles, and organizational structures — would be appropriate (although there was no one-to-one relationship between a social goal and a kind of text). In Bakhtin's (1986) words:

> When a speaker [or writer] is creating an utterance [a text], . . . the utterance is constructed while taking into account possible responsive reactions, for whose sake, in essence, it is actually created. (p. 94)
>
> Thus addressivity, *the quality of turning to someone*, is a constitutive feature of the utterance; without it the utterance does not and cannot exist. (p. 99; emphasis added)

As the children sat and composed in the official world, they often turned to each other as members of unofficial social worlds. They told each other stories about their experiences in those worlds; that is, the most common experiential source of their narratives was the unofficial social world itself — what children did and said to each other. Other common sources of narratives were vicarious experiences rooted in the popular media (e.g., retelling parts or all of a TV show or movie) or experiences in important community institutions (e.g., retelling religious narratives learned at church).[4]

The children's interest in each other was reflected not only in the sources of their spontaneous narratives but also in the themes of those narratives. Certain themes were powerful enough to be maintained over many episodes. The children would change social roles as a theme was passed along, jostled collegially between participants, or grabbed by one speaker and then another. The coming examples will include many of the themes that gave rise to lengthy conversations of five episodes (i.e., five separate narratives) or more. Among the themes inspiring such storytelling were: the exercise of teacher authority (e.g., narratives of teachers disciplining students); the exercise of personal competence or authority (e.g., narratives of children displaying their toughness); the nature of popular media figures and events (e.g., narratives illustrating their humor or scariness); the nature of encounters with God and the dead (e.g., narratives of what will happen on the day the world ends).

In the following section, I present examples of the children's social work. Given the interactional nature of that work, I organize the presentation according to key participant structures, key ways in which the children interactionally organized themselves vis-à-vis each other. These ways included: *joint constructions*, which served primarily the goal of social cohesion; *presentations with audience co-participation*, which allowed for individual performances as well as the criticism of (or defense from criticism offered by) others; and *inquisitions*, which could serve as an indirect means for criticism and defense.

The examples suggest the children's sociocultural breadth, that is, how their language varied in different social situations. While not necessarily consciously made, the children's genre choices (their choices not only of theme, but also of style and organizational structure), and the discourse traditions that figured into those choices, illustrate their emergent ability to situate themselves amidst the complex unofficial worlds. While the focus is on oral composing, I use the term *story making*, because it paves the way for the subsequent focus on writing.

Collaborative Story Makers:
Joint Constructions/Reconstructions

In the children's worlds, story making was not necessarily an individual production. A child could initiate a narrative by adopting a collaborative stance toward another (or others). If the other was willing, a *joint con-*

struction or reconstruction followed, each child participating relatively equally in reconstructing a recalled event or constructing an imagined one.

In joint story making, the children were not communicating information to an unknowing other but cueing shared meaning. Indeed, the children often acknowledged the story part just told with a "yeah" or an "I know" before offering their own contributions. Beginning those contributions with "and then" or another conjunction helped the evolving story cohere across turns, as did the use of lexical and syntactic repetition and pronominalization (Halliday & Hasan, 1976). Thus, such story making seemed to promote social cohesion, as well as to provide mutual entertainment (for similar observations of older children of diverse backgrounds, see Eder, 1988, and Goodwin, 1990).

Social Cohesion in the Peer World.   In the peer social arena, children often jointly reconstructed stories from the popular media — television shows, rock videos, movies — resulting in *narratives of narratives* (for definition of this text type, see Appendix B). In the following episode, Lamar, James, and Tyler collaboratively reconstruct a Batman movie, replaying funny or engaging moments. While the three boys were close neighborhood friends, Lamar carried on similar conversations with many children in the room. Such story making was especially common among the boys.

> Lamar, James, and Tyler are drawing pictures of a sea shell. James notices that his drawn sea shell is shaped like Batman's cape, which triggers recollection of the Batman movie.
>
> JAMES: (recognizing a Batman cape in his drawing) I'm Batman. Lamar! Look it. I'm Batman.
>
> . . .
>
> TYLER: Remember when he dropped that bottle? The smoke came out, and then he pressed that button, and the arrow went up?
> JAMES: Uh huh.
> TYLER: And then he —
> LAMAR: ⌈ Uh uh. That's not Batman.
> TYLER: ⌊ And then —
> JAMES: And then Batman went like that (dramatizing action). And that thing hooked on very tight, huh? And then Batman said, "Whatever you do, don't let go," huh?
> LAMAR: I'm talking about the part the part the part when he came down and he <u>showed</u> the Joker.
> JAMES: Yeah.

> TYLER: I like that part where he killed the Joker — he's hecka mean.
> LAMAR: I know. He's hecka mean.

"Remember when?" asked Tyler. "Huh?" said James, meaning "Isn't that right?" And, after an initial objection, "I know," responded Lamar. Such affirmations and negotiated recollections of a common experience — in "common" (Willis, 1990) or popular culture — were a way in which children declared and enacted their own social bonds.

The nonexplicit and disjointed nature of such story making did *not* indicate that the children lacked a more explicit register,[5] as observing the children across events readily revealed. Rather it reflected their understanding of the social occasion of joint reconstruction. In the midst of a similar episode about a popular media character (a doll named Chuckie), James turned to Mrs. Johnson and, in a strikingly sweet voice and in Standard English, attempted to define Chuckie for her: "Have you seen *Chuckie*, Mrs. Johnson? (Mrs. Johnson shook her head.) Chuckie is a doll that — " Mrs. Johnson, however, cut him off, as she most certainly had heard quite enough "about this Chuckie."

Another kind of joint story making involved fictional or *"story" narratives* (for definition of this text type, see Appendix B). Such collaborative stories were especially likely to occur when the children were drawing; their pictures could suggest a story character or dramatic dialogue. These stories were sometimes influenced by the popular media, but they also could incorporate official school material. In the following episode, for example, the children were talking as they illustrated their "I-have-a-dream" speeches, dictated in honor of Martin Luther King. The official class discussion of M. L. King may have inspired the collaborative story making — but so did their knowledge of horror movies.

> JAMEEL: I wish Martin Luther King wouldn't have gotten killed. And I would see Martin Luther King here. . . . [omitted data in which children talk about M. L. King as an angel in heaven]
> JULIAN: Once there was a march up in heaven. (The children have been studying the civil rights marches.)
> AUSTIN: Oh God. (laughs)
>
> . . .
>
> Or he could go down back to earth and go to march.
> JULIAN: No. He's dead and everybody would get scared.
> AUSTIN: Oh yeah.
> JAMEEL: He'd go "AH:::!" I'd be scared outa my wits.
> AUSTIN: Oh yeah. Oh yeah.

JAMEEL: He'd be, "We gonna have a march." (uses a zombie voice)
          We're gonna have a march. Oh you dead, come out.
AUSTIN: All the dead come alive.

While this chapter's focus is on children's actions in unofficial worlds, the children did initiate joint constructions in the official world too. In that world also, the playful mood and inclusive spirit of such social encounters seemed to contribute to a sense of comradery.[6] In the following episode, Louise and the children construct a fictional story about a classmate, John. They build on common experiences in the official school world (e.g., adults helping children learn their number words) and on an image found in popular or common culture (the person who "pops out" of a container).

> Louise is sitting with the first graders, who are going to write letters
> to Lynette, an adult assistant who was Ervin's special helper. They
> have been brainstorming ideas for the letters.
>
> LOUISE: How about what we've been learning about another
>   country?
> CHILDREN: HUNGARY!
> Children excitedly talk all at once about learning to count in Hungarian. John, a kindergartner from Hungary, has been teaching them
> the numbers.
> SHAWNDA: Louise! We can write a letter and put the numbers [written in Hungarian] in it.
>
>   . . .
>   I bet she won't even know what it means.
> LOUISE: I bet she wouldn't, 'cause she doesn't know Hungarian.
> HANNAH: Unless we put the number next to it.
> LOUISE: Uh huh, 'cause then she might get an idea—
> BERTO: And send John in the package!
> LOUISE: (chuckles) It'd be pretty hard to send John in the package, don't you think?
> SHAWNDA: We could put him in a big box.
> LOUISE: Uh huh.
> SHAWNDA: And he'll pop out.
> LOUISE: And then he'll say all the numbers in Hungarian!

Social Cohesion Among Community Friends.   The joint constructions discussed above were built upon the common ground provided by popular media or the official curriculum itself. But some kinds of collaborations depended on common experiences with the same children — and common ways of evaluating those experiences. These sorts of collaborations occurred only within the unofficial world the observed children shared with others from their home neighborhood; as will be detailed in Chapter 4, this was a world of more intense friendships.

For example, such collaborations occurred in joint episodes involving *"talking about somebody"* (TA) genres; two children would collaboratively construct a text involving a third, absent party (see Appendix B). In effect, two collaborating peers affirmed their own social cohesion by distancing a third peer, who became a critically portrayed character in their narrative.[7]

Such stories were only to be used when a grievance had been committed, as Shawnda made clear to Eugenie in the following episode; "talking behind someone's back" was not condoned.

> The children are coming back from a walk to Louise's house. Shawnda and Eugenie are walking together behind Lamar. Shawnda tells Lamar to "tie your shoe," which he does, and then Eugenie has some advice to offer.
>
> EUGENIE: Lamar, don't let them [the other boys] pick on you, OK? If somebody hit you, you better hit them back. See, if you just take a stick—
>
> Eugenie interrupts herself, perhaps because Lamar is no longer listening, and turns to Shawnda.
>
> EUGENIE: Let's talk about Lamar. See Lamar—
>
> SHAWNDA: Lamar is my <u>friend</u>, Eugenie. I don't talk about you, do I? So you don't talk about other people.
>
> EUGENIE: Yeah, you do be talking about me. Yeah, when we get in fights and stuff. Yeah, you do be talking about me. That's not a lie, you do.
>
> Shawnda changes the subject by talking about the "fun rides" (e.g., swings, small pedal-driven vehicles) the preschoolers in the bungalows have, compared with the bigger children. (Bungalows are portable classrooms, used for preschoolers and located behind the main school building.)

This topic about grade-level experiences restores social cohesion.

When the children did jointly "talk about somebody," their speech was fast-paced and punctuated with colloquial phrases. In the following example, Eugenie successfully initiates such story making with Monique, whose participation is particularly striking; during official school functions Monique's talk was invariably polite, soft-spoken, and standard in its grammar. Her talk with Eugenie thus reflects the close, comfortable relationships that gave rise to "talk about somebody" genres. The children's talk is composed of two kinds of TA texts—a *routine* (a text conveying a typical sequence of action) and a *narrative of experience* (see Appendix B).

> Eugenie and Monique have been discussing how someone might get
> on your nerves and cause you to worry and become angry.
>
> EUGENIE: I'm talking about, it's this girl. Her name is Jennifer. She
>   asks about everything. No, it's a different Jennifer [than a
>   schoolmate]. She goes to—she in a bungalow.
> MONIQUE: Wo::ah!
> EUGENIE: And she, and she—
> MONIQUE: I know her. She's (stupid).
> EUGENIE: And she—and she—and she wor::ies me a lot. And she
>   make me an::gry!
> MONIQUE: 'Cause you couldn't—I know her. She supposed to be in a
>   bungalow. She goes blah, blah, blah.
> EUGENIE: And she stutters.
> MONIQUE: No, she's real (). She get on my nerves!
> EUGENIE: No, I know! No, she get on my nerves too.
> MONIQUE: I say to (a child's name), "[Let's] stay by ourselves and
>   don't let her (bring that butt in here)."
> EUGENIE: Oh: Wo::ah:!
> MONIQUE: Wo:ah!

Collaborative Episodes: Beyond Narratives.   Although the focus herein is narrative genres, the children jointly constructed other kinds of texts as well. Within the peer world, children sitting together sometimes jointly recited well-known chants (e.g., from commercials), raps, songs, and other kinds of language plays. Indeed, Anthony consistently engaged in such interactions. His generic material was drawn from the children's common culture, although that material was often reflective also of African-American verbal traditions (e.g., raps). In the following example, Anthony draws Celia into an at least partially improvised chant with a distinctly Caribbean beat.

> On this day, the children have hunted for eggs that were unexpectedly hidden in their classroom. They are now drawing and writing their hypotheses about how those eggs got in the classroom. Celia is sitting across from Anthony. Her egg rolls off the table but does not break.

ANTHONY:	(adopting a rhythmic, nasal voice)
	Hey ya Ma ma
	Chick en egg
	Ya ya ya ya
	Ce li a
	Dropped her egg.
	Chick en play dough
	shaking the ba: by.
	Chick en play dough
	shaking the ba: by.
CELIA:	Shaking the ba: by.
ANTHONY:	Oo:: shaking the ba: by
	Oo:: shaking the ba: by
CELIA:	Oo:: ma ma ci ta
ANTHONY:	Oo:: ma ma ci ta
CELIA:	Oo: ma ma ci ta
	Some:: bo dy weep a
ANTHONY & CELIA:	Na na na na na na na na na na (chanted quickly with a staccato beat)

And on they went, ending in alternating cries of "R::umba!" and Louise's distinct directive from the official world, "SH::!" (In observing Anthony, I sometimes felt I was watching a 1940s musical.)

To change the beat considerably, within the social world of the children's sociocultural community joint constructions often involved expositions about religious matters, as in the following example involving Monique and Jameel.

Jameel and Berto have just jointly told a playful narrative of experience about how Edward J. fell in love with Tyler's sister. Monique, who is sitting with them, participated only minimally in that episode. Now, the talk turns to a disagreement between Berto and Jameel about whether or not Jesus is God's son.

MONIQUE:	He really Son. Uh huh. He's the Son. He is.
BERTO:	No he isn't.
MONIQUE:	Well. He's a little—He is our blood. We have only blood, I know.
JAMEEL:	And sometimes it comes out of us.
MONIQUE:	And then it goes back to Jesus.
JAMEEL:	And gets him the blood to grow up up up.
MONIQUE:	And then the babies, it goes into them.

As the above event illustrates, jointly constructed or reconstructed texts, particularly narratives, revealed the sociocultural complexity of these young children's worlds. Monique was not active in the boys' playful discussion of Edward J.'s romantic feelings, but she was intensely involved in the discussion of Jesus — in religious matters, children from Monique's and Jameel's community stuck together. Through texts grounded in shared thematic and experiential material, skilled peers could display and reinforce their sense of social belonging. Moreover, from their respective and unique places in the social world, children could define themselves as complex beings in a world crisscrossed with differences.

In the next section, I turn to a kind of social work that was not so egalitarian in underlying motive and, thus, more prone to display and to give rise to social tensions: the child as a distinctive performer.

Performative Story Makers: Presentations with Co-participation

Unofficial worlds were socially dramatic places, where children worked hard to proclaim their own uniqueness in ways that would gain the respect of the others. Indeed, children sometimes gave presentations whose main purpose seemed to be to perform, to take the stage.

In the *official* classroom world, children sometimes responded to classroom experiences with narratives of their own experiences, told in a relatively nonperformative (i.e., communicative) style. For example, a visit by Daisy's father, a nurse, prompted many such narratives about children's own hospital visits and those of assorted family members. Such stories allowed the children to voice their unique connection to the classroom topic and also allowed Louise to point out connections among the children themselves (e.g., we all get sick and need to be cared for).

In the *unofficial* worlds, though, stories were more dramatic, more performative. In these interactionally dense social arenas (i.e., places with many activities, including many conversations, occurring at once), it could take great effort to gain and maintain conversational dominance, to cast peers in appreciative audience roles.

To gain the audience's appreciation, a language performer relies not only on the lexical meaning of words but on their expressive qualities, their inviting rhythms, their vivid images. If the performer is successful, audience members allow themselves "to be caught up in [the performance]. When this happens, the performer gains a measure of prestige and control over the audience" (Bauman, 1977, pp. 43–44). On the other hand, an audience member may challenge the performance in some way and thereby deny control and withhold respect.

The observed children became co-participants in a peer's performance by providing encouragement through positive "back channel responses" (Yngve, cited in Tannen, 1984), like laughter, repetition of certain dramatic lines, and elaborations of others (e.g., brief dramatizations of what a character in the teller's story might have looked like or said). Requests for elaborations, on the other hand, were more neutral in tone. And requests about the point ("So?"), corrections, and negative back channel responses (e.g., "No!" or "You lie") generally signaled a desire for the performance to stop, as did ignoring the performer.

Sometimes co-participants responded with a related performance of their own, leading to a *round* of narratives, a series of episodes involving texts of the same genre and similar thematic material. Such rounds of stories could serve the goal of social cohesion, as Heller (1992) discusses in her study of a women's writing group. With the observed children, though, the dominant purpose sometimes seemed to be "one-up-manship," that is, to outdo one's peers.

Taking the Stage Among Community Friends. Extended narrative performances occurred primarily among community friends. Making a bid for a dominant place on the social stage involves some vulnerability on the part of the teller; thus such bids may be more likely to occur among children who are frequent companions and who share a common imaginative universe for evaluating performances. This vulnerability was most evident in the observed children's bids to tell "true stories" (see Appendix B).

Literal truth was not the point of these artful narratives; like all narratives that exploit the expressive potential of language, the "truth" of these narratives existed in the evaluative point they made, the quality of human experience they highlighted (Britton, 1992; Bruner, 1986; for a developmental perspective on this point, see Dyson, 1989b). In "true stories," these qualities were most often an ability to face and triumph in the face of adversity in the physical or social world (Heath, 1983; Smitherman, 1986).

Presented true stories were sometimes religious and often humorous; their discourse structure was repetitive and circular, their style, very dramatic. Precisely because these stories were so dramatic, they most clearly displayed the features of African-American oral performance discussed in Chapter 1. In the following example, Lamar performs a story for James and Tyler. Tyler, as will be evident, was not a good audience member; no matter who was performing, he would attempt to take the floor for his own performance before the teller was done. Because of this, in the excerpt Lamar works hard for the desired response from Tyler by repeating his "true" story until he elicits laughter.

Lamar, James, and Tyler have been discussing collaboratively God's actions at the end of the world.

LAMAR: But James, when God comes back to this world, all of us gonna be alive again. For real.

JAMES: But first we gotta die, huh?

LAMAR: Yeah. And then when God comes back we're alive again.

JAMES: When God's son comes back — when God's son comes back we can live for a long time.

. . .

LAMAR: But you can't see God.

TYLER: You can't see him. I know.

LAMAR: He's in the clouds.

TYLER: Yep.

Lamar now takes the floor for a performance.

LAMAR: And once I went up to heaven, when I was sleeping. For real.

TYLER: One time I went up to heaven —

LAMAR: And then — And then I open my eyes and then I was back at home and then I fell right back down on my bed (laughs)

TYLER: One time —

LAMAR: 'cause I thought I was flying.

TYLER: One time —

LAMAR: (dramatizes falling down flapping arms)

TYLER: ⌈ One time —

LAMAR: ⌊ I thought I could fly!

TYLER: One time I was sleeping in my dreams.

. . .

I flew up to heaven. I flew up to heaven

LAMAR: ⌈ I didn't fly up to heaven. When I was sleeping I <u>went</u> up to heaven. (responding to Tyler with reference to his own story)

TYLER: ⌊ And when — And — wait Lamar. Wait Lamar. And when I came back from heaven I fell and bumped my head on my brother's poster. I mean I fell and bumped my head on a needle.

LAMAR: (does not respond to Tyler's story but returns to his own performance) I thought I was flying. So I went like this (very high voice) "I can fly. Ain't this funny? ooooooo" (dramatizes crashing after flapping his arms) (Boys laugh.)

Lamar was a better (more artistically performative) storyteller than Tyler, who tended to imitate other children's stories. However, when Lamar had finished his story, he allowed Tyler the floor for his own "flying" story.

Lamar *then* responded as audience to Tyler, offering supportive elaborations and laughter.

Lamar was successful in taking the floor in the episode excerpted above, but performers were not always positively received. Telling true stories — with their kernel of truth, their exaggeration for dramatic effect — was developmentally and sociolinguistically demanding. For young children, there is a tenuous line between the real and the imaginary, as reported by developmental psychologists (e.g., Piaget & Inhelder, 1969; Werner, 1957; Franklin, 1983), scholars of children's response to stories (e.g., Applebee, 1978), and observant teachers (e.g., Paley, 1980) — a tenuousness that can be attested to by anyone who lives daily with a child. The kindergartners often displayed this tenuousness as they grappled with the relationships between a verbal lie, a verbal mistake, and a verbal imaginary world, for example.

> Tyler said he would make a whale but, actually, he drew a person.
> JAMES: But you say — you told a lie! Because he say he was gonna'
>   make a whale.
> ANTHONY: (to James) You say story not lie! Story.
> LAMAR: Yeah, you know what a story is, James?
> ANITA: You can't call people liars.
> ANTHONY: Don't call people liars 'cause that's not nice.

Moreover, bringing in nonliteral elements or actions demanded careful attention to the mood of one's peers and to the kind of playfulness going on. If the dialogic nature of the ongoing conversation demanded literal truth, one's story could be dismissed as a lie. Such a fate seemed often to befall Tyler. For example, in the midst of a discussion of an aquarium field trip, Tyler brought up the topic of giants.

> ANTHONY: And did you see those big ol', the big huge, the huge ol'
>   fish?
> JAMES: Yes.
> ANTHONY: Gol. Hecka big.
> JESSE: That was hecka, really, really big.[8] That could eat us.
> TYLER: Oh no. A giant could kill it.
>
>   .   .   .
>
> ANTHONY: We're not talking about gi:ants, 'cause giants aren't such a
>   thing as giants.
> JAMES: Yeah, and ghosts is not real.
> ANTHONY: 'Cause why would God make something that would hurt
>   us and tear up this whole wide world? Why, Tyler?

In one incidence, Tyler understood that an event involving true stories was occurring, but his story did not capture the essential quality being displayed. The boys were having a round of stories about facing physical danger without fear. Lamar told about how "when James choked me I didn't even say nothing. I didn't even say, 'stop that, stop that' . . . Come over here and cho—choke me James." Anthony then told about how "one time I was jumping from the slide, and I fell and I cracked my knuckle! . . . And it didn't even hurt!" Tyler told a similar story but one lacking in the punchline about defying pain.

TYLER:	One time I jumped off, one time I jumped off my daddy's roof and broke my head!
JAMES:	So? Your head ain't broke.
LAMAR:	All he does is tell stories.
JAMES:	Ye::p.
TYLER:	No, I don't.
BOYS:	Yeah, you do.
JAMES:	Your head ain't broke!
LAMAR:	He tells stories!
TYLER:	No I don't. No I don't.
LAMAR:	He does. Yes he does. (to James) You tell stories.

Indeed, they all told stories.

Presentations of these complex events involving "true stories" were initiated particularly, but not exclusively, by boys. Shawnda, for example, was a very performative storyteller. She and Jameel had a round of stories in which they told what fate befell their spurned boy friends or girl friends (e.g., being tossed "in the biscuit fire").

Girls and boys often presented narratives of experience that, although more straightforward than "true stories," still involved performative features. In the following example, Eugenie's narrative is quite performative, with its rhythmic delivery, repetition, and expressive sounds. Moreover, her major social purpose seems to be to present herself in a favorable light: She got away with breaking a rule! Monique is a responsive audience, smiling and commenting. Eugenie's narrative performance gave rise to an extended collegial discussion, marked by many narratives and the easy exchange of dominant social roles, about the exercise of teacher authority.

Eugenie and Monique are coloring pictures of dogs to illustrate their "dog" stories.

EUGENIE:	One time I had went to school with some gum in my mouth and I chewed that gum for a lo:ng time.

MONIQUE: I chewed it too after school.

EUGENIE: I chewed that gum for a lo:ng time in my mouth. And that — and I was upset Louise gonna get me 'cause I had gum in my mouth, and I () kept on chewing it. Nobody noticed. . . . [omitted talk on need for a particular crayon]

Ah huh. Ha ha ha o::h! I'm lucky I didn't get in trouble.

After a bit, Monique tells her own chewing gum episode.

MONIQUE: Louise didn't say nothing [to me either]! Louise is *so:* nice!

Coloring seemed to be, for all Louise's children, a kind of "rocking-on-the-front-porch" activity, to use a rural metaphor — a relaxing activity that generated much casual chat, including many stories.

Taking the Stage in the Peer World.   Although most extended performances occurred among community friends, the focal children did take the stage in the unofficial peer world. As discussed above, Anthony was a frequent performer of rhymes and chants. Others typically joined in on his performances, however; he seldom occupied center stage alone.

Jameel's performances, on the other hand, were designed primarily to spotlight him. (His performances in classroom worlds will be discussed at length in Chapters 5 and 6.) During the latter half of his first-grade year, Jameel often used playful language and actions to amuse his peers. Monique, Shawnda, Celia, Brett, Austin, and Daisy all served as responsive and appreciative audience members for his efforts. On the other hand, Hannah and Angie were often exasperated by his playfulness, which exasperation often seemed only to fuel his performance. As the episode excerpted below illustrates, Jameel was successful at gaining interactional control, even if his audience was less than enthusiastic.

Jameel and Angie are sitting at a table, completing a worksheet about rhyming words. Jameel's purple color rolls off the table, an event that provides him with a set-up for a joke.

JAMEEL: Where'd my purple go? It disappeared from out of space. I knew there were aliens.

ANGIE: Jameel. (exasperated)

JAMEEL: It was a joke. It was a joke. (back to dramatic voice) I shoulda known [there were aliens].

ANGIE: Why don't you look on the floor? (deadpan)

JAMEEL: If I'm not seeing things, it [the color] should be on the floor. (bends down and looks on floor) Nope, an alien. I

> shoulda known. There was an alien from outa space come
> into our planet. (large sigh from Angie) Them bad little
> aliens.

Telling jokes, reciting raps, narrating dramatic stories were all ways of
assuming interactional control over others in a playful way. Such performances involved the risk of rejection, but they also potentially offered the
respectful attention and responsive participation of others.

Voicing a Protest in Unofficial Worlds.   The observed children sometimes
presented narratives not primarily to perform, but to criticize others or to
defend themselves from others' criticism. These presentations typically
involved *confronting somebody* genres (see Appendix B). Lamar and his
friends especially told such narratives, perhaps because they were consistent playmates and had many opportunities for disagreements.

In these episodes, similar to disputes described among older boys by
Goodwin (1990), the teller casts an audience member as a character in his
or her narrative, a character who errs in some way. Such stories sometimes
evolved into rounds of counter-accusations; in the following episode, however, James does not respond in kind to Lamar's confrontation but, rather,
accepts his friend's criticism. Tyler, who is listening, works to establish
social cohesion with Lamar by joining in and contributing the moral, as it
were, of Lamar's story.

> Lamar, James, and Tyler are discussing the fact that there would be
> no sweets for lunch today.
>
> LAMAR: We not getting no sweets today. We getting some sandwich.
> TYLER: Oh::.
> LAMAR: No sweets.
> TYLER: No sweets today.
> JAMES: Lamar, but—
> LAMAR: And don't cry 'cause I—see, remember yesterday you hit me
> with that plant?
> JAMES: Yeah.
> LAMAR: Because I wouldn't give you none of my fruit snack.
> JAMES: Yeah.
> LAMAR: 'Cause I forgot. I <u>forgot</u>! James, you couldn't just slap me
> with that plant.
> TYLER: Lamar, 'cause you can't hit nobody.

All focal children and their friends expected each other to share equally
special foods. Lamar excused his own failure to share ("I forgot!") and
criticized James for his deliberate offense ("you couldn't just slap me . . . ").

While Eugenie and her friends most often directly confronted younger children, rather than each other, Eugenie presented a striking exception to this one day when she confronted Hannah. In my view, Louise's, and the children's, Hannah was a child who had a tendency to whine under stress. On this day, the children were composing, a situation that Hannah found particularly stressful, since she had great difficulty spelling. Hannah was sitting at a table next to Eugenie and, next to Eugenie, Vera. As the children worked, Eugenie, who was left-handed, inadvertently bumped Hannah with her elbow, making Hannah "mess up" her paper. Hannah began to complain tearfully and, to retaliate, bumped Eugenie's elbow. Whereupon Eugenie delivered a very fast-paced, rhythmic performance that left Hannah seemingly stunned and Vera in stitches.

EUGENIE: You ate my mama my daddy my sister my brother my
          granny granny goose and I don't care.
          'Cause you don't hurt me and I don't care if you do.
          'Cause if you do girl your head too is gonna snap off like
          a cracker jack.

Scholars of African-American verbal art might refer to Eugenie's performance as an example of signifying or "talking negatively about somebody through stunning and clever verbal put downs" (Smitherman, 1986, p. 82). A child skilled in such play might defend him- or herself by trying to top Eugenie (as in the related playing of the "dozens" or trading of insults about someone's mother, in fun or in anger). Hannah, however, was completely silenced, giving Eugenie great satisfaction, or so suggested her smile.

In sum, through narrative presentations, the focal children managed complex social relationships, taking the floor for artful performances or for effective social management. Artful presentations in particular illustrated the vulnerability of the performer, who puts forward not simply a text, but the self. A positive or negative reaction from the audience is a response to that self, a granting or withholding of respect. The meaning of a particular reaction, though, is not necessarily the same for performer and audience. Hannah may not have meant her silence to signal respect, but Eugenie may so have interpreted it. Similarly, although Angie did not seem to appreciate Jameel's joke, she did not ignore him and, moreover, she offered responses he could play with — gain control of.

In the next section, I consider episodes in which a child exploited the vulnerability of story makers and their desire for control and social respect. While not as common as collaborations and presentations, the discussed episodes dramatically revealed the sociocultural intelligence of the focal children, their implicit knowledge of the social work entailed in story making.

The Controlled Story Maker: Inquisitions

Narratives were primarily a way of taking or sharing control, of shaping a symbolic world in which the children themselves were in control. This controlling story maker contrasts sharply with the controlled story maker now discussed. In these episodes, narrative meaning was not shared among child participants or presented in a deliberate way by a child teller. Rather, the teller responded to a series of questions by the addressee, who became a sort of inquisitor, demanding specific information for his or her own purposes. And the dominant purpose seemed to be social regulation.

The inquisitor typically initiated the episode by indirectly criticizing the teller, thereby forcing that teller to defend him- or herself by telling an unflattering story. These episodes were thus a way of taking control of someone not regarded as a superior. In the following example, James seems to begin the inquisition simply to tease Anthony; taking the lead from Mrs. Johnson, who inadvertently set the stage for the episode, James asks a deceptively direct question designed to highlight Anthony's tendency to suck his thumb: "That's why you sucking your *thu:mb*?" James may extend the exchange out of curiosity, but he is clearly undeterred by Anthony's reluctance.

Anthony is sucking his thumb as he draws. Mrs. Johnson, the instructional assistant, asks Anthony if he has sugar on his thumb, to which James replies that Anthony is always sucking his thumb.

ANTHONY: Something happened when I was a baby.

MRS. J.: Oh, I see.

JAMES: That's why you sucking your <u>thu:mb</u>? (sings last word in a teasing way)

ANTHONY: Something happened to my <u>mom</u> when I was a baby, not me. (with finality)

MRS. J.: Mm:. OK. (Mrs. J. begins attending to another child.)

JAMES: What happened? What happened, Anthony?

ANTHONY: None of your beeswax.

JAMES: What?

ANTHONY: None of your beeswax.

JAMES: She die?

ANTHONY: No!

JAMES: She pass?

ANTHONY: No.

JAMES:	She had a heart attack?
ANTHONY:	No. <u>My mother didn't die.</u> (very firmly)
JAMES:	Well, what then?
ANTHONY:	When I was born something happened bad. They gave her kinds of drugs. *Go:lly.* (irritated with James)
JAMES:	Why they gave her that?
ANTHONY:	I don't know, 'kay <u>James?</u> (still irritated)
JAMES:	Drugs'll kill you, huh? Different kinds a drugs. Not all drugs'll kill you, huh?
ANTHONY:	No, they didn't smoke cigarettes, or some beer or cocaine. It was some other drugs.
JAMES:	Dope?

The conversation continues until Anthony quite firmly says, "Not those kinds of drugs." However, as soon as this episode ends, Anthony retaliates by dragging a story out of James. His inquisition begins with the question: "Why do you like to go pee on your mat? Golly."

The above episode was unusually long. James's response to Anthony's inquisition was more typical. After a quite explicit attempt to explain his "accident," he deflected Anthony by telling a narrative in which he was the competent older brother of a baby sister who "*always*" wets his mother and father, a funny story, from Anthony's and James's points of view.

THE SOCIOCENTRIC CHILD AT WORK AND PLAY

Tizard and Hughes's (1984) remarks about the British 4-year-old girls they observed seem perfectly suitable as well for the closing section of this chapter.

> Interest in other people — both children and adults — was a characteristic feature of most of the children in the study and manifested itself in many different topics: their friends, other members of the family, growing up, birth, illness and death, what people did for their living and so on. . . . It is sometimes supposed that children of this age have special, childish interests, mainly to do with mothers, babies, dolls, teddies, and animals, and such a view would be reinforced by most of the picture books published for children of this age. The conversations in our study suggest that, on the contrary, all human experience was grist to their intellectual mill. (p. 128)

And so it was with the children in Louise's classrooms. They not only talked about unofficial social worlds, however; they actively constructed them. The children were not egocentric communicators incapable of anticipating an audience's needs and reactions (Piaget & Inhelder, 1969); rather, the children were able to act in socially sophisticated ways, based on their understanding of the "human sense" of these familiar social arenas (Donaldson, 1978, p. 17). "Why do you like to go pee on your mat?" said Anthony, a masterful social manipulation from one kindergartner to another.

Through such actions, the children positioned themselves within different kinds of social relationships, drawing on different kinds of textual material, different sorts of cultural resources. Their oral texts emerged from a distinctly sociocultural process: Certain kinds of textual sense evolved amidst certain kinds of responsive relationships with other people. Stories told to perform for an appreciative audience were different in substance and in appropriate response from those told to enlist the collaborative efforts of one's peers, which were different from those told to satisfy a persistent inquisitor (see Table 3.1).

This chapter has not exhausted the social work of the children; for example, in future chapters focal children will be depicted assuming the role of teacher and, using a communicative style, delivering expositions or describing routine happenings to needy friends. However, the major work accomplished through the children's narratives was not explicit teaching but establishing social linkages, marking their own distinctiveness, and defending their honor, often in playful, humorous ways.

As the children carried on their social work in unofficial worlds, they

TABLE 3.1.   Key Participation Structures of Child Narrative Use

Structure	Sample Genre	Dominant Purpose	Addressee Role	Text "Sense"
Joint construction	NN	Social cohesion	Involved collaborator	Shared
Presentation with co-participation	TSTR	Artful performance	Appreciative audience	Artful
Inquisition	EXP	Social regulation	Inquisitor	Explicit

Note: This is not intended as a comprehensive chart; it is intended to illustrate the contextualized meaning of words like "audience" and "sense."

also engaged in activities in the official school world. The children's initial efforts in one important activity, the crafting of written texts, was strongly influenced by the children's social work in unofficial worlds. The children's writing did not initially have the functional power of their talk, nor was it in any simplistic way similar to that talk. But the children were writing as they sat among their peers; gradually, as in a previous project (Dyson, 1989a), the children's writing would become an important tool for official and unofficial action. Their written texts became tools for social action — not the action of experienced adult composers, but the action of experienced participants in children's worlds.

Indeed, at the end of the year, as a small group of first graders looked back at the writing they had done throughout the year, they remembered with uncanny accuracy the social life that had surrounded the production of varied products.

EUGENIE: (finds her illustrated dog story in an old writing folder and remarks to Vera) See, mine's [my drawn doggie] is a girl. Me and Monique made the same.

. . .

BRAD: Ah. This is when I was copying offa Shawnda [i.e., trying to draw what Shawnda was drawing]!

Eugenie and Vera laugh.

VERA: [How about] the one where he was trying to copy offa Eugenie!

BRAD: I don't have that one.

. . .

VERA: Me and Shawnda did this one together.

EUGENIE: Remember this one when I made — Vera, with Shawnda?

VERA: Yes. Uh huh.

In the next chapter, then, I focus on the four focal children in Louise's K/1 both as social players *and* as beginning crafters of written words.

CHAPTER 4

THE CASE STUDY CHILDREN
Social Actors and Literacy Users

The chief problem presented by the sheer phenomenon of aesthetic force, in whatever form and in result of whatever skill it may come, is how to place it within the other modes of social activity, how to incorporate it into the texture of a particular pattern of life. . . . [This problem gives rise to talk] about how it is used, who owns it, when it is performed, who performs or makes it, what roles it plays in this or that activity. . . . To study an art form is to explore a sensibility [and] such a sensibility is essentially a collective formation [and its foundations] are as wide as social existence and as deep. . . .
— Clifford Geertz, *Local Knowledge*, 1983, pp. 97–99

The "chief problem" that writing presented to Lamar, Anthony, Eugenie, and Jameel was "how to place it within the other modes of social activity, how to incorporate it into the texture of a particular pattern of life." The children approached this "problem" as distinctive, contributing classroom members. Their unique social places influenced and, in turn, were influenced by their emerging control of written language, particularly their use of written language for creating symbolic worlds of words. Thus, understanding their writing development in school begins with understanding the "texture of a particular pattern of life" and, more particularly, with gaining insight into each child's social work in the classroom.

In this chapter, I allow Lamar, Anthony, Eugenie, and Jameel center stage, introducing each in turn as a social member of the intersecting unofficial and official classroom worlds. As part of this introduction, I describe each child's initial use of writing during the opening four months of school. As a backdrop for those introductions, though, I first discuss the theoretical links between children's social work and their literacy learning efforts in school.

THE SOCIAL WORK AND SYMBOLIC TOOLS
OF CHILD COMPOSERS

As illustrated in Chapter 3, the children's social places in classroom worlds were negotiated, at least in part, through their discourse — through the themes, structures, and styles of their story making and language play; their oral texts drew upon both popular (e.g., pop songs) and folk genres (e.g., "true stories"). The children's writing, too, would come to reflect their diverse cultural resources, but not in any simple or straightforward way. That is, the children did not simply begin to write the sorts of stories, chants, and songs they told, recited, and sang. In learning to write, children make use of their entire symbolic repertoires, not simply their ways of talking (Dyson, 1989a, 1991; Gundlach, 1982; McLane & McNamee, 1990; Vygotsky, 1978).

In fact, young children's school social lives are enacted primarily through symbolic media that are direct, rather than "second order" — through symbols that rely not only on the sounds of their own voices, but also on the movement of their own bodies, the lines and curves drawn with their own hands. Initially print may simply be an interesting object to investigate or a useful prop for dramatic play. Children may explore the physical nature of letter shapes and page arrangements as print-like forms are sprawled across a page; given an interested other, children may "read" or invent a hidden message (Clay, 1975). Or children may enact writing's functional possibilities in the adult world as telephone messages are taken, grocery lists made, and newspapers produced in their dramatic play (Morrow & Rand, 1991; Schickedanz, 1978); their messages are not precisely encoded but swiftly indexed through marks and swirls.

When children first begin to use written language to symbolize their ideas, print may continue in a supplemental role. For example, they may write stories by "symbol weaving" (Dyson, 1986), by intertwining written words with talk and drawing (see also Harste, Woodward, & Burke, 1984; Newkirk, 1987).[1] Their written words may be words in, rather than the essential stuff of, their symbolic worlds. That is, the words may be labels for drawn objects or perhaps the sounds of drawn and dramatized events (e.g., BOOM) or of pictured characters (e.g., "NO!"). The children's major functional work — the representing of meaning, the expression of an attitude toward the world, the engaging of another person — happens through other media, not through writing.

Thus, children's writing cannot be studied separately from their talk and drawing; to separate media is to separate *form, sensibility,* and *social existence,* to use Geertz's terms; that is, it is to destroy the integrity of children's symbolic worlds — and the possibility of understanding a critical aspect of development (i.e., how children differentiate writing from other kinds of symbol making). Moreover, children compose — organize — such multimedia worlds to accomplish important social work; thus, their composing must itself be examined within specific activities or events involving participants, goals, and specific actions and values.

The central importance of activity to the development of a symbol system — and of a symbol system to the enactment of human activity — was a critical theme of Vygotsky (1962, 1978), whose sociohistorical approach to development has influenced current scholars (e.g., Bruner, 1986, 1990; Ochs, 1988; Rogoff, 1990; Scribner & Cole, 1981; Wertsch, 1985, 1991). In his view, children acquire symbolic knowledge and skill as they assume varied social roles and engage in valued cultural activities. For example, children acquire oral language as they use speech to act in the social world; the acquisition of linguistic knowledge and the acquisition of social knowledge are inextricably linked.

Vygotskian scholars have illuminated the importance of social activity to children's development as symbol users, including as writers — but they have not attended to the specifics of writing, to craft. Bakhtin (1981, 1986) provided just such attention. In his view, speakers and writers learn to linguistically enact varied social roles by listening and responding to the voices of others. In assuming new roles, composers use those already spoken utterances as working material. That is, to accomplish certain kinds of social work, they select words "from *other utterances* . . . that are kindred . . . in genre, that is, in theme, composition, or style" (Bakhtin, 1986, p. 87). Thus, child writers do not simply learn to draw speech, as Vygotsky (1978) emphasized; they learn to craft voices: Guided by a history of past conversations, the child responds to the present social situation by drawing words on paper. Those words give voice to the child's intentions — but they are used words, linked to other voices in the child's worlds.

The four K/1 children were just beginning to control the slow, deliberate process of writing. Their written words, if any, were embedded in talk and, usually, pictures. Still, they used certain experiential and thematic material, structured in some way, and infused with a particular style, to achieve a particular relational goal. That is, the children's graphic composing, like their oral composing, was a sociocultural process that reflected their complex worlds. It is the beginnings of their entry, through writing, into the school literacy dialogue that I illustrate in this chapter.

BEGINNING PORTRAITS

In introducing Lamar, Anthony, Jameel, and Eugenie, I concentrate on the daily open-ended composing time. As illustrated in Chapter 2, under Louise's guidance the children wrote for many different purposes; as a class, they composed lists, charts, letters, and recipes. But, in the beginning of the year, what seemed most important to Louise, as to many early childhood teachers, was that the children use whatever resources they had to begin writing in whatever way was comfortable for them. Louise made suggestions (e.g., writing labels, descriptions, wordless picture books, chapter books, and so on), and kept options in front of them by helping them name their daily efforts, but her curriculum was permeable—it allowed space for children to define their own agendas, their own goals.

For each K/1 focal child in turn, then, I typify the nature of their social stances in classroom worlds and also the nature of their official composing during the opening months of school. By the end of November, the children seemed to be distinctive social actors on classroom stages. However, major changes in their social actions and particularly in their composing were to come. Thus, the presented portraits provide an orientation for the stories in the chapters ahead of how the children changed. As I move from Lamar, the first child to enter the spotlight, to Jameel, the last, I will simultaneously move from their use of writing primarily as a supplement to symbolic activity to the use of writing as an important mediator of school life.

Lamar: A Collaborative and Collegial Social Actor

"Biggest thing about Lamar is his head," or so remarked Ayesha, the third-grade focal child. Lamar *was* short, even for a kindergartner, but he was sturdily built and walked with a kind of definiteness. He wore a silver earring in one ear and had a neat "flat top" haircut. Four years and eight months old at the beginning of the study, Lamar lived with his brother Lamont, his cousin Mona (like Lamont, a second grader), and his parents, who divorced during his kindergarten year.

From Lamont, Lamar said, he had learned about animals, from prehistoric dinosaurs to present-day birds, from tiny ants to huge whales. A former student of Louise's, Lamont gave Lamar previews of all study units. Lamar knew about the "biggest whale," the "strongest dinosaur," animals that could regenerate appendages, that are blind, and on and on. Lamar's knowledge of and interest in animals figured not only into his factual discussions but also into his fictional stories in both official and unofficial spheres.

In all classroom encounters, Lamar's most pervasive characteristic as student, peer, and friend was his social responsiveness, the ease with which he responded to and incorporated others. In the following sections, I illustrate this quality as I discuss his social stances and language use in official and unofficial worlds.

A Cooperative Literacy Learner.   Lamar's older brother was a very good student, and Lamar also wanted to do well. Lamar sometimes "got in trouble," as the children say, from attending to peers in rug-time meetings, rather than to Louise. But, most of the time, he was attentive and quiet on the rug and cooperative in small group activities.

In the beginning of the year, Lamar mainly listened during many literacy activities, including the joint reading of rhythmic picture books, discussions about the spellings of words for social studies and science charts, and brainstorming pictures to draw for one page or another of the alphabet book (e.g., *B* words for the "B" page, *L* words for the "L" page). He did not venture forth with suggestions — at first. He seemed, mainly, to be paying attention, getting a sense of what was required here. He knew about half of the alphabet letters but did not display a clear grasp of the alphabetic principle. When composing, he sometimes named one letter ("[I'm gonna make a] *C*") but actually made a different one. Nonetheless, given brief sentences whose precise wording he knew, Lamar could work to match exactly voice and print (Clay, 1979, 1991; Ferreiro, 1978); that is, he had some sense of spoken and written word units.

During composing time, Lamar explored lines, colors, and shapes, trying to draw something that was recognizable. When asked about his efforts, he willingly supplied a caption or narrative focused on action: "A seal was in the ocean and the daddy seal had to go get him." "The seal was capturing spiders." "The colors came and the colors went away." Similarly, Lamar wrote the letters of his name and made letter-like forms, which he would sometimes read, if asked: "[This says] The seals were gone."

Figure 4.1 presents an early composition. It contains both letter-like forms and the representational use of drawing and writing: Lamar drew a sun, a rainbow, and flying insects, and wrote letter-like forms and his name (upper right-hand corner).

A Collegial Peer.   Like all the focal children, Lamar interacted with children outside his network of close friends, primarily during school tasks that allowed for informal peer talk and, thereby, for the intersection of official and unofficial work. The daily composing time offered just such tasks: While Lamar drew and wrote, he also talked with his peers. During the early part of the year, Lamar's social life primarily surrounded his graphic composing; he seldom engaged others through the discursive *substance* of his efforts (i.e., through the themes, styles, or organizational structures of told, drawn, or dictated stories). But Lamar did construct the *procedures* of composing time in collegial, even collaborative, ways.

For example, in an early assigned writing activity, the children cut out

FIGURE 4.1. Lamar's Early Composing

magazine pictures for their own "topic" or "all about" books. Sitting with Austin at a two-person table, Lamar looked through magazines for pictures of dogs, his chosen topic — *and* for pictures of cars for Austin's book. Austin had not asked Lamar to do so, nor did he look for dogs for Lamar. Lamar constructed his activity to include Austin matter-of-factly ("Here's another car for you") and consistently. On another occasion, when first grader Brad admired a fly he had drawn, Lamar adopted a helpful and collaborative stance toward the older boy.

LAMAR: Make a circle. (Brad does so.) You did it! (with enthusiasm) I'll make it [another circle] up here. You put the wings on it.
BRAD: Right here?
LAMAR: No, in the back. (Together, the two boys complete the drawing.)

I have portrayed Lamar as a cooperative student and a collegial peer, which he was. However, Lamar's social stances were more varied, his language resources much richer, and he himself much more complex than this. Lamar's sociocultural breadth, and the richness of his social and cultural resources, was most evident in the social life he constructed through talk with neighborhood friends.

A Collaborative Friend.   Lamar's collaborative and collegial stances were enacted dramatically in his story making with close friends: James (his best friend), Anthony, and Tyler. Readers might recall Lamar's collaborative narrative about the movie "Batman" and the rounds of "true stories" about flying up to heaven and about defying physical danger (presented in Chapter 3). Lamar not only initiated stories with ease, but he also served as a responsive audience for others. For example, one day Anthony told Louise about the fate of his grandparents' little dog, who once ate a cigarette.

> ANTHONY: She won't grow 'cause she ate a cigarette.
> LOUISE: Mm::. That's amazing.
> Louise turns to talk to another child. However, Lamar, sitting by Anthony, responds.
> LAMAR: Dog can't grow, he out here, "I wish I was a *big* dog like my brother."

Lamar thus offered a performative elaboration, co-participating in his friend's narrative.

Although he was collegial and collaborative, Lamar was also a social leader who could assume positions of relatively higher status. For example, he offered help to apparently needy friends.

> James is threatening Tyler but, unfortunately, he is stuttering as he does so.
> JAMES: Me me me and Lamar — we gonna follow you outside.
> LAMAR: "Me me me." Take your time, James.
> JAMES: Me me me.
> LAMAR: Take your time.
> JAMES: (slowly and in a quiet voice) Me and Lamar are going to walk you outside. Wherever you go we gonna follow you and see what you doing.
> LAMAR: Yeah. (Lamar now aligns himself with James.)

Lamar also closely monitored the social activity of his friends, recalling typical routines and offering commentaries and critiques. Most of the time, his analyses were accepted. (Readers might recall the confronting somebody narrative, in which Lamar chastised James for hitting.) Moreover, his approval was regularly sought ("Isn't that right, Lamar?"). But, sometimes, his friends did protest, as James does in the following event excerpt; Lamar's response displays his own social and language sophistication.

> James, once again, has arrived late for school. Lamar announces his
> late arrival to the class, which is meeting on the rug. James glares at
> him, upset that Lamar has "called" him late. Lamar defends himself.
> LAMAR: I ain't calling you late. I'm just telling you late.
> JAMES: I know I'm late.
> LAMAR: I know you're late too.

"I'm not criticizing you, my friend," Lamar seemed to say, "I'm just presenting the facts."

In addition to his ongoing social work with his male kindergarten friends, Lamar often interacted playfully with the older girls from his neighborhood, particularly Vera, whom he liked ("looked at," as Vera put it). In addition, he was the willing recipient of help from Shawnda and, less often, Eugenie, who made sure his shoes were tied, his nose was wiped, and his body was where it was supposed to be.

Lamar's intense social work with his friends, especially his collaborative and collegial story making, contributed to the transformation of his composing behavior, particularly his drawing, into an important mediational tool in the kindergarten. However, as will be illustrated in Chapter 7, the social stances that seemed to support Lamar's academic "success" in the kindergarten also seemed to contribute to his academic "failure" in the first grade.

Anthony: A Collaborative Player and a Social Critic

"Can you make him stop saying that?" complained a giggling James to Mrs. Johnson, "'Cause he making me laugh." A master of language play, Anthony was indeed one who could make them laugh. His keen sense of language play, however, was combined with a propensity for social criticism, for making them defensive, as it were.

Anthony was taller than Lamar but thinner, a wisp of a child with cropped hair and a big lopsided grin. Five years and four months old at the beginning of the project, Anthony had a soft, quiet voice — which he could easily turn into a high-pitched shrill when he felt no one was listening to him. He lived with his mother, but he spent long stretches of time with his grandparents in Utah. He sometimes told his friends stories of the dogs, raccoons, and ducks on his grandparents' place, which may be where he first acquired an interest in nature, an interest he shared with Lamar.

The time spent in Utah may also have contributed to Anthony's relatively less intense involvement with neighborhood friends. Anthony did not, for example, construct narratives designed to confront or talk about his peers, as Lamar, Eugenie, and, eventually, Jameel did. Because Anthony was less involved in classroom social work, his experiences were less theoretically informative, and he will be in the background of the chapters to come.

Nonetheless, Anthony's easy play with language, seemingly rooted in African-American verbal traditions and in those of popular child culture, contributed to my focus on children's artful discourse. Indeed, the earliest demonstration of Anthony's powers came in reaction to my own inadvertent request for a performance. Unsure of Anthony's sense of voice/text match, I asked him to "play" around with writing with me, a researcher ploy that Anthony took quite sincerely. I wrote out a sentence on a piece of paper ("The baby dropped the bottle"), read it, and asked Anthony to reread. Moving his hand back and forth over the print, Anthony read:

> The baby dropped the bottle
> And the baby said
> Oh what a honey honey thing I did
> Ding a ding, ding a ding.

"Huh?" I said, and Anthony gave me another verse:

> The baby said
> Wah wah wah
> Get me a noth er
> clean ol bot tle
> That's what you need
> for you and me.

Such playful exchanges were common in Anthony's case, as was the serious assertion of his own sense of competence and control. In the sections to follow, I detail Anthony's participation in official and unofficial classroom worlds.

A Presentational Student.   One day, as Louise held up a book about birds, Tyler yelled out, "HOW COME IT HAS A LONG TAIL?" Anthony leaned over, tapped him on the shoulder, said "Shhhh," and sat up very straight. However, in the midst of another bird book, Anthony joined other children in pretending to fly as Louise's head was turned to the book. When Louise looked back at the class, everyone had stopped flying—except for Anthony, who sat there grinning at his peers and flapping his wings, all by himself. This seemed to be the way with Anthony. He had an enormous desire to be competent, a respected student, although at times his enjoyment of peer play conflicted with that goal.

In official class discussions, Anthony often made brief presentations, offering commentaries or questions, always with a seriousness of purpose—even though the more experienced first graders did not always take them seriously. During an oceans study unit, for example, Anthony told a straightforward narrative of experience about "a little baby starfish" that came out of the drainer when he was in the tub, a story that left Shawnda in stitches (to Anthony's distress).

In literacy activities, Anthony was attentive and, before the end of the fall semester, he joined in on rhythmic readings of books and poetry. He had a good ear for the music of language, as should already be evident. He was participatory as well in the kindergarten alphabet book activities; he, like Lamar, knew about half the alphabet letters but displayed no evident sound/symbol knowledge.

Also like Lamar, Anthony primarily explored drawing and writing at the beginning of the year. As suggested by Figure 4.2, he drew familiar shapes—"humans," suns, and fish—and manipulated letters, especially letters from his full name (which included not only A but also M and R). Unlike Lamar, however, Anthony did not invent narratives for his pictures and letters but straightforwardly gave them labels (*shark, snake, D*). He clearly aimed to do "nice work" and presented his efforts in a positive light to Louise (e.g., "My picture's gonna be nice").

A Performative but Critical Peer. Anthony had many playful interactions, not only with neighborhood friends, but also with Jesse, Sonya, and Celia, who enjoyed his jokes and language plays. Many of these drew on popular culture, for example, Batman rhymes, Knock knock jokes, and popular songs. (Readers may recall Anthony and Celia collaboratively constructing the "mamacita" chant. [See Chapter 3.])

In the peer group as a whole, though, Anthony tended to adopt a critical stance toward others' social behavior. (This especially irritated the first graders, who "know more than you," as Eugenie pointed out.) Anthony protested for children he felt were being mistreated. He stood up for first grader Brad, whose temper tantrums made some children laugh ("That's not funny, you guys," Anthony would say, adopting Louise's voice). He watched out for kindergartner Ervin, who had cerebral palsy and, as a result, great difficulty handling a marker. When other children would tell

FIGURE 4.2.   Anthony's Early Composing

Ervin where to draw his lines, Anthony would proclaim Ervin's competence: "Don't tell him what to do! . . . He knows!" And he defended
Anita, a kindergartner who joined the class in January and did not initially
have any friends: "Don't tease her, you guys!"

As in Lamar's case, Anthony's interactions in unofficial worlds seldom
involved the substantive (e.g., thematic) material of his compositions.
However, products themselves were important props, things to declare his
own competence. Anthony viewed any comment on his work that was
potentially critical as an insult, as "not nice," and said so. His defense of
Ervin, in fact, centered primarily on protecting him from other children's
comments about the uncontrolled nature of his marks.

A Collaborative Player.   Anthony adopted the presentational and critical
stances discussed above with neighborhood friends. In the midst of collaborative discussions of God or nature, Anthony would present what he
viewed as important facts.

"God can make the wind pick up this whole world, huh?" commented
James one day.

"That's called a hurricane," responded Anthony.

Moreover, Anthony's comments about the competence of his products — and his rejection of any criticism as impolite — were useful social material for his friends. Tyler, his closest classroom friend, often used Anthony's declarations about his work as opportunities to work for social cohesion.

> Louise is circulating as the children compose.
> ANTHONY: (to Louise as she walks by) My picture's gonna be nice.
> LOUISE: Sure is nice.
> TYLER: I know. Anthony is my best friend. I play with him in the big yard [the older children's playground]. I always do.

On the other hand, Anthony's propensity for social criticism often led to counter-accusations and social unrest. Anthony played regularly with his neighborhood friends, and they knew well that he himself was not always "nice." The attentive Lamar, for example, pointed out that Anthony was "the nastiest one." With his quickness for rhyme, Anthony could turn innocent alphabet book activities into scatological or "bathroom" humor, much enjoyed by young children. Lamar's "nasty" comment suggests the children's awareness that Anthony was no perfect child by adult standards. Further, James noted that Anthony, who often screamed at others "don't hit," would hit children on the playground who "messed" with him. It's hard to take the moral high ground with those who know one well.

Lamar, James, and Tyler did not react to Anthony's comments only with angry or serious rebuttals, though. In fact, their responses could lead to extended, playful episodes. "Be qui:et, be qui:et!" sang Anthony to a loud James. "Be si:lent, be si:lent!" sang James right back. Indeed, the most pervasive social stance Anthony adopted outside official circles was a collaborative one involving jokes, language plays, songs, and raps; he also sometimes took the floor for a performance of the same. His language plays could thus serve a range of social work, from presentations of self in a way that captured others' attention and respect, to playful exchanges of insults and counter-accusations, to social cohesion as a group enacted a well-known chant or collaboratively built a rhythmic exchange.

When Mrs. Johnson, for example, complained that her back hurt, Anthony performatively recited this rhyme for his table partners:

Then go home
Mama moan.
Then go home
some and moan.

In the following example, Lamar joined in on Anthony's play with the identity of his mother, but Anthony got the upper hand quickly.

> Lamar and Anthony are playfully threatening to beat each other up. Lynette, an adult assistant, calls out to them from another table.
>
> LYNETTE: Anthony, how you doing over there?
>
> ANTHONY: (in a sweet voice) Fi::ne I a:m::. Ma ma Mama. A::H!
>
> LAMAR: (laughs) Oh! There's your mama right there. (pointing to Lynette)
>
> ANTHONY: Where — There's your mommy right there. (pointing to the door; Anthony was almost taken in by Lamar but caught himself and returned the play)
>
> LAMAR: Uh uh. (grinning)
>
> ANTHONY: Uh huh. For real. Ain't his mommy right there? (to me) Yeah. Yeah. O:::! Look! Bye! Bye! Bye! There she goes.
>
> LAMAR: Stop! (amused)
>
> ANTHONY: O::! That was fresh. (He's commenting with satisfaction on his own play.)

As with Lamar, Anthony's breadth of social work and language use, from communicative narratives to performative language plays, was most evident when he was viewed across complex classroom social arenas. Moreover, Anthony revealed a link between respect for self and respect for one's compositions, a link that will become more evident as I turn the spotlight on the two key first-grade children: Eugenie and Jameel.

Eugenie: A Collegial Child in Need

"Shucks," said Shawnda to Eugenie, "I erased that whole row [of writing] and I'm doing it over. (Eugenie giggles.) I don't care if it is recess time. I'm gonna do it over and I might do it over 10,000 times. I mean that."

"O::, I know how you feel, gir::l!" responded Eugenie with great conviction. "I KNOW, HOW, YOU, FEEL!"

This brief exchange, from March of her first-grade year, was hard won for Eugenie. Eugenie worked to achieve social connections with others, connections rooted in shared personal experiences and feelings: "I KNOW, HOW, YOU, FEEL!"

Eugenie's out-of-school life was itself rooted in webs of relationships. A tall, strong child with a sweet smile, Eugenie was 6 years and 7 months old at the project's beginning. She lived with her mother, who, near the end of the school year, gave Eugenie a baby brother. Eugenie and her mother sometimes stayed with her grandfather, and she also had aunts and neighbors she knew well. Eugenie not only knew by first name the parents of children in her neighborhood, but she remembered as well the names of every mother and father who visited the classroom. Collegial connections to adults and children were important to her.

In her efforts to establish collegial relations, the daily composing time was initially a source of both great satisfaction and great frustration, as I detail in the sections below. As in the opening portraits of Lamar and Anthony, I begin with the official school arena and add unofficial layers. But, with Eugenie, this organizational pattern will have much fuzzier boundaries, as the generic material of the official composing activity figured in important ways into unofficial social work.

Conflicting Stances in the Official World. In the official world of teacher-led activities and monitored tasks, Eugenie was both a collegial student, who often presented her efforts with pride, and a needy student, who presented her work with self-depreciating comments.

Eugenie went beyond being cooperative to seeking apparently collegial, mutually responsive relationships with Louise. In all teacher-led activities, large group or small, Eugenie tended to fill Louise's pauses with responsive comments.

"I looked at your writing books last night," said Louise.

"Did you look at mine?" asked Eugenie.

"And Eugenie wrote a long story about things she liked," responded Louise, directing herself to the class as a whole.

"We have new writing books with lined paper!" announced Louise next.

"But what if you want to use the markers and they might go through!" responded Eugenie, collegially generalizing her own speech to include the generalized "you" of all class members.

In small group sessions on reading, Eugenie's collegiality, her desire to verbally signal her involvement, her willing attentiveness, was again evident, as was her sensitivity to human relationships. Early in the year, Eugenie read primarily by relying on her strong auditory memory, inventing or skipping what she could not remember. She needed much teacher support to tackle the text, to reread to decipher unknown parts through context and attention to graphic cues. Despite her initial difficulties, she was an active and eager participant in reading groups, perhaps sustained by her enjoyment of reading group talk. As illustrated in Chapter 2, Eugenie made many unsolicited comments, particularly, evaluative comments about the characters in her stories (e.g., she remarked about the little rabbit who believed the fox was a frog, "A frog go ribbet, ribbet. He might tell the difference from a frog. . . . They [mamas] could tell the difference 'cause they grown, but the child is not grown").

In the opening months of school, Eugenie's compositions were primarily "art notes" (Dyson, 1989a), texts that expressed her positive feelings about her pictures (e.g., ILVH [I like this house]). She did, however, write an expressive piece directed to Shawnda:

Shawnda
i LOVEYOU
ILIPUSNF
[I(I) like (LI) to play(P) with you(U) Shawnda(S) It(N)'s fun(F).]

Eugenie drew primarily houses and little girls. However, she never simply made a girl but made girls with intricately patterned dresses. She never simply drew a house but made houses with striped doors and multi-colored roofs. As she said "I always make such beautiful things." She presented her drawings with pride to Louise.

Unlike drawing, writing, particularly spelling, was initially quite difficult for Eugenie. She worked laboriously to sound out words. As suggested by the examples above, she did not initially spell alphabetically but listened for letter names as she slowly pronounced words. When reading, Eugenie had a good sense of "word-space-word" matching (i.e., that each oral word should be matched with a written one [Clay, 1991]); since she did not necessarily represent every spoken word in her writing—only those words in which she heard letter names—she frequently became muddled when rereading her work. In the midst of such muddles, she would adopt a needy stance toward Louise and other adults. "I don't know how to do it," she would tearfully complain, a comment that almost inevitably led to a "Sure you do" and helpful guidance.[2]

And, indeed, early in the year, Louise's explicit help seemed to ease Eugenie's entry into the complex encoding process, as did Eugenie's superb memory for words she had frequently read or discussed in afternoon word study sessions. In the illustrative interaction in Table 4.1, Louise calls Eugenie's attention to the distinction between a letter name and a sound; the interaction occurred as Eugenie wrote a caption for the picture in Figure 4.3.

An Appreciative, Helpful Peer.   Eugenie interacted with peers beyond her close network of friends primarily in overlapping unofficial and official worlds. With her peers, Eugenie's major social work involved regulating others, but in much more positive ways than the critical Anthony. Within the network of peers, Eugenie aimed to be a supportive, helpful person.

For example, despite her own difficulties with spelling, she did not adopt a needy stance toward *peers*. Rather, she took advantage of opportunities to help others with their own encoding. Her strong memory allowed her to do so, even as she was grappling with the nature of the system. In the midst of her own struggles to encode "My house is so pretty" (MHESP), she helped others correctly spell *like, me,* and *the.* Sometimes she did so when children did not need help, which they unfailingly told her ("I know").

To further illustrate, during the morning sharing time on the rug, Eugenie made collegial, appreciative comments about shared work, just as Louise did. "That's a good story," she said after Lamar's piece was shared. "Them is pretty," she told Peter, whose work followed. Drawing, then, was a useful object for both eliciting and offering compliments.

As was evident in Chapter 3, Eugenie would stick up for herself if she felt someone was not treating her fairly, as in her performative teasing of Hannah ("You ate my mama my daddy my sister my brother my granny granny goose . . . "). Her typical stance, however, was to be a helpful, appreciative person. Her needy stance was directed primarily to Louise and other adult helpers, not to peers.

Searching for Social Cohesion. As with Lamar and Anthony, Eugenie's most intensive social work occurred among close neighborhood friends: Monique, Vera, and Shawnda. She worked to establish and maintain strong social ties with them, as she engaged in joint reconstructions of narratives, sometimes focused on particular children (the "talking about somebody" genres), and rounds of narratives, in which she and her friends shared similar experiences.

Moreover, from the beginning of the year, Eugenie sought collegial, even collaborative, relationships in doing tasks with her friends. "*We* have to put *our* names," she commented to Vera, after she noticed that her own name was not on her paper. However, such relationships were problematic with Shawnda, the peer she most admired, but one who did not treat her as an equal. The more confident Shawnda treated Eugenie in the same helpful way as she did other peers, but she would not allow Eugenie to help her back. Moreover, she expected appreciative comments from Eugenie but did not return them.

Eugenie and the children are completing their "topic books." Although it is October, Eugenie's is about toys and candy and other "Christmas things." Shawnda's is also about toys, primarily dolls, but she does not call hers a "Christmas book." Shawnda wants to see Eu-

TABLE 4.1.　Eugenie's "My House" Event

Eugenie's Text	Composing Code*	Comment
		Eugenie is writing an art note for her picture of a house. She has remembered the spelling of "like" and, with Louise's help, sounded out me ["my"] has ["house"]. She continues as Louise watches:
M	OV	"My"
H	OV	"House"
E	OV	"is"
S	OV	"so"
P	OV	"pretty"
	RR	"is so pretty I like my house" (rereading first line)
		. . .
B	OV	"Be"
	OV	/k/ [cause]
		. . .
C		
E	OV	"it"
	OV	"is"
	IS-T	Eugenie:　Another E?
		Louise:　Think about it.
		Eugenie:　/i/ /i/ S-N
		Louise:　Eugenie, what makes this sound: /i/?
		Eugenie:　I
		Louise:　And what letter makes the sound /s/?
		Eugenie:　S?　Z?

Eugenie's Text Composing Code*	Comment
	Louise: I-S. S̲ makes that Z̲ sound too. Now try i̲t̲. /i/
	Eugenie: I̲
	Louise: i:t̲
	Eugenie: T̲ (smiles)

---

*D̲i̲a̲l̲o̲g̲u̲e̲: IS-T-- interruption solicited from teacher.
M̲o̲n̲o̲l̲o̲g̲u̲e̲: OV--overt language; RR--reread.

genie's. She is not sitting with Eugenie, and so she loudly calls across the room, "Eugenie, let me see yours." Eugenie gets up, walks over, and shows Shawnda her book. Shawnda is not appreciative.

SHAWNDA: Christmas is way back, baby. You got to do something dif-
           ferent. Okay? Next time you do a book like this, you got to
           do a different one. Sure is, Christmas is WAY back.

Eugenie does not respond but takes her book back to her seat. She just sits down, and Shawnda gets her attention again.

SHAWNDA: Eugenie, look at this dressing gown. Eugenie, look at this
           dressing gown. Look at this. (Eugenie is writing in her
           book and not moving.) Eugenie, you better see this dress.
           Eugenie, you better get over here and look at this book.
           I'm gonna () you. (Eugenie gets up and goes over and
           looks at her book.)

Shawnda also playfully insulted Eugenie's work, which Eugenie accepted with good humor and, moreover, without offering a rebuttal or counter-attack. For example, one day Eugenie commented that she was making "Frog and Toad's" house, a decision influenced by Lobel's (1970) book. Shawnda commented, "That house is burnt and wasted." Eugenie just chuckled.

Not only did Shawnda insult Eugenie's products, she also did not respond to Eugenie's efforts to gain appreciation. Eugenie worked hard for compliments, which she greatly valued. However, Eugenie and her friends did not value "bragging." So, to get the longed for appreciation,

FIGURE 4.3. Eugenie's House with Doors

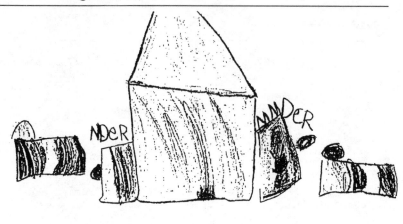

Eugenie would make self-depreciating comments about her pictures; the appropriate response was to offer a compliment. (This strategy is similar to the one Eugenie used in the official world to gain supportive comments from Louise.) Shawnda, however, did not respond appropriately. On the other hand, Daisy, who was not a close friend but who was a very responsive child, always did. Indeed, Eugenie's first acts of defiance or protest to Shawnda came after just such responsive comments from Daisy, as illustrated in the following event excerpt.

> Eugenie is sitting with Shawnda and Vera, drawing Frog and Toad by their house. Her two friends get up to use the restroom. While they are gone, Daisy sits down.
>
> EUGENIE: Don't laugh at my frog. I can't make my frog any good. And people laugh at that. I'm making Frog and Toad.
>
> DAISY: It's cute.
>
> EUGENIE: Thank you.

Shawnda now returns.

SHAWNDA: Vera was working here, Daisy. Vera was working here,
           Daisy. She's coming back.
EUGENIE: (to Daisy) Get a chair and put it here [right next to me].
SHAWNDA: There's only supposed to be three people.
EUGENIE: So?
SHAWNDA: Vera is working here. So shoo, turkey, shoo.
(Eugenie moves over and makes room for Daisy, who brings over a
chair from another table and sits down. [Score 1 for Eugenie.]) . . .
EUGENIE: I can't make my frog any good. And people laughing at it.
           My frog. (Nobody is laughing at Eugenie's frog.)
SHAWNDA: I'll draw you a frog, Eugenie.
EUGENIE: NO::::. Not nobody mess up my picture.[3]

In addition to being a useful prop for eliciting compliments, Eugenie's
drawing was beginning to serve as a useful *mediator* of social relationships. That is, the substantive material of the drawings (e.g., their thematic content) could be deliberately manipulated for social ends, particularly for social cohesion. In the following exchange, Vera casts both herself
and Eugenie as central figures in her drawing about their experiences in
Farm and Garden. Moreover, Eugenie is as much collaborator in, as audience for, Vera's composing, as she tells Vera both that she would like to
be in her picture and how she would like to appear.

Eugenie and Vera are sitting side-by-side. Eugenie is drawing a picture of her mother's house, Vera a picture of Farm and Garden,
where both girls spent time this morning.

EUGENIE: Vera, you gonna make me in the picture?
   VERA: I'm doing the hair.
EUGENIE: You make my hair different colors? (Eugenie's talking
           about her barrettes.)
   VERA: That's all my hair. This is pretty. You're gonna be prettier
           than me. (Notice how Vera softens her self-complimentary
           remark.)

           Look how I made me.
EUGENIE: O::. That's cute.
   VERA: Want you to look like that?
EUGENIE: Yeah.
   VERA: Oh.

           That's you in Farm and Garden.

Later, when Vera's piece was shared on the classroom rug, it entered into a more complex network of social regulation. "That's me and Vera," said Eugenie with pleasure.

"EUGENIE!" whispered Shawnda very loudly to Vera, "Why didn't you put me?"

Eugenie seemed intent on Vera's picture and gave no sign of having heard Shawnda's comment, but Vera just shrugged.

As already noted, early in the year Eugenie's writing was not itself a major tool for social interaction with peers and friends, although appearing competent — at least as competent as others in encoding her own messages — was important to her. (The one exception was her written declaration of affection for Shawnda.) However, the "Farm and Garden" event illustrates the complex social work that multimedia composing could do, both in its enactment with friends and on the classroom stage. Moreover, Shawnda's reaction previews the complex and unofficial social work that official written composing can accomplish; by third grade, written texts could assume the social complexity of oral "talking about somebody" genres.

As will be seen in Chapter 7, Eugenie's involvement in the network of friends and her simultaneous desire to be a competent, helpful peer and a collegial, attended-to student fueled her progress in the first grade. But, similar to Lamar's case, her unofficial social work also allows some insight into her academic difficulties in the second grade.

Jameel: A Joyful Performer

"Jameel should be a songwriter," commented Monique one day, "'cause he writes songs." Moreover, as Monique also pointed out, "Jameel is good." Such respect for his performative powers, given late in the year, was a major social goal for Jameel.

Early in the school year, though, Jameel was not a person with close or particularly positive connections with peers or classroom friends. Still, from early in the year, Jameel did make evident his performative powers — not in his unofficial and oral story making, but in his official and multimedia composing, where he gave voice to his own ideas by borrowing, by crafting, the voices of others.

When Jameel arrived at school each morning, however, he seemed anything but a lively performer. A long-legged, thin child, Jameel began most days quiet, thumb in mouth. Six years and five months old at the project's beginning, Jameel and his mother were homeless, and early in the year they lived at the Salvation Army Shelter. Midyear, they stayed with a cousin in a neighboring city, and then, near the end of the year, they moved to the home of a friend within that same city. School bus transportation was provided only for children within the attendance zone. So, for much of the year, Jameel began each day with a long city bus ride to within a few blocks of the school, got himself off, and, if it was a lucky day for him, met up with Louise as she walked to school. Sometimes he arrived too late for school breakfast. As the other children gathered on the rug, he'd sit at the back table, and Mrs. Johnson would fix him and anybody else needing breakfast a bite to eat. (Louise had a refrigerator and a large sink right in her classroom.)

Jameel seemed to gradually wake up each morning in the midst of opening songs and routines. He'd sway in time to the music, although, with his thumb firmly in his mouth, singing was out of the question. By the end of the morning opening, however, he found it difficult to sit still. In his words, "I'm not used to sitting down . . . I just gotta jump up. I end up popping up." That "popping up" was particularly noticeable during the morning composing time, when Jameel's performative powers were dramatically displayed.

A Student Both Serious and Playful. Jameel typically paid attention during whole class activities on the rug. He could become completely mesmerized by a storybook, but he was equally mesmerized by the social and physical world around him. "Did you know I was into science?" he asked me one day. His manner was often serious, his language style communicative, his stance generally cooperative, sometimes intensely inquisitive. During a discussion of early Native American customs, Jameel repeatedly questioned Louise until he understood the idea behind animal-hide rugs.

> Louise has been talking with the children about how Native Americans traditionally used animal fur for blankets and rugs.
> JAMEEL: How did they cut it off? But how did they cut the fur off?
>   (Notice how Jameel himself makes his own question explicit.)
>   JAMES: But if you cut it off, how do you get it back together to get a blanket?
> JAMEEL: But it's not enough. But it's not enough, except for a baby.

Jameel was typically attentive but quiet in small group reading activities. Like Eugenie, early in the year he relied primarily on memory to read trade books and his literature reader; however, he worked hard to match voice and print, particularly in sections with repeated verses, using both orthographic and context cues to correct errors in matching. This seemed to be his preferred way (and, ultimately, a very successful way) of learning to read; he asked a young adult helper one day, after she had been directing him to sound out each word, "Can you read it to me all in one good sentence?"

The depth of Jameel's intellectual involvement in both science and story came into view only when he took center position on the classroom stage. It was as performer, not as collaborator or colleague, that Jameel's intellectual and language powers were seen in their fullest.

During class composing periods, Jameel constructed a social stage for his performances by casting Louise in the role of major audience. Jameel did not ask for help during composing. He wrote standing up, and when he thought of a particularly funny idea, he would "pop up" and run off to find Louise. Early in the year, she was an unfailingly appreciative audience, one who laughed heartily at his texts.

Jameel's writing reflected his enormous enjoyment of pattern books and other kinds of literature with rhythm and rhyme, like the Dr. Seuss books, the poems of Shel Silverstein (1974) — even linguistic readers (textbooks that gradually introduce phonic patterns), which he labeled "joke books" and considered enormously funny. Jameel used known written words, words copied from the board or from a book, and words whose spelling he could "sound" out to create a variety of constructions — wordless picture books, rhythmic chants (e.g., "cats man cats man cats man"), stories composed largely of dialogue, and jokes (e.g., "What do you get when you get cat? You get the bat with the cat" — and, indeed, in Jameel's "joke books" one does find cats that, for the sake of phonogram practice, have bats).

Jameel's texts thus contained stylistic features of rhythm and rhyme, structural ones of dialogic, question/answer sequences, and thematic ones of talking animals and clever "tricks," or jokes played by one character on another. Written stories, however, were not the only sources of these features. Some of the generic "stuff" of Jameel's composing clearly came from the popular media and, particularly in its performative language and presentational stance, some came from his folk traditions as well. Jameel's "Circle Man" story provides a good illustration.

The story was actually dramatized orally and drawn; only spoken chants and dialogue were written, as was his usual procedure. Inspired by a shape bulletin board, Jameel drew a ship of "shape" aliens landing on the planet Mars. (See Figure 4.4, Figure 4.5.) Table 4.2 illustrates how, becoming quite playful, he broke into performance as he wrote this story.

During the next composing period, Jameel continued in this performative style. He transformed the "I can. Can you?" monologue of the pattern

FIGURE 4.4. Jameel's Shape Aliens Approaching Mars (Swirls in Background Represent Mars)

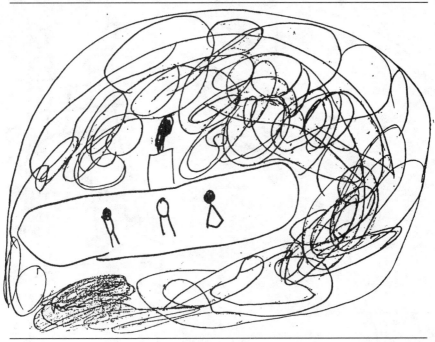

books and linguistic readers into a dialogue among the shape people (*I can see circle man. So CAN I. HP HP [Help Help]*). He even transformed his own dramatic story into a joke, claiming that the giant "didn't really eat Circle Man. It was a joke. And Circle Man wasn't even a man. He was a girl (laughs)." In the last part of the story, Jameel has Circle Man yell out "Mama Mama Mama," explaining, "Circle . . . he love to talk. He run his mouth real good."

Thus, Jameel constructed his text from a myriad of voices, transforming math bulletin boards into space aliens, men into girls, stories to jokes, and patterns from beginning reading books into the dialogue of space aliens. The world became unglued and then glued back together in interesting ways by a child who himself "run[s] his mouth real good," a phrase reminiscent of Abrahams's (1972) descriptor of highly respected African-American "men-of-words" (p. 215). Further, Jameel's use of chants and repetitive phrases allowed for a fluent performance in which he was in control.

FIGURE 4.5.   Jameel's Giant Attacking Circle Man

A Coexistent, at Times Protesting, Peer.   In the midst of his Circle Man story, Jameel remarked to Louise, "O::! I'm so anxious to read." From the beginning of the project, Jameel greatly looked forward to and valued the daily sharing time, when he, like Louise, could read stories to the class — *his* stories. His peers would become his audience when he took over on the classroom stage.

However, during composing itself, Jameel often seemed to simply coexist with his peers. On rare occasions he offered spellings to children or chatted about what they were trying to draw. But most often, as Berto noted, "Jameel always wanta be by himself." He enjoyed having his own space at a work table, his own packet of (school) markers, his own scissors, paste, and tape — and he worried that others were not following classroom rules, not allowing him his turn, his place, his things.

Jameel was not at all a competitive child — indeed, as will be illustrated in Chapters 5 and 6, he appreciated the artful productions of other children. But he was a watchful child. (Perhaps being homeless contributed to Jameel's wariness about his turf.) For example, one day, as he complained that a small group of children were not giving him his turn in a board game, Anthony told him firmly: "You got it wrong, Man. You can't force people to do things you want them to do." Jameel soon left the group and began working a puzzle by himself on the rug. Tyler accidentally tripped over his legs, and Jameel immediately reacted angrily, punching Tyler until Louise pulled him away.

A Presentational and Collegial Child Friend to Adults.   Jameel initially seemed to prefer the company of adults to that of other children; he sought out teachers outside his classroom as friends with whom he could visit. In time, Jameel also became a friend of mine, someone he enjoyed presenting his reading and writing to, but also someone he could be quite considerate of. Once when he was explaining to me how thrilled he was to be going to a pizza party at someone's home, he stopped himself and commented in a sweet voice, "I wish you could come but I don't think you're invited."

Among the adults outside the classroom whom he visited were the school music teacher and the reading resource teacher (who did not work with first graders but who visited all classrooms and had struck up a friendship with Jameel). One day he asked the reading teacher if she was friends with the music teacher, since "you both let people visit and you're both White." (The reading teacher was actually biracial.)

Jameel's question suggests his own awareness that most (but by no means all) close friendships in his school were among children who were of the same race. As already discussed herein and in Chapter 3, Eugenie,

TABLE 4.2.   Jameel's "Circle Man" Event

Jameel's Product	Jameel's Interaction*	Comment
WS circle [Once circle] LAPT ON MUA [landed on Mars]		Jameel writes ws, copies circle from the math bulletin board, and, with Louise's help, sounds out "landed on Mars."
	L: Now tell me what happened when the space ship landed.	
		After Louise leaves, Jameel draws a square, a triangle, and a circle with faces ("shape aliens") and two small trees.
	J: It was a sma:ll world. It was a sma:ll world that they landed in. It was a sma:ll world they was in. It was small. Belie:ve me. 'Cause you can see little trees.	Jameel now adopts a performative style in presenting his world (e.g., note the repetition and vowel elongation).
circle		Jameel draws a giant and then rushes off to tell Louise that a giant will soon eat Circle Man. When he returns, he draws a conversational bubble next to the giant and writes circle. (See Figure 4.5.)
	J: He yelling out "Circle" cause he picked Circle up. He yelling, "CIRCLE, CIRCLE, CIRCLE."	Jameel begins talking excitedly, taking the role of the giant.

Jameel's Product	Jameel's Interaction*	Comment
	(voice change) "OH GOD! He ate Circle! . . . Yes, he's eaten Circle Man. OH NO! He ate Circle Man. OH GOD! O::H!"	Jameel now takes the role of a shape space alien who has witnessed the eating of Circle Man.
He ut circle		Jameel begins to write: As if he can't quite contain himself, he rushes off to tell Louise that Circle Man has been eaten! She responds with suitable amazement and encourages him to return to his seat to finish the sentence, which he does.
man	"EE:OW! He' ate Circle Man." (laughs) "He ate Circle Man. So he ate Circle Man."	Jameel begins dancing around the table, continuing the performance. [During tomorrow's composing period, "Circle Man" will become "Circle Dudt [Dude]."
ho nos [Who knows] so ho nos		Jameel now writes again. He sounds out "Who knows, so who knows," and then rereads the repetitive text in a suspenseful voice. Next comes a chant:
circle man circle man circle man		He rereads his text in a rhythmic way.

*L: Louise's speech; J: Jameel's speech.

Anthony, Lamar, and their neighborhood friends shared particular genres (e.g., true stories, kinds of language plays, narratives dependent on close relationships, like confronting somebody and "talking about somebody" genres) and topics (e.g., religion). Jameel had access to these conversations; that is, the children assumed his inclusion in such language events. Initially, though, Jameel was seldom responsive.

In time, his relationships with both his teacher and his peers would change. To guide his writing, Louise would have to negotiate new roles beyond audience; moreover, his peers would themselves come to serve roles as playful colleagues and trusted confidants. All of these social changes were mediated in explicit ways by the use of literacy, as will be seen in the next two chapters.

ON CHILD COMPOSING AS SOCIAL WORK

As discussed in this chapter's opening, the child's emerging control of any symbol system is simultaneously the child's increasingly active participation in a cultural dialogue, for symbol systems contain a people's way of organizing and responding to experience. Thus, the development of written language is dependent on social interaction and inextricably linked to cultural membership, that is, to an "imaginative universe within which their acts are signs," to again use Geertz's (1973, p. 13) phrase.

However, as also discussed, the development of the written medium does not proceed in a linear way. Children learn to "mean" (Halliday, 1977) — to fulfill certain kinds of intentions or functions — through particular forms that will later be served by other media. Gestures, spoken words, drawn pictures may all be used in ways that foreshadow the use of the distinct symbolic medium of written language. And so it was with Lamar, Anthony, Eugenie, and Jameel. Their early writing efforts were surrounded by and interwoven with other media.

As the children participated in the culturally complex social arenas of the classroom, they learned how the written medium itself could accomplish valuable social ends. Within culturally valued and child sensible activities, they observed others use the written medium and, moreover, began to use it themselves, eliciting the social responses of others to their own efforts. In such ways, they began to understand the possible relationships to others and to reality that can be enacted through manipulating the elements (and thereby the words) of written language.

However, the children's composing and their resulting products could reverberate differentially in classroom worlds. Their social ends — their attempts to establish social connections, to regulate their social worlds, and to take the interactional stage—could both support and make problematic their entry into the official literacy dialogue (the communication chain of child writing and official response). In effect, the children had to do more than differentiate the functional limitations and possibilities of writing—they had to negotiate the diverse imaginative universes in which their efforts were interpreted.

In Chapters 5 through 7, I focus on the social work and writing use of Jameel, Eugenie, and Lamar. Each child was a distinctive individual whose composing drew in complex ways on diverse cultural resources. Collectively, however, they illustrate (a) the richness and diversity of children's cultural resources for learning to compose, (b) the social processes inherent in such learning—that is, the differentiation and negotiation among sociocultural worlds entailed in learning to compose in school, and (c) the ways in which teachers and peers support or constrain children's learning. In brief, I look in detail at each child's efforts to incorporate writing "into the texture of a particular pattern of life" (Geertz, 1983, p. 97).

CHAPTER 5

JAMEEL

Staking a Claim on the Official
Literacy Curriculum

That life is complicated is a fact of great analytic importance. . . . Such acknowledgement complicates the supposed purity of gender, race, voice, boundary; it allows us to acknowledge the utility of such categorizations for certain purposes and the necessity of their breakdown on other occasions. It complicates definitions in its shift, in its expansion and contraction according to circumstance, in its room for the possibility of creatively mated taxonomies and their widely unpredictable offspring.

— Patricia Williams, *The Alchemy of Race and Rights*, 1991, pp. 10–11

From the very beginning of the year, Jameel was a child who defied any simplistic ways of defining boundaries, of putting separate boxes around supposed distinctions between the "oral" and the "literate," the "popular," the "folk," and the "literary." Indeed even his own aspirations suggested "creatively mated taxonomies and their widely unpredictable offspring": Among many ambitions, he hoped to be a "singing scientist" when he grew up.

As discussed in Chapter 1, images of cultural bridges from home to school seem inadequate for understanding children's, including Jameel's, challenges and triumphs in school, for there are no neat boundaries between home ways with words and school ways. Nor does the supposed boundary between "oral" and "literate" styles make clear their efforts. In Jameel's "Circle Man" story, the composing example described in Chapter 4, circles and triangles sprouted feet and commandeered space vehicles. As Circle Man was attacked by a giant, his comrades recited a pattern inspired by beginning reading books ("I can see Circle Man. So can I"), and then Circle Man himself "ran his mouth real good." Jameel intermingled voices from diverse social arenas as he constructed a graphic product of oral dialogue to perform on the classroom stage.

Jameel's approach to language and story revealed an oft-cited quality of childhood—its joyful irreverence. Indeed, many child observers— teachers, parents, and researchers—have described this playful spirit, which seems related to one Bakhtin found in the Renaissance carnival. A carnival was a time when people wore language like a mask, freely using the words of monks and poets, scholars and knights. In this way, wrote Bakhtin, people entered into the "free laughing aspect of the world with its unfinished and open character, with the joy of change and of renewal" (Clark & Holquist, 1984, p. 301). The street songs, anecdotes, and sayings, the parodies of the language of the elite, all suggested a freedom from cultural hegemony, a celebration of the world's variety and its capacity for surprise and for "violat[ing] natural boundaries" (Clark & Holquist, 1984, p. 304). Carnivals were a time, in Williams's (1991) words, for "wildly unpredictable offspring" (p. 11).

Children too are boundary crossers. The master early childhood teacher Vivian Paley (1986a) writes of her children at play, "Themes from fairy tales and television cartoons mixed easily with social commentary and private fantasies . . . [to form] a familiar and comfortable world" (p. 124) for them (see also Garvey, 1990 [especially Chapter 6]; Jenkins, 1988; Opie & Opie, 1959). Children seem to "attune," to assume or spontane- ously construct links between texts adults might consider generically very different, including texts from different social arenas. Readers may recall, for example, Jameel's assumption that linguistic readers were joke books.

And yet, the spontaneous alchemy of childhood composing takes place amidst potential classroom social borders (see Figure I.1). As children participate in the complex worlds of school, they may learn new ways of relating to others through language—new "genres" (Bakhtin, 1986). In the process, as genre themes, styles, and compositional structures figure in different ways into their relationships with others, children also learn about the diverse social values accorded cultural material.

Jameel's case will introduce the social processes through which children differentiate and negotiate among these intersecting social worlds. By ex- amining how he used varied kinds of language art forms and traditions to participate in varied social spheres, I illustrate that these social processes go beyond the mere differentiation of contexts in which different ways of using language belong. Rather, they involve crossing boundaries and intermingling texts in ways that bring together official and unofficial worlds, supporting children's efforts to be "at home" at school. In effect, these social processes yield an "intertext," as the literary theorists would say, a reverberation of connections.

Thus, in analyzing Jameel's experiences, as with all the focal children's experiences, I emphasize not only his ways of participating in events—his social stance toward teacher and peers, the mood of the events, the kinds of oral and written texts he deliberately formed—but also his ways of linking events. By studying the ways in which his evolving texts were generically linked through theme, style, or structure to texts produced in other events, both official and unofficial, I aimed to understand something of how children become "subjectively located in language and culture" (Meek, 1988, p. 35). Against a landscape of shifting social boundaries (Figure I.1), Jameel positioned himself amidst the breadth of possible relationships; at the same time, his public words—his used signs—linked that present historical moment to past ones in the depth of sociocultural space and time (Figure 5.1).

As Jameel's case unfolds, his ways of using diverse cultural resources to

FIGURE 5.1.   Composing as a Sociocultural Process: Its Horizontal and Vertical Dimensions (Breadth and Depth)

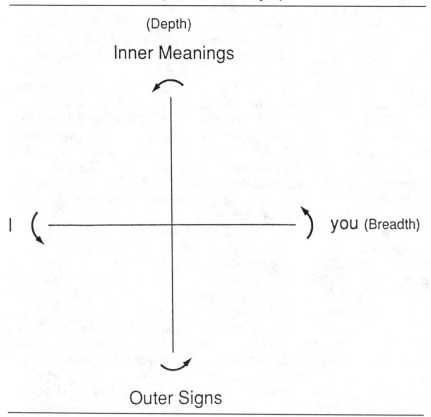

negotiate important classroom boundaries will seem increasingly deliberate. The nature of his official classroom community, with its emphasis on naming and connecting, may have provided "scientific" concepts (Vygotsky, 1962) — labels for kinds of texts and their parts — for discussing his own "spontaneous" use of diverse texts. Thus, while Jameel will be in the foreground in this and the foregoing chapters, in the background will be his interactive partners — Louise, his attentive adult friend (me), and, particularly in Chapter 6, his classmates.

Jameel, as may already be evident, was an unusually verbally skillful child, and his social situation was particularly hard, as he was homeless. I tell his story first not because he is somehow "typical" — he is *not* — but because he allows such insight into the social processes involved in composing a place for oneself in classroom neighborhoods.

JAMEEL: THE CASE OF THE SINGING SCIENTIST, PART I

Jameel bumps his head hard on the table as he comes up from picking a pencil off the floor. He is momentarily stunned and then remarks.

JAMEEL: Guess what? It's not hurted. Cause my head is hard as metal. That's what I always tell people. If they ever break me in a challenge fight, breaking a table at a time with metal on top of it, I can break right through it. 'Cause my daddy can do that. And he raised me like that, like breaking through that.

This comment suggests significant themes in Jameel's school life. Having banged his head on the table, Jameel transformed this jarring event into an occasion of competence and control, and he did so by means of language that was at once sensitive to human dramas and performative in its expression (e.g., use of hyperbole, analogy, and rhythmic delivery). Indeed, Jameel had not seen his father in what he viewed as a very long time; a number of his jokes were about his father ("My mama . . . can't find my daddy. He's somewhere in Los Angeles. No wonder they call it Los Angeles" [hearty laugh at his own pun; Jameel's pronunciation of *lost* was homophonous with *Los*]).

Jameel's way of participating in school literacy activities throughout the school year suggested his delight in performance, in change of identity, in costume and in mask, and in the humor of the unexpected. Through the artful use of language — through its rhythm and rhyme, its structural capacity for dialogue, its semantic possibilities for metaphor and exaggeration — he transformed his ordinary self into a performer who was in control and deserving of others' respect (Abrahams, 1972; Bauman, 1977; Foster, 1989; Hymes, 1975; Simons, 1990). He seemed, then, both in search of control, of a secure place for himself, and, at the same time, in need of space to explore, to cross boundaries.

However, as discussed in Chapter 4, early in the year Jameel was not a person at home among his peers; most often, he merely coexisted with them. For Jameel, part of truly belonging in the classroom would involve negotiating, through language, new kinds of relationships with his teacher and within the complex network of peers. In the beginning, though, what seemed to matter most to Jameel and to his teacher was that he "attune," that he view his language and his experiences as perfectly compatible with the official experiences of school.

Attuning to the Music of Language in and out of Books

It's recess, but Jameel has decided to stay in and read some books, including Shel Silverstein's (1974) *Where the Sidewalk Ends.* "How about a few rhymes?" he asks me, as he thumbs through the book. "I wonder — where is that 'Lazy Jane' [poem]? That's a good one." Jameel reads the poem easily and then searches for another, giggling at the silly drawings accompanying the poems.

During the opening four months of school, Jameel's composing, as in the "Circle Man" event, often seemed fueled by a spontaneous alchemy — by an attuning to the language about him. His texts reflected his sensitivity to the music and drama of language — in whatever "story" it might be found, whether a picture book or a Saturday morning cartoon. Of the 22 written texts collected during the opening four months of school, 17 (77%) were composed of patterned language (repetitive and rhyming words, phrases, and/or sentences) and 5 (23%) contained two voices engaged in dialogue.

From the very beginning of the year, Jameel would take the essential "trick" or "joke" of a shared story and transform it into another imaginative and, from his point of view, funny story, a story he would eagerly perform for his favorite audience, Louise.[1] For example, the first graders read a story about a dog who sold a cat a hat that was way too big for him. "You look good!" the dog told the cat; so the cat wore the hat, even though, as he said, "I can't see." Jameel transformed that situation into his own construction-paper book. Jameel drew a tiny person with huge glasses (see Figure 5.2) and wrote:

FIGURE 5.2. Jameel's Tiny Person with Huge Glasses: "Me I can't see."

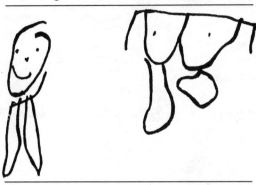

Me I can't see.
Me I can't see.

He read the lines rhythmically (<u>Me</u>, I can't <u>see</u>. <u>Me</u>, I can't <u>see</u>); then, on the next page, he drew the person looking in a mirror (Figure 5.3) and wrote:

Me see me.

Jameel laughed heartily at his story, with its twists of language and actions. Completely delighted with his "book," he ran off to show Louise.

The children not only read about a cat with a big hat but also about a big cat with a hat, the cartoon-like *The Cat in the Hat* (Seuss, 1957), which is composed of repetitive, often rhyming language patterns, like the poetry of Jameel's favorite author, Shel Silverstein, and the "joke books" called linguistic readers. Jameel drew tiny pictures of cats in hats and hats on cats and wrote accompanying rhythmic lines ("The cat sat on hat. The hat sat on cat").

His play with cats and hats and rhythmic, rhyming verse foreshadowed his most revealing story making event, the "911 for cat" performance. That event, which occurred near the end of this period of early attuning, suggested the unstable social stage upon which Jameel was performing. As a child performer, Jameel cast others in appreciative, co-participative roles, and, in so doing, he contributed to explicit "negotiations" — "arguments" may be more accurate — about the rights and responsibilities of composer and addressee in the official classroom dialogue.

FIGURE 5.3. Jameel's Tiny Person Finding Himself in a Mirror: "Me see me."

The "911" Event.   Jameel introduced his "911" story to the class by sharing his drawing and reading the accompanying text to them, as they all sat along the edges of the classroom rug. Jameel's text, like that produced in the "Circle Man" event, captured in chants and dialogue key moments of his story.

> Sat on Cat. Sat on Hat.
> Hat Sat on CAT.
> CAT GoN. 911 for CAt
> (all punctuation added to indicate Jameel's pauses between utterances)

"It's sort of like a poem," responded Edward G. appreciatively.

"It's sort of about a car crash," explained Jameel.

Mollie, as readers may recall from Chapter 1, was not impressed. "It doesn't make any sense," she said. As with all texts, though, the "sense" of Jameel's story lay, in part, "behind the words" (Meek, 1988, p. 20), in the textual material he had drawn upon.

To begin, the story's thematic inspiration was a class discussion of an accident that had occurred just as school was starting. A car had rammed into the playground fence, injuring a woman on the street, and 911 had indeed been called. In addition, there were thematic links to anecdotes Jameel sometimes told about his cat, Panther, now lost, whom he feared had been killed by a car (like his dog). In addition, there were clear thematic links to real storybooks, including *The Cat in the Hat*, although Jameel's text was more tightly rhythmic and repetitive—so much so, in fact, that its style and structure reminded Edward G. of a poem.

Moreover, Jameel's story included a "zooming robbers" theme, perhaps inspired by the popular media. Jameel had begun his story by drawing small pictures on the bottom of his paper: the smiling friends, Cat and Hat, alternately sitting on each other, and four "speeding robbers" zooming past. (As Jameel said when he began drawing them, "That car is rolling. He he he he. That car is *ro*:lling!") It was those robbers that ran over poor Cat. After drawing those images (see Figure 5.4), Jameel wrote:

Sat on Cat Sat on Hat.
Hat Sat on CAT
CAT GoN

He repeated the last phrase rapidly in chant-like fashion, "Catgone, catgone, catgone" (shades of "Circle Man, Circle Man, Circle Man") and then wrote the last line:

911 for cat.

FIGURE 5.4. Jameel's Ill-Fated Cat, His Friend Hat, and the Destructive Speeding Robbers

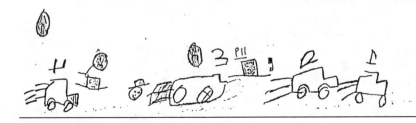

Given his attunement to the performative power of language, Jameel had every reason to expect an appreciative, respectful audience and, moreover, to assume that his role, should confusion exist, was to be helpful — to explain his story. (This, after all, was what Louise did when the stories she performed [i.e., read] were confusing.)

Thus, to go back to Jameel sitting on the edge of the rug, when Mollie commented on his story's lack of sense, Jameel tried to explain his text. Evident in his efforts to explain this sense are varied intertextual connections, among them the morning discussion about the accident and the importance of calling 911, his anecdotes about Panther, and the reading of picture books. Moreover, the conversation that evolved between Jameel and Mollie illustrated the different participation structures each assumed. While Jameel was trying to explain his story to his audience, Mollie was trying to help a needy peer. To maintain control, Jameel used questions to place Mollie herself in the needy student stance and then interpreted her directives as requests for help.

JAMEEL:	What part of it doesn't make sense?
PEER:	(unidentified) It makes sense to me. You can tell with his picture [of the cat on hat, the hat on cat, the "speeding guys," and the crying faces].
MOLLIE:	It doesn't make sense.
JAMEEL:	If your mother got hit wouldn't you call 911? Wouldn't you call 911? Would you call 911? Would you call 911?
MOLLIE:	That's where it doesn't —
EDWARD G:	It makes sense!
PEER:	Yeah!
JAMEEL:	If a car was passing by — and then you were by the house and then a car was going past and then you got hit — I'm talking about the hat and the cat got hit.
EDWARD G:	It sounds like a poem.
MOLLIE:	It doesn't make sense.

Louise asks Mollie and Jameel to talk the problem over by themselves at a side table. As they talk, Mollie adopts a directive stance, but Jameel resists, playfully manipulating her language and intent to try to maintain control.

MOLLIE:	Read that story.
JAMEEL:	What don't make sense?
MOLLIE:	Read it to me again.
JAMEEL:	OK. You can read all these words.
MOLLIE:	No I can not. They're smashed together.
JAMEEL:	(laughs) Don't you know [how to read]!?! (asked with mock amazement)

But Mollie does not laugh. Jameel tries to explain his story to Mollie, but she is indeed having difficulty, in part because she assumes that his phrase *cat gone* is *cat goes* and that *911 for cat* is the last part of the phrase. (Indeed, the *s* on *cat gon* in Figure 5.4 was added by Mollie.)

MOLLIE: The cat goes 911?

JAMEEL: The <u>hat</u> goes 911. Now the telephone right here. (adds a telephone to his picture)

MOLLIE: Jameel, now look.

JAMEEL: I don't get it. She <u>don't</u> get it. I don't got no more friends. I don't got no more friends.

Mollie suggests he write a story about his own cat.

JAMEEL: This IS about my cat. I ain't writing about no cat. I'm writing about MY cat 'cause I don't know if he died.

MOLLIE: But it doesn't make sense. Cat goes 911.

JAMEEL: It DOES MAKE SENSE. (yelling very loudly)

Mollie leaves, and Jameel laments.

JAMEEL: Why she tell me—I did it the way I wanted it. And now they want me to do it how they want it. But it's my decision.

If Jameel had not resisted, Mollie would have turned his performative presentation into an inquisition. Having decided that his story made no sense, she wanted to help him write a narrative of experience about his cat. She was, from Jameel's point of view, attempting to drag a text out of him that he did not want to tell. Inquisitions, intended or not, are power plays that deny control, a very upsetting experience for Jameel.

Mollie, however, felt that, as a member of Jameel's audience, she had a perfect right to demand literal sense. And, indeed, Jameel's story *was* quite different in sense from the sorts of stories Mollie wrote about pets, which told in a relatively straightforward, communicative style what the pets looked like or what an imaginary pet might do. In contrast, Jameel had used performative tools to capture the rhythm of an experience, embedded comfortably in a series of pictures (as, indeed, did many of the classroom picture books). Further, he felt a member of the audience had no business seeking to teach him about his own story. Mollie was not according him, as performer, proper respect.

Jameel had not deliberately introduced themes, stylistic language, or organizational structures that were unexpected. However, the ground was being laid for such claims or, more accurately, the social ground of the classroom was becoming less stable, as his assumed attunement was being challenged, his respected place questioned.

On the Importance of Sense. Jameel's response to Mollie suggests that he could adopt a presentational stance that was serious, not playful, and that he could present an exposition or explanation rather than a story of some type. His focus was clearly on the literal sense of what was being communicated, even though his text was "like a poem."

This way of participating in activities seemed to occur whenever Jameel was speaking as an expert to a relatively ignorant addressee. His presentations were at times performative and, at other times, straightforwardly communicative. The first evidence of Jameel's abilities to produce lecture-like discourse came when he began explaining classroom reading texts to me during the morning recess. These sessions were initiated when I asked Louise about Jameel's reading progress, and she, in turn, asked Jameel if he would like to spend his recess that day reading to me. Jameel did so with great pleasure. From his point of view, I did not know the books in the room. He adopted a presentational, playful stance as he performed the books for me; he chose books with "jokes" in them or those based on songs (e.g., *Old McDonald, A Huntin' We Will Go,* and *Abiyoyo* [Seeger, 1986]; Jameel commented about the latter, "I hope you will like it. It's got a rhythm. That's why I choose it a lot").

Jameel sang books based on songs and, for all texts, carefully attended to repetitive print and simple sentences, reading with great expression; he made up sensible text for the more difficult parts. He sometimes elaborated upon the meaning in intentionally funny ways, infusing his own style into the given words.

> JAMEEL: "Who will eat this cake?" said the little red hen. [And, after
>   a litany of "I will"s,] But the little red hen ate every, last,
>   one, of those darn-it crumbs.

However, Jameel not only performed the books, but he also explained them, much as Louise did during class choral readings of favorite books. For example, he commented on character variation in folktales after reading *The Little Red Hen*.

> JAMEEL: You know *The Little Red Hen* that we just read? They got the
>   dog in it sometime. They got another book of it. They got the
>   dog, the cat, and the, the, um, the mouse. They got different
>   characters than this book. They got different kind of people in
>   different kinds of books. But sometime they don't.

It was clear, then, that Jameel was not unaware of the demands of communication, nor was he unwilling to explain his point of view in certain contexts. During "story writing," however, he was uncomfortable sharing control of that text in explicit ways with his audience.

This discomfort, displayed in the "911" event, led to classroom tensions. Although Louise discussed with the class the author's ultimate right to determine her or his own story, she was also trying to establish a writing workshop in her classroom. To implement such a workshop, Jameel's written stories would have to become "drafts," and his audiences — his teachers and his peers — would have to become "editors" of those drafts, editors who (however subtly) critiqued his sense and offered help (Calkins, 1986; Graves, 1983). Thus, Louise began to redefine Jameel's classroom stages for performance, that is, she began to change her own role as interlocutor in his social dialogues, as revealed in the next section.

Staking a Claim in the Official School World

During the winter months, Jameel continued his play with the performative possibilities — the performative masks — of language. But some of these masks were *deliberate* claims on classroom life. That is, in his early attuning, Jameel had spontaneously constructed links between texts from official and unofficial worlds. As the official and unofficial social spheres became more clearly defined, deliberately crossing their boundaries became a possibility.

Key in this defining of social spheres was Louise's more demanding stance. After the experience with "the cat goes 911," Louise introduced the concept of a "draft," that is, a text as first effort to be edited for sense and for spelling with an adult "editor" or helper. Although she remained appreciative, she also gradually adopted a more inquisitive, helpful, and, at times, directive stance toward Jameel, underlining her role as teacher and the social requirements of the official school world.

This change led to complex negotiations as Jameel and Louise worked to define their rights and responsibilities as author, audience, and helper. Moreover, Jameel himself began to deliberately play with his role as student in the official school sphere and, thereby, to deliberately assert some control. These assertions, illustrated in the "Rich Dog" event to follow, foreshadowed Jameel's claims on the official curriculum itself, that is, on the kinds of texts included.

The "Rich Dog" Event.   Jameel wrote a number of versions of his "Rich Dog" story. Following is the one displayed on the bulletin board:

One daY The RiCh dog WaS locked Up and The dog "said I got Some mone"y an he Said I am free To go"

The "Rich Dog" is atypical for Jameel in that, structurally, it is a report of an event rather than a dramatic construction of chants and dialogues, perhaps because of its direct link to a trade book with a relatively straight-forward prose style. Louise had introduced the topic of "dog" stories by reading Ezra Jack Keats's *Whistle for Willie* (1964) to the children as they all sat on the classroom rug. The plot of Keats's book is summarized below.[2]

A little boy named Peter is playing outside one day when he sees a boy whistling for his dog. Peter decides that he would like to whistle for his own dog Willie. He hides in a box and tries to whistle when he sees Willie walking down the street. But he cannot manage a whistle, and so Willie walks right by him. Peter heads home. On his way, he picks up a piece of chalk and draws a long line right up to his door. There he puts on his father's hat and tries, unsuccessfully, to whistle. When his mother sees him, he pretends to be his father. Eventually, Peter succeeds in whistling, Willie runs to him, and his parents are very proud. The book concludes with Peter returning home from a trip to the grocery store for his mother; he is whistling, and Willie is trotting along right behind him.

Jameel enjoyed the book greatly. Peter's "good trick," in Jameel's words, of pretending to be the father and the presence of the dog Willie struck thematic chords with Jameel. Later, back at his seat, he told me a story about his own dog. He began by telling me that he was not going to write about his dog, even though many children in the class had responded to the book by saying, "I'm gonna write about my dog."

JAMEEL: I don't want to tell anybody [peers] about my dog because it got ran over. His name was Coco.
DYSON: That's a nice name.
JAMEEL: Some people call it Coco Pops. **And every time I saw it he go walk walk and walk until I whistle.**
DYSON: He was what?
JAMEEL: He can walk and walk— He walked all <u>DAY</u>! **And when I draw with a piece of chalk, like that (drawing a wavy line with his pencil), and this was my house (drawing a house)** — anything like that— he () home, and then he will come rac- ing and just lick up all the chalk, just like that (following along with his finger on the line) until he sees the house, and he go, "Patooey." And when he eat his dog food he go, (makes a disgusted face) "My taste buds are yeck!"

DYSON: Your dog said, "My taste buds are yuck"? (amused but incredulous)

JAMEEL: (laughs) Uh huh. 'Cause he licked up the chalk and the chalk stayed on his tongue. So we had to put water in his mouth. Then we have to punch his tummy like POW! Like that, until it pops out. And at the end [of his meal], he will always say (making sad expression). His eyes go like that when he want some. He never hardly drink water. He only drinks milk.

        It wasn't a girl. It was a boy. He got ran over two times. The first time his leg broke off. They have to put another leg on him. And the second time his leg broke — the other leg broke off. And he died. That's why, I don't wanna tell <u>nobody</u>, <u>about</u>, <u>my</u>, <u>dog</u>. (with definiteness) (Sections in bold are related in a literal, thematic way to *Whistle for Willie*.)

Jameel's story, which he labeled a "true" story, was about his dog Coco Pops, but it contained clear intertextual links to *Whistle for Willie*. Coco Pops, like Willie, would walk around the neighborhood, and Jameel, like Peter, would whistle for his dog. Also like Peter, Jameel drew lines with chalk right up to his house door, but, in Jameel's story, Coco Pops would lick up that chalk, which led to a very bad taste in his mouth.

In telling this story, Jameel wove his own experiences into the classroom dialogue about dogs and stories. His own story was in a performative style, in his own accent as it were. Jameel's "Coco Pops" tale was filled with dialogue and exaggerated action (a dog whose expressions spoke). But the funny episode about Coco Pops and the chalk eating was only part of a larger story in which Coco Pops was run over on two separate occasions and died.

Jameel's story was performed for me, a rather passive observer but a very good audience: I was unfailingly attentive, I laughed, and I made lots of back channel comments. Still, I wasn't "anybody." Jameel did not compose sad stories for the "somebodies" in the official school sphere. Jameel, in fact, rarely wrote about personal experiences. He preferred to perform funny stories on the classroom stage. His decision not to compose a story for the whole class about Coco Pops suggested an emerging deliberateness in his sociocultural decision making and a sensitivity to the public nature of official texts. In his words, "I wanted to make [my story] funny."

Jameel's funny story was about a cartoon-like dog who lived in a town of rich dogs. One day he was taken to the "pound" — it's "like the dog's jail," Jameel explained. As will be detailed below, Jameel's rich dog was no little puppy sent to the grocery store in a world of daddys, houses, and money for errands. For this rich dog, the jail was like a grocery store, and he himself was a commodity. The dog bought himself and thereby became "his own master" and shouted "I'm free!" as Jameel explained. Jameel often used such metaphoric language play, a kind of play Smitherman (1986), in her discussion of Black verbal art, describes as "metaphorical-imagistic . . . [with] images rooted in the everyday, real world" (p. 121).

Jameel's funny story, though, like the 911 story, did not meet with universal appreciation. To illustrate, after beginning his rich dog draft, Jameel popped up and ran to perform for Louise, as was his usual procedure. He read the draft.

> The Rich Dogs
> mun Da Thir Yus   [One day there was
> a Rich Dog Lot up   a rich dog locked up.
> mun Da Tha Sad   One day they said]

Now, he explained, he would write "one day they said 'Oh. I got some money. I can buy something from the grocery store.' And so he bought himself!" Jameel laughed heartily, and, I believe, expected Louise to laugh too, which she had reliably done until now.

> Louise, however, offered advice.
> LOUISE: OK. That part needs to come now. You've got your rich
>   dogs. "One day there was" — that's where I got stuck — "a
>   rich dog. They were locked up. One day they said" — that's
>   the part where I got stuck.
> Louise explains to Jameel that quotation marks would help clarify his
> text.
> LOUISE: That'll be my cue that the dogs are talking.
> JAMEEL: There's only dogs there. (exasperated) This is a world where
>   dogs live, where no people are.

Louise did not comment on Jameel's humor, use of metaphor, or transformation of the Keats book. (A relatively relaxed observer — Louise, not I, had responsibility for 27 children — I did not appreciate these aspects of his text either until I was home in the peace of my living room.) The imaginative universe informing process pedagogy does little to encourage teachers of young children or children themselves to appreciate nonliteral sense, including metaphor. The focus is on clarity of explicit information — which was not Jameel's focus, nor did he want advice from his audience.

Eventually, both Louise's inquisitive and directive stance about his text and the implication of that stance — that he was in need of help — became an object of Jameel's deliberate manipulation. As he worked, he periodically slapped his forehead, announced dramatically that he was "stuck," having forgotten his story, and then rushed over to Louise to report his problem. He would recite his story when he "remembered it."

JAMEEL: One dog says, "Hey, I got some money. I can buy myself from out of this roughy store. And I can get rich and rich and rich and rich." And the jail start rocking and started tumbling over. He go wooh BOOM! Wooh BOOM! And he got upside down. (pause) Oh. I just forgot again. (laughs) [Note the metaphoric connection between jail and store.]

Jameel's loss of control was *just* play, however. At one point, Jameel ran out of writing space and began to staple a small piece of construction paper to the bottom of his writing paper. I asked if he thought he would then have enough room. Jameel responded in a performative style, explaining his competence with repetitive structures and questioning.

JAMEEL: Uh huh. I'm positive. If a man doesn't know what he was doing he wouldn't do it. See if he wouldn't know what he was doing — see if you didn't know what you was doing you would have to think. And see I thought — I thinked it and then I got it. 'Cause see, don't you see all that room right there?

Jameel had changed his mask from presentational storyteller to needy student — but he was still in charge; he still was "a man who knows what he's doing." Loss of control itself could be transformed through playful performance into control. And this use of playful performance is how Jameel ultimately dealt with the need to treat his "dog" story as a draft.

The next writing period, Louise asked Jameel to revise his draft to make clear who was talking: one dog or many. (Jameel had written "they said," but, as in the oral version of his story, only one dog was talking.) Jameel at first attempted to present an oral exposition of his story. He, however, became quite protestant when Louise remained understanding but firm in her revision request.

JAMEEL: But I wanted to say it like this.

            .   .   .

            But I wanted to make it funny.

LOUISE: Making it funny's OK but people have to be able to understand it.

. . .

Who bought himself?

JAMEEL: The dog.

. . .

But see I'm working with only one dog. Thousands of dogs in this town are rich.

Eventually Jameel "revised" his text. Without looking at his old text, he wrote a new one that eliminated the reference to the town of rich dogs but also eliminated the *they/he* confusion ("One day the rich dog was locked up and the dog said . . . "). Louise was pleased. Jameel proclaimed his love of story writing and happily began recopying his paper to make a "neat" copy for display. However, in doing so, he copied a word wrong and, then, began to play with the whole notion of "making sense," turning the "final copy" of the story into a playful performance—and a funny text.

Jameel has just copied *in* instead of *and*, at which point the performance begins.

JAMEEL: But it doesn't make sense to me no more. OK, you want it to make sense. You got it. You <u>got</u> it. Now. There's your *and*. Let's see. It's silly. She told me to make it funny. This is funny.

In erasing the *in*, Jameel rips his paper and begins on another sheet. He decides to write yet another piece, this one beginning, "The dog he like to be rich"; moreover, he starts writing on the bottom line of the page and works up.

JAMEEL: Yeah. He he he. This is funny. If they turn it up like this, it's upside down.

. . .

She wanted it funny. She said I can make it funny. So it is funny. (laughs)

Jameel unintentionally makes a squiggly *m*, and he incorporates it into the play.

JAMEEL: Let's make more squigglies. Mm mm mm mm m. She said make it squiggly. She said make it a little squiggly. And I made it squiggly. And funny.

Laughing very hard, Jameel goes and puts the revised version of the story and his "final copy" in the "in" box. (Later, Jameel's revised version is displayed on a classroom wall; the "final copy" is filed in his writing folder.)

The "Rich Dog" event exemplifies Louise's and Jameel's changing relationship during class composing periods. Given Louise's concern with having a strong writing workshop program, her adoption of a more active stance as "editor" seems very reasonable to me. The literature on process pedagogy does not discuss a contradiction between the roles of audience and editor/helper — or audience and teacher, for that matter. The teacher is to convey her understanding of the child's message and ask questions about the information in the child's piece. If the child is able to spell and print with some ease (which was the case with Jameel by this point in the school year) and if the child's personal investment in the piece is high (which also was the case for Jameel in almost all story writing events), then the child should want to revise when the teacher (or peer) "audience" reveals that a discrepancy exists between the child's intention and what the audience understands (Graves, 1983). This was not the case with Jameel. As Louise became more inquisitive and helpful, he became more protestant.

Jameel and Louise's difficulty in these exchanges over his stories was not the result of any simple unwillingness of Jameel to receive help from others. Louise, in fact, helped Jameel throughout the school day, checking his math work, helping him figure out words during reading, answering his questions during science. Taking explicit help from his "teacher" was not problematic. But taking explicit help from his story "audience" was problematic.

Moreover, a lack of "academic" or "literate" language on the part of Jameel also was not, in any simple way, at the root of Jameel's and Louise's difficulty. As previously discussed, Jameel's writing reflected the performative features of African-American oral art forms, features that might lead some scholars to assume that Jameel did not control a more explicit discourse style.[3] But, as also discussed, Jameel's explanations of his own stories were elaborate. Further, while Jameel participated only minimally in "expository" writing activities during study units (e.g., writing "I liked the aquarium"), he continued to present extended lectures to me during recess. The lectures expanded to include study unit topics. Jameel's expositions on these topics were often straightforward, his language syntactically complex, his concern for clarity and precision clear. The following excerpts from Jameel's lectures on birds and barnacles are illustrative.

ON BIRDS

JAMEEL: We got lots of bird books. Would you like to read one of 'em?

                           . . .

           (Jameel gets a bird alphabet book; he skips the pages Louise read that morning because "these are the things you already know about because you was here.")

This bird is very interesting. It eats little kinds of beans.

. . .

Let's see. This one is a dentist. [The dentist metaphor is Jameel's, not Louise's.] This is a crocodile bird that cleans out the little stuff stuck up in his teeth. [This assertion is accurate.] The crocodiles will never eat him. They will never eat their dentist.

. . .

Now this, is a duck.

. . .

It's a member of the duck family.

ON BARNACLES

JAMEEL: See, you see them little shell things? (Jameel points to a barnacle.) See um when the tide is low um first the tide is high and then it opens the shells and these little webby things— them web feet catches the food. And then when um when um when it's low tide it covers its shells real tight so the water won't get out unless it will die.

Jameel was capable of being sensitive to his audience and of using the syntactically "integrated" language (e.g., the nominal complements, the subordinated clauses) associated by some with the academically "literate" (Chafe, 1982). But "story writing" was not for him the occasion for such language.

As appreciative, undemanding regard from his favored audience ended, and as his own notion of "sense" became questioned, Jameel began to straightforwardly take some control of the curriculum—to show that he was thinking. And the texts he was thinking about were increasingly performative; they were, in fact, based on dramatic performances, as detailed in the following section.

Cartoon Events.   "All I'm writing about [now] are cartoons," remarked Jameel to me one day. Jameel's "cartoon stories" were about characters like "Chip and Dale" Rescue Rangers, Mad Cat, Inspector Gadget, and Doctor Claw.[4] For example:

Vis" is" My" Book" vat Jis	[This is my book.
Can't Be JorS DoKro clKoy	That just can't be yours.
and Mad Cat	Doctor Claw and Mad Cat]

In the accompanying picture (Figure 5.5), "Doctor Claw" is sitting on a stage in a cartoon "studio." Mad Cat is entering stage right, and Inspector Gadget is entering stage left. Mainly their feet are visible. Inspector Gadget is objecting to Dr. Claw, his agent Mad Cat, and their "mad book," which Doctor Claw hopes will help him "take all the money in the world."

The cartoon genre, and the out-of-school event of watching cartoons, clearly influenced the "cartoon stories," which were filled with dialogue, cartoon characters and their typical actions, and an exaggerated, slapstick style. But Jameel linked his cartoon stories to more than just television shows.

Jameel's cartoon stories were the first clear instance of the social process I refer to as "staking a claim" on the official school curriculum. That is, this was the first known instance of Jameel explicitly using a genre (or generic features) that he *knew* was not a normal part of the official scene in the classroom but that he felt *should* be. That is, he was able to articulate perceived links between cartoon stories and more common official genres.

FIGURE 5.5. Jameel's "Toons" in a Cartoon Studio: A Dialogue Between Doctor Claw and Inspector Gadget

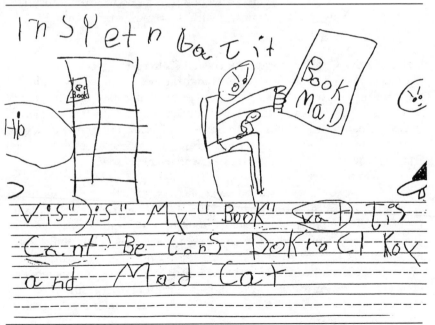

Jameel explained to me that some people considered cartoon stories "nonsense" ("That's the problem with cartoons"). In explaining their sense, he referred both to classroom literature and to the popular movie *Who Framed Roger Rabbit?* The latter is a sophisticated blending of cartoon and human characters in which cartoon performers, "toons," are exploited members of a segregated community. As Jameel explained to me, "Cartoon characters . . . they call 'em toons if they <u>not</u> inside a TV. They call 'em cartoons if they <u>inside</u> a TV."

In cartoon stories, the toons function, not in a television studio, but in a *drawn* studio, just as do characters in picture books. Jameel explained.

JAMEEL: OK. Look. See the whole point is. OK. Just like you were in school. (Jameel gets a book from the classroom library.)

.   .   .

I just want to show you this little picture [in the picture book]. Don't worry about that [his cartoon story]. Look. Don't you see the thing? The picture gotta go with the words and the words gotta go with the pictures.

.   .   .

For instance, OK, I put, *A Chair for My Mother* [title of picture book]. Do the pictures go with the words? (I agree that they do, and Jameel now points to his own cartoon story.) Now do the pictures go with the words here? (Again, I agree.)

Cartoon stories, Jameel argued, were not so hard to "get." I, as reader/ audience, needed to use the pictures and the words, just as I would use the pictures and the words if I "were in school" and had to read picture books by professional authors. Indeed, I might add, many of those picture books are composed heavily of humorous, sometimes rhythmic dialogue; in fact, some books consist *only* of pictures and quoted speech, with no framing devices (e.g., "she/he said"). Moreover, there are many picture books that are illustrated in a cartoon style, like those of Dr. Seuss.

Perhaps because I was listening so attentively—I had not yet seen *Roger Rabbit* nor heard the term "toons"—Jameel talked about the special quality of toons, the featured characters in cartoon stories. As earlier noted, Jameel viewed toons, who are considered "fake," as actors with "real" existences. In fact, he drew his "toons" on a *stage*. He seemed intrigued with the idea, presented so vividly in *Roger Rabbit*, that characters and objects have real existences, even though within certain frames—on certain stages—they are "fake." He pointed out that a toon was like other objects in the classroom.

JAMEEL: 'Cause see, it's just like a feather. (Jameel points to a fake
           feather among the displayed real bird feathers the children
           have been studying.) See this one is fake. [Amidst the real
           feathers in the display, this one is "fake" but it is still real—
           it exists.]

           Fake is really real. Now you get it? Just like a toon in a car-
           toon. If you ever forget that, and the other—another kid try
           to tell you, you just play your tape and you'll know what he
           means or she means.

Jameel's cartoon stories might well be deemed nonsense by readers unfamiliar with the cartoon genre and also by those who evaluate children's
written texts by examining the clarity and completeness of the information
given. But undergirding the "nonsense" was much child wondering about
fictional sense and about the use of multiple media (pictures and words)
to create that sense. (Later in the year, Jameel began referring to characters in books who did ludicrous things as "toons.")

Indeed, Jameel's analysis is reminiscent of Meek's (1988) discussion of
Come out of the Water, Shirley, John Burningham's (1977) picture book
about a little girl's experiences at the beach. The central character's real
(but of course unreal) experiences and imaginative (but of course just as
real) experiences are depicted in side-by-side illustrations. What's real or
not depends on the rules of the game: "Shirley does not bring her [pirate's]
gold back to her mother. She knows which things are appropriate in which
contexts" (p. 18).

As Meek (1988) notes, learning the rules of the game, language or otherwise, is something children seem to be rather good at—the stuff of child
culture is filled with "alternative versions of nursery rhymes, Christmas
carols, national hymns, which never find their way into books" (p. 18).
And, indeed, Jameel had learned rules for manipulating voices from cartoons. He knew how characters build on one another's talk and how they
use their voices to create emotion. In fact, he sometimes wrote "interrup-
tions" (his word) in his cartoon stories, since characters break into each
others' conversational turns.

Moreover, Jameel sometimes dictated extended versions of his cartoon
stories to Louise. Intrigued by her writing—and her talk about punctuation—he became fascinated with quotation marks. (His experimentation
with them is evident in Figure 5.5.) When Jameel dictated a version of
the Dr. Claw story to me, he spontaneously framed some of his dialogue,
revealing an interest in, and emerging understanding of, how certain as-

pects of the oral medium (e.g., voice changes, pitch) might be captured through the print medium (e.g., "he yelled").

> "This is my book."
> "This just can't be yours because—can you share it?"
> "No way, Jose."
> "Please!" he yelled.
> Doctor Claw got mad. "You better give me that book or else
> I'll crush you into metal."
> Inspector Gadget said, "But I am stronger than that."
> "I'll get you some day," Dr. Claw said.
> The End.

Some of Jameel's cartoons could be quite artful, as illustrated by his "clock" cartoon story. The text and picture were so unusual that they captured the attention and admiration of the peers at his work table. He drew a large clock, a crying face, and two smaller figures running that he labeled "toons." He then wrote:

> "I love My Friend. So Do I" But I Don't Hav Tim "Stop Tim iS Runen ut" [Quotation marks are Jameel's]

Jameel performed this piece with a desperate, expressive voice as he reread while writing. He elaborated on his meaning in a similar style.

JAMEEL: The time is running out. We've [the two toons] only got 'til nothing hits there. Nothing hits there. It's [the clock's] mov-ing. (in soft, suspenseful voice, with a deliberate cadence) It's moving forward. It's moving. It's moving forward. It's moving slowly. (then in a desperate voice) Time is running out!

SONYA: I like your clock.

JAMEEL: HELP! (writes *Heep* on picture)

When Jameel finishes his piece, he turns to Brett, who is interested in Jameel's ideas. Jameel adopts a playful, presentational stance and per-forms a magic trick for Brett.

JAMEEL: See the pencil trapped in there (a piece of rolled up paper). And I can magically make it come out. Da daaaa. I put the pencil in here. And then I rolled it up. And now! (Brett laughs)

JAMEEL MIDYEAR:
NEGOTIATING A CLASSROOM PLACE

By March of his first-grade year, then, Jameel's talent with words was clear. Equally clear was his need to exercise those verbal skills for his own sense of control over his world. Moreover, his classroom reading program seemed well-suited for his strengths, given the program's emphasis on literature with rhythm, rhyme, and dialogic patterns; its abundance of humorous, playful books; and Louise herself, who was a superb reader of children's books (in my judgment and the nonverbal judgment of her attentive audience, who smiled, laughed, and read along with her). Indeed, Jameel was gaining control over the written system. Not only were his texts becoming longer and his spelling more conventional, he was beginning to skillfully manipulate voices in varied contexts, including stories, jokes, and cartoons.

At the same time, however, learning to write was not a simple matter of developing new skills; it was a matter of entering an ongoing conversation. In taking his position on the classroom stage, Jameel most often became not a teacher, or a colleague, but a performer. His situated interpretation of the story composing event, and of the kinds of discourse strategies it demanded, drew on a complex of voices that reflected not only his sociocultural past — the oral traditions of his community — but also his sociocultural present, including cartoons, jokes, and the rhythmic prose and poetry of the most socially valued children's literature and of his everyday world.

And yet, despite his attention to the language around him, the official school dialogue had an interactional rhythm and underlying reason that sometimes left him seeming out of tune. Questions of what makes sense, of who has the right to help, of valued genres and assumed roles all arose. Undergirding the official conversations was an imaginative universe that assumed explicit prose as *the* valued "developmental" end goal, and presumptive audiences as important aids to that end goal. In his power struggle during the "911 event," Mollie, not Jameel, was attuned to, and innocently aligned with, the discourse practices enacted through and embedded in institutional structures like curriculum guidelines, assessment procedures, and academic definitions of development and progressive pedagogy (Foucault, 1977).

There was, however, social space for negotiation. Louise was puzzled by Jameel's texts and his protests, but she listened as he began to name his texts and to explain the sense of "cartoon" stories and "jokes" and "rhymes." She did not demand "emotional masquerading" (Gillmore,

1985, p. 115) or passive acceptance of the status quo. Still, if she was to teach him, she and Jameel would have to enact social dialogues in which she assumed a teaching role, not simply an audience role.

Gradually, as the official classroom sphere became more clearly defined, Jameel began to change his classroom social place. For example, notable in the discussion of "toons" is the absence of the continual "jumping up" to perform his texts for Louise, which no longer occurred with such frequency by the winter months. Indeed, as the playful magic trick for Brett suggested, Jameel had gradually begun to move into the peer network, and his performative powers had a clear role in this move. Jameel's products and performances were noticed by his peers.

Jameel's negotiation of a place in the peer group was not easy, however. Peers sometimes cast him in collegial or collaborative roles he resisted. Moreover, he continued to be sensitive about others' responses to his products. In the next chapter, I continue this examination of Jameel's negotiation of a place in official and unofficial classroom worlds; Jameel will be portrayed "making inroads" in peer worlds and, most important, constructing textual "crossroads" amidst worlds, that is, texts that allowed him to accomplish social work in the diverse and sometimes contradictory worlds of school.

CODA: ON BOUNDARIES

"Life is complicated," wrote Patricia Williams (1991), "a fact of great analytic importance" (p. 10). And this was what Jameel was learning — and what Jameel implicitly was teaching me too, as he changed from performer to teacher, from story maker to exposition giver. The "tyranny of conceptual dichotomies," so prevalent in discussions of literacy (Graff, 1987, p. 24), is revealed as just that, a tyranny, an attempt to put cultural traditions, language, and, indeed, children in neatly labeled boxes. Realizing that "oral" is not the opposite of "literate," that the "artful" does not negate the "scientific," is essential if educators are to open up curricular space for children and, at the same time, organize social situations that reveal the breadth of a child's language repertoire.

This all has to do, to conclude with Williams's (1991) words, "with a fluid positioning that sees back and forth across boundary, which acknowledges that I can also be black and white, male and female, yin and yang, love and hate.

Nothing is simple. Each day is a new labor" (p. 130).

CHAPTER 6

JAMEEL

Claims, Inroads, and Emerging Crossroads

When I read with inexperienced readers I find that their difficulties lie not in the words but in understanding something that lies behind the words, embedded in the sense. It's usually an oblique reference to [another text,] something the writer takes for granted that the reader will understand, so that the [new] text will mean more than it says. . . . Those who know how to recognize bits and pieces of other texts in what they read find it is like the discovery of old friends in new places. They feel they are sharing a secret with the writer. . . . They become "insiders" in the network.

— Margaret Meek, *How Texts Teach What Readers Learn*, 1988, pp. 20–22

Child composers, like adult composers, declare themselves as social "insiders" by the very nature of the writing act. Through the genres they use, the discourse traditions they draw upon, and the social stances they adopt, composers enact their roles as social players, anticipating the responses of their listeners and readers. And yet, the dialogue between composers and addressees occurs against a backdrop of other voices — already uttered texts — without which the composers' own voices cannot "sound" (Bakhtin, 1986).

For example, Jameel's "Coco Pops" story would be read differently by those who know Keats's *Whistle for Willie* than by those who do not know that book. Similarly, it might resonate differently for readers familiar with oral performance traditions than for those not so familiar. Texts are heteroglossic, as Bakhtin (1986) argues, existing amidst a matrix of social and historical forces and thus open to diverse readings.

At the same time, however, each newly uttered text can also bring people together in the local context, as it calls forth their memories, imagi-

133

nations, and feelings. In this way, it may contribute to a shared imaginative universe, to an evolving culture. As Bruner (1986) argues:

> [A] culture is as much a *forum* for negotiating and renegotiating meaning
> and for explicating action as it is a set of rules or specifications for action.
> . . . It is the forum aspect of a culture that gives its participants a role in
> constantly making and remaking the culture—an *active* role as participants
> rather than as performing spectators who play out their canonical roles ac-
> cording to rule when the appropriate cues occur. (p. 123)

Participating in a cultural forum—participating in the construction of
shared ways of interpreting texts—is, in fact, inherent in our humanness
(Langer, 1967). We are social creatures who gather together around
shared symbols, whether graphic marks on a page or oral sounds in the
air.

In Chapter 5, Jameel was portrayed as he began to influence the official
school world, its imaginative universe, by staking claims on the kinds of
generic themes, structures, and styles that might be used therein. He was
beginning also to participate more actively in unofficial worlds. In the
next section, I examine Jameel's efforts during the winter months (January
through March) to compose a social place for himself in unofficial worlds.
Then, I turn to Jameel's closing months of school (April through June),
when new kinds of written genres emerged—beyond cartoon productions
and joke stories—that served as crossroads, or common dialogic ground,
for bringing together diverse social worlds.

JAMEEL: THE CASE OF THE SINGING SCIENTIST, PART II

As suggested in Chapter 5, early in the year Jameel often seemed oblivi-
ous to his peers, his stance coexistent. He seldom answered questions peers
directed to him about his work. "Don't ask me. Ask the story!" he would
say, if he responded at all.

Jameel's most consistent conflicts, as well as his most collegial interactions, occurred with community friends. Jameel's greatest problems were
with Edward J., who, in fact, seemed to admire Jameel. From the very
beginning of the school year, Edward J. had chosen regularly to sit by
Jameel during composing, perhaps drawn in part by their shared ethnicity
and gender. Edward J. offered interested comments on Jameel's work,
which Jameel steadfastly ignored. Edward J. also talked playfully about
and at times insulted Jameel's work, which Jameel did not ignore but
protested angrily and, sometimes, tearfully—in marked contrast to the

other focal children, who tended to respond in kind or with laughter to such insults.[1] The most dramatic such incident involved Jameel's own transformation into a "toon" (a cartoon character).

> Jameel is returning to the classroom from a visit with the school reading teacher. He walks in with a very pleased expression on his face. He is dressed like a "toon." He is wearing his sun glasses and a paper "costume" taped over his regular clothes — a paper shirt and two pairs of pants, one taped over the other for a "quick change." He saunters over to an activity table where Edward J., Brad, and Monique are working. He picks up a math worksheet, which contains a hidden pumpkin to be revealed when certain numbered portions are colored.
>   Misled by his sun glasses, Jameel picks up a red, rather than an orange color, and starts working. Edward J. points out his error. "That's why you should TAKE THOSE STUPID SUN GLASSES OFF," he yells.
>   Jameel immediately begins to sob. Monique, who has been anxiously watching, tries to comfort him, "They not stupid. They good," she says. Brad asks with interest about his costume, but Edward J. proclaims it "stupid" too. Still crying, Jameel gets up and stuffs his costume into his cubby. "I thought they would like it," he sobs.

This event suggests Jameel's sensitivity, his vulnerability to others' comments about his constructions. The intense sadness of his reaction on this day was atypical; he more often responded with angry protests: "You got no right to talk about my story" or other sort of creation. But the sense of affront, of denied respect, was clear.

As also suggested by the above event, Monique and her close friends Vera, Shawnda, and Eugenie looked out for Jameel. They worried about his behavior, especially his physical fighting, which, according to school policy, led to discussions with the principal and notes or phone calls home.

> MONIQUE: (noticing that Jameel is involved in some incident across the room) Oh oh. I know what gonna happen now!
> EUGENIE: Jameel gonna go to the office again! Yeah.
> MONIQUE: I hate for him to go to the office.

While they would sometimes fuss at Jameel about his behavior (which directives he at first ignored and then gradually took with good humor), these children also regularly and matter-of-factly included him in their discussions. Gradually, he began to interact in more extended ways with

them, sometimes in performative ways, often just collegially, as in the
following exchange.

> Jameel is sitting by Eugenie as he works.
> JAMEEL: Achoo! (sneezes) I told my mom that I got a cold and all
>   she do is she (say), "No! Why didn't you call [me from
>   school] if you were so sick?"
> EUGENIE: She don't believe you, huh?
> JAMEEL: (with a grand sigh) Mothers never believe their sons.

Jameel's comments to the girls suggested that he knew their social networks, including boy/girl pairings, even though, on the playground, he
seemed to watch more than talk with them.

> JAMEEL: (to Eugenie) You got a boy friend. I'm glad it's not me.
> EUGENIE: I know. I already got somebody. It's not the (). It's some-
>   body else.
> JAMEEL: He used to like you. Now they hate you. I do too! AH:::!
>   (makes a face)
> EUGENIE: (laughs) Look at him.

During the winter months, Jameel began to establish more collegial
relationships with the peer group generally. However, as in the official
classroom world, his powers of oral performance were both his greatest
resource for participation and a potential source of conflict, as I detail in
the following section.

Making Inroads in Unofficial Worlds

As the official classroom sphere became more clearly defined, Jameel
began to engage in collegial discussions and playful dramatizations with
others, although those joint constructions were not directly related to his
written or drawn products. These episodes typically involved joint constructions with boys based at least in part on popular culture. However,
common ground among the children was found, not only in experience
with unofficial school material (e.g., popular horror movies), but also in
official school material. Just as Jameel could stake a claim on the official
curriculum by infusing it with *un*official generic material, so too could he
use *official* school material in unofficial worlds, thereby "making inroads,"
another kind of social process for connecting worlds. While "staking a
claim" contributed to the evolving official school world, inroads contributed to the evolution of a peer culture.

A Successful Inroad.   One example of such an inroad involved a heavenly peace march that became a march of the zombies. (This episode was followed immediately by another, in which Jameel, Austin, Julian, and Berto enacted varied scenes from Michael Jackson videos.) The heavenly peace march episode was related to, but not directly involved in, the children's official composing activity.

The assigned activity was to dictate an "I have a dream" text. The thematic content, discourse structure, and linguistic style of Jameel's text seemed influenced by the Martin Luther King tapes the children listened to; but the content reflected his own experiences as well.

> I have a dream that everyone would live in peace. Let the homeless
> get homes. And let us people live in peace.

An elaborated account of the child talk that followed Jameel's dictation, talk first presented in Chapter 3, is given below.

> Jameel draws a picture to accompany his text. As he does so, he comments about Martin Luther King, seemingly addressing himself to no one in particular.
>
> JAMEEL: I wish Martin Luther King wouldn't have gotten killed. And
>   I would see Martin Luther King here.
>   JOHN: You know what? Martin Luther King Tweet tweet tweet
>   tweet tweet tweet tweet tweet. (waving arms in angel-like
>   fashion as he dances around in a circle)
> JAMEEL: Uh huh. He's a angel.
> Jameel then does a "tweet, tweet, tweet" routine to the tune of Twinkle, Twinkle, Little Star and another to the tune of The Farmer in the Dell.
>   JOHN: Once there was a march up in heaven.
> AUSTIN: Oh God. (laughs)
>
>   .   .   .
>
>   Or he could go down back to earth and go to march.
>   JOHN: No. He's dead and everybody would get scared.
> AUSTIN: Oh yeah.
> JAMEEL: He'd go "AH:::!" I'd be scared outa my wits.
> AUSTIN: Oh yeah. Oh yeah.
> JAMEEL: He'd be, "We gonna have a march. (uses a zombie voice)
>   We're gonna have a march. Oh you dead, come out."
> AUSTIN: All the dead come alive. (laughs)
> Jameel begins to walk around the table, arms stretched out, legs stiff. Other children join in — until Louise calls off the march.

In collaboration with his peers, Jameel reframed the official school material on civil rights within the unofficial genre of a horror story. Jointly turning the official world on its head—reciting a nonsense rhyme while reading a picture book, making a scatological rhyme during a phonics activity—is a way of conspiratorially sharing a secret, in Meek's sense. Such play, long a mainstay of childhood in many parts of the world (Opie & Opie, 1959), helps children articulate a shared imaginative universe, a shared way of interpreting their position as the "governed," the "ruled," the people whose time has not yet come.

Moreover, presenting a performance for one's peers by casting official material in a generically inappropriate text can also be a way of assuming control, a respected place, in an unofficial sphere. However, just as Jameel's claims on the official world did not always play well, his inroads in unofficial worlds did not always play well either. As earlier discussed (Chapter 3), Jameel's playfulness with official school tasks could be a source of great exasperation to Hannah and Angie, both of whom were quite serious while working. Indeed, at times, it could exasperate his peers generally, as in the "cooperative" science event that follows.

A Bumpy Inroad.   On this day, the class completed an experiment in which doll clothes were washed and hung outside to dry. Small groups were now to discuss how the clothes would get dry on such a gray, cool day. Jameel, Anita, Edward G., Sonya, and Vera, the assigned group leader, were all in one group. As the discussion began, Jameel was in a serious mood; his stance was collegial and, at times, critical. He used a communicative style to explain his point of view to his peers.

> JAMEEL: Um see the <u>air</u> goes inside the thing [the clothes] and then it pushes the water out and then it's dry.
>
>   .   .   .
>
> SONYA: The <u>heat</u>.
>
>   .   .   .
>
> JAMEEL: It's too cold out there. So it's gotta be the wind, go inside it, push the water out.

Edward G. and Anita now also speak for heat. So Jameel reiterates his point of view. Finally he becomes performative, although still quite serious. He assumes the role of a lawyer, or perhaps a political leader. He argues that heat and wind are "the same thing" (air, I infer) so everyone really is "going with"—agreeing with—him. But Sonya again says that *heat*, not wind, will make the clothes dry.

> JAMEEL: I object. <u>She</u>'s [Sonya's] going with me. He's [Edward G.'s] going with me.

. . .

SONYA: What are you talking about? (i.e., "I'm not going with you")

JAMEEL: Because heat and wind are the same thing, but heat is hot and wind is cold. So they both can push, and then it's the same thing.

VERA: Jameel. Jameel. Jameel. And don't talk when someone else is talking please.

Vera says she's going with heat.

JAMEEL: So you're going with me. It's final.

. . .

EDWARD G: He's driving me bananas.

SONYA: Yeah, me too.

ANITA: Me too.

VERA: Jameel. Do you know about this, 'cause you didn't do this last time? (Jameel was absent when the children first formed "cooperative" groups to discuss an idea; Vera here defends Jameel from others' criticisms.)

Sonya then suggests that the only way the clothes will get dry outside today is if they put a clothes dryer out there; then they'll have heat. Jameel, clearly unable to garner the "cooperation" of his peers, takes control with a repetitive, rhythmic story, filled with exaggeration and humor — a kind of "true story."

JAMEEL: [Sonya's clothes dryer] will start a fire. And then the clothes will burn up. There'll be a big fire. And then the whole school will go bananas. And then a few of the kids might get killed like that. So we shouldn't, we shouldn't make a machine and put it out there and BURN UP the school. (said with dramatic urgency)

. . .

The school will burn to pieces,

. . .

to pieces. And then [name of school] will be finished. Finished, finished, finished, And then everybody — all kinds of kids — WILL, BE, DEAD!

VERA: Jameel. Jameel. Jameel. (trying to get him under control)

JAMEEL: I MEAN DEAD.

Jameel thus performed a story, incorporating into it both thematic material from the day's science lesson and the complaints of the other children about his behavior. Through these inroads, he reframed the official school material with an unofficial genre — fictional, not expository — and made a bid for control, not over the official curriculum, but over his peers. Indeed, when Louise approached the group, Jameel abandoned his story and returned to his communicative style and his assertion that "the wind is gonna push the water, and push the water out, and then it's gonna fall out . . . it's gonna evaporate."

As skillful as it may have been, Jameel's story was not appreciated by his colleagues, who were frustrated with his attempts to take over the activity. His playful verbal performances did not allow him to situate himself comfortably here in the egalitarian cooperative groups. His peers did not want to be an appreciative audience for his presentations; they wanted to be joint participants in solving the science problem.

By the end of the winter months, then, Jameel's playful, performative use of language helped him to participate in and to construct the diverse, intertwined social spheres of his classroom. Not only did new kinds of genres appear, among them "cartoon stories" and "true stories," but he began to stake claims and make inroads. His performances, however, were not always well-received in the social spheres of school, and his sensitivity to poor reviews was high.

The Evolution of Textual Crossroads

During the last three months of the school year, Jameel's collegiality with his peers continued to grow, particularly during playful, informal talk. In part, Louise and the children had simply shared many engaging experiences and now had more common memories, all formed in a classroom in which respect for the individual and social responsibility to others were stressed. Further, both benefiting from and contributing to Jameel's social place was his use of new genres in the official school world, genres that allowed for both Jameel's performative style and his concerns for social acceptance and respect. Among these new genres were a play, a game, and, most significant, songs, the latter two genres introduced by Jameel himself. These genres afforded common dialogic ground for Louise, Jameel, and his peers; for all class members, they required oral presentation of text and an appreciative, participative audience.

In one sense, the enactment of these genres involved varied sorts of claims by Jameel on the nature of the official curriculum. That is, they were ways in which he introduced generic material into the official imaginative world. In another sense, however, Jameel's texts could be the basis of inroads; they were appealing to his peers and allowed him entry and influence in unofficial worlds. Thus, Jameel's texts could function as a kind of crossroad; they flowed from, and allowed him to take action in, diverse social worlds.

In the next sections, I illustrate how Jameel's texts could potentially be situated amidst diverse social dialogues. I begin with the "whale of a tale" event. This event did not involve a new genre for Jameel, but rather a kind of joke. However, this was the first event in which Jameel's official text evolved through a kind of collaborative play; indeed Jameel and his three peers wrote variations of the same text, which they happily performed later on the rug for their classroom audience. This event highlights the critical role of playful, responsive peers in the evolution of crossroads. Then I turn to the events involving new genres; these events highlight not only the role of peers, but also the critical role of a responsive teacher.

The "Whale of a Tale." In this event, the children were each to write a "whale of a tale." Jameel's completed text (see Figure 6.1) is as follows:

Did you ivr seen a shock borck.
[Did you ever see a shark bark?]
My my my
did you ever see marck row deer steer. steer deer.

FIGURE 6.1. Jameel's Whale of a Tale

[Did you ever see a mark (intended but did not actually write *sark*),
deer steer, steer deer?]
(a picture of a shark saying) Borck Borck [Bark Bark]

This seemingly simple text grew out of a complex of language events, some official, some unofficial. Officially, it was thematically linked to many events in an ongoing science unit on oceans and their creatures. It was linked as well to the children's book, *Did You Ever See?* (Einsel, 1980), which includes among its fantastic possibilities barking sharks and steering deer and, stylistically, is filled with rhythm and rhyme.

Structurally, however, Jameel had converted the book's series of questions into a written dialogue, in which an amazed person utters "my my my" in response to the "bark bark" of the shark. (Indeed, such dialogues had characterized Jameel's texts throughout the year.) As will be illustrated, that "my" line had a complex history. During the morning rug time, the class had been chorally reading *Little Fish Little Fish*, a class text modeled after Martin's (1982) *Brown Bear, Brown Bear*. During these readings, Jameel had been leading a small group of children in quietly echoing "me me me" after the repetitive line "I see a [ocean creature] looking at me," using the book's pattern as a kind of inroad to surreptitious peer play; the "me me me's" evolved into cartoon-like opera singing of "my my my" on the held notes of the daily song *This Land Is Your Land, This Land Is My Land*.

Jameel revealed these connections as he moved among varied social arenas to produce his "whale of a tale." His strikingly easy movement among spheres seemed supported, in part, by playful, responsive peers and by the nature of the official event itself, which, unlike the science activity, was quite playful. Moreover, all group members were privy to both the official and unofficial intertext of Jameel's story (i.e., to the Einsel book and to the morning chants) and thus were appreciative of his cleverness.

Jameel is sitting at a table with Monique, Berto, and Daisy, all playful, socially responsive children. Monique, a particularly attentive friend, turns to Jameel.

MONIQUE: What can I write? What's the name of the title going to be? What is the title going to be? WHAT'S THE TITLE GOING TO BE? (Monique persists, and eventually Jameel responds.)

JAMEEL: The sharks with a bark. Hey, that's a good story. The shark with a bark with some — TIMber gonna (fall) on his lark!

(laughs; Jameel seems to be playing with the double meaning of "bark")

MONIQUE: Lark! Or, "have you ever seen a shark bark?" (Monique enjoys Jameel's rhyme ["Lark!"], co-presenting with him, and then adds her own variation; both children now laugh.)

And Jameel writes, *Did you ever see a shark bark?* Jameel continued in a collegial, even collaborative way. In sharp contrast to his behavior at the beginning of the year, he performed his evolving text for his peers, much as he once had for Louise. His text was situated amidst both official and unofficial dialogues: As author, Jameel was responding to Louise's assignment and to his peers' playfulness; his peers, in turn, presented their work to him.

JAMEEL: (draws a shark and says playfully) Bark, bark, bark, bark, bark.

DAISY: Make it say, "bark bark."

Jameel *does* so, writing the words *bark bark* as if they were coming directly out of the shark's mouth. Then he listens as Daisy reads her text, laughing appreciatively.

DAISY: The whale ate the snail but the snail ate the whale.

. . .

JAMEEL: That snail must be humongous right now. (giggles)

MONIQUE: Yeah!

BERTO: I know.

Jameel returns to his own work, drawing a line under his picture of the shark. He writes, "My my my," saying the word repeatedly. Monique asks what he is doing and, in response, Jameel sings the morning chant.

MONIQUE: Oh no! (with exasperation)

JAMEEL: My my my. My my my. My my my my. (with an amazed expression, as someone would who had just seen a barking shark)

Mrs. Johnson comes by to check on the group. She worries that the children are copying the book *Did You Ever See?*

"We're just making up our story," they protest.

All four children thus became a "we," a group of students in the official world. After Mrs. J. left, Jameel once again became a performative "I" in unofficial spheres, teasing and making brief jokes. Some of this play incorporated aspects of his official text and, thus, was an inroad.

Monique has just told Jameel to be quiet as he continues to chant words. He responds with a teasing retort, based on a cartoon-like rendition of the *Did you ever* pattern.

JAMEEL: This is my mouth and I can say whatever I want to.
MONIQUE: Why don't you shut up?
JAMEEL: You're gonna get a licking, outside. Watch. (said with a smile)
MONIQUE: Right, Jameel, right. (sarcastically)
JAMEEL: And you're gonna say, "Did you ever see twinkling stars?"

At this point in the year, Jameel engaged in this kind of "tough teasing" only with the first-grade girls sharing his cultural background.[2] Jameel next aligned with Berto in a "boys'" playful discussion of "women of my dreams" and then with Monique in expository talk about religious beliefs, a topic commonly discussed only by African-American children in this class (see Chapter 3).

During this event, Jameel moved in and out of social arenas, transforming diverse thematic, stylistic, and structural material. His resulting text was at the crossroads of diverse social spheres, its complex intertext including both "official school material" (Einsel's book) and unofficial peer play (the "my my my" chant). Jameel was transforming material from diverse social spheres more deliberately than was evident at the beginning of the year. He played with the text's meanings in different ways for different others. With one and the same text, he could be a playful performer, a collegial peer, a dutiful student, and a tough teaser.

The "Singing Fish" Event.   In just over a week, Jameel's "barking shark" reappeared as a singing fish, as Jameel introduced a new genre into the official school sphere. The "singing fish" text, even more so than his "barking shark," illustrated how a text could serve as a kind of crossroad, supporting and being supported by Jameel's participation in different social arenas. In staking a claim for the popular song, Jameel made use of a genre that played well throughout diverse classroom neighborhoods. Not only was singing an important part of official classroom life, but in our common culture a skilled presentation of a popular song, by definition performative in style, gives rise to an appreciative stance by others and, perhaps, even a participatory response.

Jameel's song, previously presented in the Introduction, was actually only part of his text. On the top of his paper was a drawn fish with four large bubbles coming out of its mouth. (These are both comic-like and air bubbles — a visual pun.) In each bubble is a "tune," that is, the words being sung by the fish. The bottom half of the page is an exposition of the fish, written in a performative style, with paired, contrastive variants of a sentence (see Figure I.2).

Sitting on the rug during sharing time, Jameel presented his piece in a poised manner. He was performing, using stylized language, but he was not being ostensibly playful.

> JAMEEL: The first time I'm going to say it. I'll say it two times. The second time I'm going to sing it to you. (Jameel reads the piece.)
>
> AUSTIN: Now sing it to us. (The entire class — with no exception — is focused on Jameel. Most children are grinning, wide-eyed.)
>
> JAMEEL: (He sings in a crooning voice, like Bing Crosby or Nat King Cole. His singing is presented below in phrase groups.)
> M-Y-M-Y: (sings each letter in a smooth, rising tune, elongating the last Y; he has written periods after each letter [e.g., M.Y.M.Y.] to indicate that each is to be sung separately.)
> M-Y-M-Y: (sings similarly)
> M:-M: (continues on the high pitch with elongated M's)
> me me me: (even pitch)
> you you you: (even but higher pitch)
> my my my: (even but higher pitch)
> M-Y-M-Y: (as before)
> I: lo::ve (elongated and with a rhythmic drop and then rise in pitch)
> you, to, boop boo bee do (syncopated)
> M-Y-M-Y: (as before)
> That fish isn't any ordinary fish. It's a singing fish. (reads in an announcer's voice; note the repetition and variation in sentence structure)

Jameel had combined his interest in rhythmic, poetic, humorous prose with his interest in exposition, and he had brought together his enjoyment of cartoons and jokes with his fascination with the ocean study unit.

> JAMEEL: [I wrote it] 'cause I love singing. Then I started loving animals. And then I thought, "I'll make 'em singing a song. A singing fish."

The song's closest generic link — thematically, stylistically, and structurally — was his own barking shark story. Not only had the central character become a singing fish, but the amazed expressiveness of the implicit ob-

server (the "my my my's" of the surreptitious morning chants) had become
the melodic expressiveness of the fish itself.

The exposition that followed the song made Jameel's text, once again, a
dialogue. Each voice in this dialogue was distinctive — the singing fish
answered by an "announcer," as Jameel explained. Moreover, Jameel had
made a stapled pocket on the bottom of his song. This, he said, was for
the money donations — the next dialogic turn — that would surely follow
when Jameel took his singing fish to the streets.

> JAMEEL: [People will] pay money for it, the fish. But it's gonna be me
>   [taking the money]. And I'm only give the fish a itsy bitsy
>   piece of candy. And I'm gonna keep the money.

On the "streets" of his own classroom, Jameel's peers were overwhelm-
ingly appreciative. In the afternoon following his morning performance,
many of his classmates decided to write songs themselves. Louise, also
appreciative of the song's verbal cleverness, promised to tape their efforts.
As the children set to work, many laughingly but appreciatively sang "me
me me" and "my my my" as Jameel's text reentered the peer world. Some
even filled their songs with "me me me's" and "my my my's." Moreover,
the children at Jameel's table, including Mollie, Monique, and the two
Edwards, all clambered for a copy of his song. (The next day, at Jameel's
request, I made him photocopies for distribution among his classmates.)

The "singing fish" event illustrated most dramatically the kind of audience appreciation and involvement Jameel seemed to work toward with
his rhythmic, humorous texts. Indeed, it seemed to be a "turning point for
Jameel," to use Louise's words, that is, one that solidified his performative
role and gave him widespread recognition and admiration from his peers.

Jameel went on to write many more songs, including the one excerpted
below, which is also inspired by a science study unit — the study of space
and, particularly, gravity.

> I love rockets and ships, too.
> I love space
> Do you, too?
> I love space
> because it's fun
> I love space cause you bounce around
> It's just like in Chucky Cheese
> I just love, to, bounce around,
> Bah bah bah bah bah bah bounce around. [transcribed]

Indeed, Jameel's reputation as a good songwriter seemed to give him increased and positive visibility in both official and unofficial spheres. His morning compositions (drawings, texts, and paper constructions) were more often commented on by other children. He, in turn, sometimes responded (to the boys only) with "Hey babe's" and fancy walking, as he enjoyed the attention. Most notably, Jameel's newly emerged collegial and presentational stances with peers seemed to support his successful play with Edward J., as illustrated in the following event.

The children are doing a board work task.

JAMEEL: I gotta have some music! Excuse me! I gotta sing some music. (Jameel goes to his cubby to get another song he has written.)

EDWARD J: Make me one [a copy]?

. . .

Jameel offers to trade the song for something, *if* Edward really wants it.

JAMEEL: I gotta check and see if you really like it. Cause I might give it to you. See if you like it. That hurt? (Jameel taps Edward's knee with the eraser end of a pencil, "checking" his reflexes as a doctor would.)

EDWARD J: No.

. . .

Jameel taps Edward on the head. He then decides Edward doesn't really like the song since "nothing hurts." Edward then says, "Ow!"

JAMEEL: That hurt. Well, let's see, what's the final check. Now your neck. I'm gonna cut your neck off! Yeah, yeah.

EDWARD J: No, no.

JAMEEL: Gonna cut the nose off. You don't need that nose! You don't need to smell. Cut the eyeballs off. You don't need the eyes. Cut the ears off. You don't need the ears. I'm gonna cut his brains out!

Edward runs to Mrs. Johnson, ostensibly for protection.

JAMEEL: Yeah? Oh yeah? I'm gonna scare the pants offa him! I'm gonna scare the pants offa him! I'm gonna scare the pants off you! (playfully)

Edward chuckles.

Jameel did not hit Edward in the above episode, but he playfully threatened much worse. This teasing "tough" talk signaled the emergence of a more peaceful existence with Edward. A key element in the emergence of

Jameel as a recognized and skillful performer, both in and out of the "official" school world, was the renegotiation of Jameel's classroom place, accomplished in part through the intertext of a "singing fish." That song was an inroad to playful "tough teasing" with community friends, to collegial interactions with peers generally, as well as a claim to official recognition as a skilled performer.

The Permeable Curriculum in Action

In presenting the "singing fish" event, I have emphasized Jameel's interaction with his peers. However, Jameel's entry into diverse social and text-mediated dialogues would not have occurred, if not for the permeable curriculum established by Louise. Louise responded to Jameel's song by incorporating the song and its participation framework (i.e., its performer and audience roles) into the official classroom world. Such incorporation stretched the boundaries of the writing program to include musical meaning and, moreover, a social stage for artistic performance.

Moreover, as was Louise's strategy, she used professional or "scientific" language to establish links between the children's efforts and those of the wider world and, just as important, to provide tools for reflection. For example, Louise explained the necessity of taping their songs; without special writing skills, taping would be the only way that their tunes could be remembered. She brainstormed with the children other books they had read that contained tunes whose graphic features they could study, and she consulted with the school music teacher, who talked to the children about how music was written. Jameel also talked about song writing with Louise's husband, a musician, during a class visit.

As Jameel's song writing became a part of the official business of the classroom, he himself adopted a critical reflection on his own efforts, reflection that had proved problematic in teacher and peer writing conferences. Although Jameel's popularity as a songwriter pleased him, it also brought about increased pressure to perform. Jameel began to consider how his songs would sound when performed and how others might respond. He tried his songs out and changed words if he did not like the rhythmic or rhyming effect. That is, he treated his text as a draft. The following event excerpt illustrates Jameel's concerns.

Jameel has been writing a new song at a table filled with other "songwriters." As the children work, many positive compliments are given about Jameel's fish song. Monique, for example, declares, "I like Jameel's. Jameel is good." Jameel himself has written "Me me my we

see we see we got a bee." Louise is curious about his song, but he
won't sing it to her yet.

JAMEEL: I can't sing it. I don't know if it's the right tune yet.

.   .   .

I don't know if it's gonna work. When I write songs I gotta
check it first. [That is, he wants to sing it first to himself,
which he then does.]

A Presented Play.   A similar increased reflectiveness was evident in another closing-of-the-year event in which the curricular processes of action
and reflection were linked to an activity involving performance, in this
case, the performance of a play. Moreover, this event, like the singing
fish, became a kind of crossroad, since it allowed Jameel to make a claim
on the official curriculum and, at the same time, also allowed him a
playful inroad into peer worlds.

Louise organized the children into small groups, each of which produced a puppet show based on *Where the Wild Things Are* (Sendak,
1963). The groups performed their shows for each other and for another
classroom. In his group, Jameel played the lead character, the naughty
child Max. In doing so, he elaborated on the basic text, aiming to be
funny; more specifically, he introduced thematic and structural material
based on cartoons.

For example, he adopted a cartoon-like voice and moved his puppet in
the slapstick style of a toon. He even referred to his Max puppet as his
toon costume. Moreover, he added humorous "jokes" to the text. One of
Jameel's favorite added jokes was an ad lib to the book's closing, when
Max smells good food from back home and decides to leave the land of the
Wild Things. In a performance of his group's play for a kindergarten
class, Louise, the group's narrator, read that Max smelled good food, and
Jameel ad libbed, "Chicken?" in a perky voice, a delighted expression on
his face. On the way back to the classroom, Jameel's cartoon puppet,
liberated from its original story, engaged in numerous small, slapstick
performances with other children's puppets.

The play event, like song events, articulated in its very unfolding a
distinction between text and performance and between written and oral
language as interrelated communicative and artistic — sensible and musical — tools. Moreover, in the official play event, as in the song events,
appreciative audience was clearly separated from collaborative peers and
helpful teacher. Jameel manipulated these diverse concepts in class discussions before and after the kindergarten performance. Before that performance, Jameel had asked explicitly if "we can do it funny" — if the group

could elaborate on the basic text. Louise responded that they should stick closely to the written text, because the kindergartners would be less familiar with the story and thus might not "get" the jokes.

Jameel, however, could not resist being "funny." After the performance, he engaged with pleasure in an extended class discussion of the performance. He felt that the kindergartners were able to "get" his funny acts, since they laughed at his cartoon voice (which they did) and his "chicken" remark (which fewer children "got"). He was also able to appreciate the aspects of his peers' performances that generated applause, laughter, or expressive "ooohs" and "ahhs."

When Jameel's audience could choose to participate responsively (by singing along, by laughing) but did not seek to control his text (as he perceived Mollie doing), he reflected on the seemingly more familiar, more comfortable social dynamics of text production and performance. For Jameel, the most comfortable social structure for reflection involved privacy or interaction with collaborators who were not simultaneously his audience.

An Involved Game.   Finally, I turn briefly to Jameel's participation in the school science fair. The series of events involving Jameel's entry illustrated not only the permeable nature of Louise's curriculum, its capacity for incorporation, but also the feeling of classroom community, of connection among children, that it seemed to support.

Jameel himself showed me the science exhibit in the school auditorium. He led me down one aisle and then another, looking for his entry, his "invention." Although he could not initially find it, he could, he maintained, smell it. As I followed him, notebook in hand, he pointed out other children's exhibits with pleasure. "This is Hannah's. There's James's right here. There's Jesse's . . . O::! You should see Brad's . . . I'm gonna show you Brad's! It's real neat."

Brad's was a giant box painted black. If you peeped through a tiny hole on its side, a galaxy of stars appeared. It was very neat, I agreed. It also was, like most projects, made with a parent's help.

Finally, we found Jameel's. His invention was a game made from a cardboard box pulled from a garbage can. (The box formerly contained *Playboy* magazines.)

"People at my house thought it was ugly," he explained. "When I first made it they said, 'That ain't nothing but a piece of junk,' 'cause I made it out of garbage."

The game, stored in a shoe box, was composed of cards on which Jameel had written either *yes* or *no* or drawn a happy or sad face. Jameel's invention was, he knew, a rather atypical one. He had made it out of boredom over spring vacation. When he brought it to school, however, Louise gave him time and space to explain the game to his classmates, which he did with great precision in a communicative style. He had thought through the rules carefully.

> JAMEEL: If you get a card with a picture on it, you keep that card. If you get a card that's got a *no* on it, you gotta' put a card back. If you don't got one, when it's your next turn, you can't get a turn because you lost one of the games. . . . Whoever get the most cards [wins].

Louise not only made social space for the children to play the game, she also suggested Jameel enter it in the school science fair because it was, after all, his invention. And so he did, as just illustrated, with pleasure. Jameel's game was respected — even if it was "just junk" — within the official culture of the classroom, a culture much richer now, infused as it was with the language, experiences, and inventions of the children.

This event suggests an old wisdom, one borne out by human experience as well as scholarly research (e.g., Curry & Johnson, 1990). A sense of competence and respect for self and for others comes from successfully meeting challenges, from transforming potential adversity into advantage — with, of course, the respectful help of other people. In his classroom, Jameel's efforts were incorporated — named and connected to the efforts of his peers and the larger world around them; Jameel's acknowledgment of others' performances ("Wait until you see Brad's!"), which occurred more often in the closing months of the academic year, suggested he was indeed more connected, more at home at school.

SUMMARY: FINDING A SOCIAL PLACE AT SCHOOL

During his first-grade year, Jameel did make clear progress in learning to write. His texts became longer, his spellings more conventional. Early in the year, his text meaning had been more in drawing and playful talk than in his writing, as is typical for young children. And, also as is typical, it was the quality of experiences (the nature of an action, of a spoken utterance), the unfolding of an event as experienced by the characters involved, that was missing from his brief texts ("Cat sat on Hat"). But, supported by his interest in patterned language and in dialogue, Jameel's texts did capture the rhythm of an experience more than typically has been found in first-grade writing (see, for example, discussions of child writing in Newkirk & Atwell, 1988).

As the year progressed, Jameel continued to rely on patterned language and on dialogue, but he became more skillful, more deliberate in organizing his words and phrases in diverse genres. (In the last six months of the school year, 43% of collected texts [N = 35] contained patterned language, and 43% contained dialogue, compared with 77% with patterned language and 23% with dialogue in the opening four months of school.) Jameel branched out as well to new kinds of written discourse, including more explicit written prose. (Consider, for example, the "Circle Man" story with its chants and unframed dialogue and the more explicit "Rich Dog.")

However, learning to write involves more than the construction of a product — it involves learning to participate in diverse social dialogues. By detailing Jameel's ways of participating in varied events, both official and unofficial, I hoped to illustrate the social work that engaged Jameel as a composer. His major aim during classroom composing activities seemed to be to perform through artful, playful language for a responsive and appreciative audience. That intention made sensible not only his genre choices (his jokes, cartoons, and pop songs) but also his views of the rights and responsibilities of story makers and their audiences and helpers.

Certainly there were dialogues not yet entered through writing. As I will discuss in Chapter 9, he showed only minimal involvement in expository writing activities during study units (e.g., writing "I like the aquarium"), despite his interest in those study units and his ability (and pleasure) in assuming the interactional stage to deliver expositions (especially to me). Still, he had entered into school literacy, and he had done so with much enthusiasm. He seemed to me to have made a good start.

In addition to illustrating Jameel's social intentions, I aimed in this chapter to reveal the complex social processes through which Jameel, and the other focal children, situated themselves in the social spheres of the classroom. Although Jameel learned a great deal in the official school curriculum (e.g., ways of naming and discussing his work and visions of the range of possible texts that could be written), he also staked claims on that curriculum, most dramatically through his songs. In addition, the common curriculum, including his own contributions, became an inroad into unofficial school worlds. The child who "always wanta be by himself" found common ground with diverse others. Composing was not the only tool for the establishment of this common ground, but it was an important tool.

In time, Jameel's texts began to function as crossroads, supporting and being supported by his actions in diverse social spheres. That is, in learning to write, Jameel did not cross a metaphoric bridge from his "home" culture into the "school" culture but, rather, worked to make a coherent world, a "home," in school. That is, he worked to negotiate a role for the complexity that was Jameel — an artist, a humorist, a sensitive person, a scientifically wondering child, a boy, an African-American — a first grader in Louise's classroom in a school that sits amidst the ethnic diversity and political complexity of urban America.

Said boldly, "Jameel constructed crossroads through writing, a social place for himself in a complex world," the accomplishment seems too grandiose for a young child. But this was not something accomplished as a deliberate act by a lone child; this was accomplished by a child as he interacted with others in the course of the school day, motivated by "his everyday concerns and involvements" and acting within the social activities that were his "normally available resources for organizing [his] behavior" (McDermott & Hood, 1982, p. 234).

Jameel found support in a classroom with a permeable curriculum, one open to individual children's language and experiences even as it introduced new language, new experiences. And a classroom in which the teacher consciously worked to create a community of children.[3] His first-grade year was not without its tensions, but tensions are to be expected when people are forging new relationships and learning new skills.

In the next chapter, I turn to two of Jameel's classmates, Lamar and Eugenie. In their cases, I play out the basic concepts — children's social work, their sociocultural resources, the negotiation of diverse social worlds — to the rhythms of other children's lives.

EPILOGUE

It was my research goal to follow the children's progress for two years. And indeed, Jameel returned to the school for the second grade. But, a few days after school began, he disappeared. As it happened, Jameel had been put in a foster home in an adjacent city, the first of three different homes that year. Given the bureaucratic complexities of Jameel's life — and of gaining entry into different social settings as a researcher — I was not able to stay in touch with Jameel.

Louise, however, did have telephone visits with him during the year and she also talked with one of his new teachers, who described a scene for Louise, which Louise described for me, and I now describe for my readers. The scene was of a second-grade Jameel walking about on a playground in a new school. Jameel had been in a fair amount of trouble during recess in this school, seeming to his new teacher to run to her time and again with complaints about one child or another. (This was called "tattle telling" in the new school, rather than identifying a "problem to be solved," as in the old.) Jameel was frustrated about not being listened to. He asked his teacher for a notebook and a pencil. Then, like an adult friend he had had the year before, he walked around the playground with that notebook, writing down what happened so he could remember. Later, he would use that notebook as a meeting place, as something to gather around with his new teacher.

As an adult member of our society, I must worry about the many young children, like Jameel, who are burdened with economic and social circumstances that they had no role in creating and have no power in fixing. Those circumstances and the power to confront them have sources beyond the classroom walls. And yet, as an educator, I also must have faith in the power of classrooms to contribute in positive ways to the present and future well-being of children. And, most immediately, as a friend of Jameel's, I must have hope for a child with such a sense of agency and negotiated possibility and belief in the potential power of schools to continue to give him access to useful tools for composing his life.

CHAPTER 7

LAMAR AND EUGENIE

From Textual Crossroads to
Curricular Side Roads

From long sitting, watching and pondering (all so unprofessional) I have found out the worst enemies to what we call teaching. . . . The first is the children's interest in each other. It plays the very devil with orthodox method. If only they'd stop talking to each other, playing with each other, fighting with each other and loving each other. This unseemly and unlawful communication! In self-defence I've got to use the damn thing. So I harness the communication, since I can't control it, and base my method on it. . . . They teach each other all their work in pairs, sitting cross-legged knee to knee on the mat, or on their tables, arguing with, correcting, abusing or smiling at each other. And between them all the time is this togetherness, so that learning is so mixed up with relationship that it becomes part of it. What an unsung creative medium is relationship!

—Ashton-Warner, *Teacher*, 1963, pp. 103–104

Ashton-Warner's comments are echoed by other teachers and observers of young children, who find, in Vivian Paley's (1986b) words, that what many children "most wan[t] to learn [in school] will be revealed by other children, not by me" (p. 32); and what they want to learn is how to connect socially with others. As argued throughout this book, developmental and social theories also suggest the importance of making positive use of children's interest in each other. In Vygotsky's (1978) words, writing should be taught as a "complex cultural activity" (p. 118) with roots in children's social lives and symbolic tools (e.g., speech, drawing, play).

In this chapter, I continue the focus on children's social lives and writing use with two of Jameel's classmates, Lamar and Eugenie. In the first part of the chapter, I illustrate the diverse kinds of social work they engaged in and how that work influenced their early ways of writing. As in

Chapters 3 through 6, the official curriculum of Louise's K/1 will remain in the background, providing a pedagogical frame for the children's actions.

In the latter half of the chapter, I turn to the children in their 1/2 classroom. I provide a brief pedagogical frame for the social work and language use that occurred in that room. But the interpretive process through which I constructed this frame, this vision of the official curriculum, was different from the process used in Louise's K/1.[1] I did not gradually adjust my own interests and questions to the new classroom's daily activities, as I had in Louise's room. Rather, I visited the 1/2 classroom to do "follow-up observations" on Eugenie and Lamar. Moreover, I was following as well the intellectual trail of my own emerging understandings; I was intrigued by the social processes I had begun to identify — the interactive work through which children might stake claims, make inroads, and, most important, use texts as crossroads. Thus, my interpretations of Lamar's and Eugenie's experiences in their new classroom do not reveal the social and intellectual texture of that place. Rather those interpretations reveal a new dynamic, a new social process, in the texture of my own study, a process I refer to as composing on curricular side roads. For in the new classroom, the children's social work did indeed seem to become an "enem[y] to what we call teaching," as Ashton-Warner (1963, p. 103) put it; that is, it seemed to lead them away from the curricular main road.

As a whole, the chapter should reveal changes in the kinds of negotiation among multiple social worlds that occurred during composing as Lamar and Eugenie moved from one room to another. Similar to other situated studies of schooling, this chapter presents no more but no less than an examination of one context — the classroom composing time — for learning, or not learning, what the school wants to teach (Diaz, Moll, & Mehan, 1986; Trueba, 1988; Wertsch, 1985).

YEAR 1:
TOWARD TEXTS AS CURRICULAR CROSSROADS

Like their classmate Jameel, Lamar and Eugenie had rich language repertoires, rooted in diverse, intersecting cultural traditions, including the themes, styles, and discourse structures of popular and folk traditions, as well as material from the official school world. And, as seen in Chapters 3 and 4, both children adopted diverse stances toward others. With their friends, they adopted roles as collegial audiences for, and collaborators in, jointly constructed stories and rounds of narratives. Too, both could be performers, presenting narratives that emphasized their own competence in unofficial worlds—their own ability to stand up for themselves. They told stories in which they recounted verbally bumping another when necessary (or, to paraphrase Eugenie, getting up in somebody's face when need be).

Lamar and Eugenie also worked hard to be competent in the official world, and these efforts too were reflected in their language use. For example, when Louise gave detailed directions for dictated stories, Lamar tried hard to follow them exactly. He often produced texts that were strikingly different from his performative tales (like the repetitive "going-up-to-heaven" story; see Chapter 3). He dictated relatively straightforward texts with features of mainstream written narratives—third person voice, adverbs, reported speech, and a linear structure (Purcell-Gates, 1988; Tannen, 1982). When Louise requested that the children draw and dictate about a class trip to the symphony's performance of "Peter and the Wolf," Lamar did just that, producing the following text to accompany his drawing of a story scene.

> One day Peter was lonely. And he heard something flapping. And he looked up in the tree and saw a bird. And suddenly the bird fell down. And he looked down at the bird and he said, "How am I going to put him back into his nest?" Peter saw the duck and he had a pond. So the duck swam in the pond.

The first graders seldom dictated, but Eugenie displayed her sensitivity to the official world in other ways, most notably, when she taught needy others about official information. For example, one day Louise asked the children to pick a shell from a large basket and then draw the animal they imagined might have lived in that shell; she stressed that their texts did not have to be true. As Eugenie and Vera worked side-by-side, Eugenie took the lead and, in adopting the guiding role, also adopted Louise's language, much as Jameel did when teaching me.

VERA: Now what <u>does</u> live in this shell?

EUGENIE: This is not fact. This is fiction. (Note the use of the school terms "fact" and "fiction.")

          Do you think a clam might be living in here? See, like a clam might be living in here. But he left his color of this spot to let us know. It might be a little clam. (Note the so-called literate qualities of Eugenie's language: the putting forth of a hypothetical statement, the linking of that statement to a previous observation [that the shell had a brown spot].)

VERA: That's true.

. . .

EUGENIE: Mrs. Johnson, come here. Me and Vera made a decision. We thought that a clam might live in the shell. (Note the explicit reference to making "a decision"; such reference was common in Louise's talk to children [see Chapter 2], but not common in the children's unofficial talk.)

Performers, colleagues, collaborators, teachers, and students — Lamar and Eugenie were complex social actors in classroom worlds, and their language reflected this complexity. Like Jameel, Lamar and Eugenie did not draw on the breadth of their language repertoire in beginning to compose, but the dominant rhythms and routines of their social and language life supported their composing.

The beginnings of this process were detailed in Chapter 4. In the following sections, I reenter the children's school life in January, focusing on the daily composing period. For each child, I examine key moments that were particularly revealing of the interplay between the child's social work and his or her graphic efforts. As will be seen, in their story making, Lamar and Eugenie used drawing as a major social mediator, while written language itself was still primarily a supplement. But both children were moving toward using texts as crossroads, as a means to take action in official and unofficial worlds.

Lamar: An Intent Learner and a Collaborative Player

The kindergartners are drawing and labeling pictures for the "L" page of their picture dictionaries. James is having lots of difficulty drawing a lion and decides to trace a small toy lion.

LOUISE: Oh, I wouldn't bother to trace it. I'd just remember what a lion looked like.

LAMAR: Me too.

JAMES: I can't draw a lion!

LAMAR: James, just draw a lion. Learn, James!

In the kindergarten, Lamar seemed to move easily among official and unofficial worlds. Seldom did the worlds seem in conflict for him. Moreover, Lamar's propensity for collaborative play was useful for his entry into literacy — as was his attention to Louise's directions and advice.

Lamar's social work and composing growth were revealed most dramatically in a series of events involving an important theme for him — danger lurking in the water. This theme was rooted in Lamar's own experiences, but, in his multimedia stories, it became interwoven with generic material from the popular media and from the official school world as well. Once, on a fishing trip with his family, Lamar's father accidentally knocked him into the water, or so reported Lamar and also his older brother Lamont. Lamar often drew stories about a child falling in the water and then, unfortunately, being attacked by a killer shark or "Jaws," a popular movie well-known by Lamar and his friends. That fallen child might, fortunately, be swallowed whole, as was the old fisherman in Lamar's favorite storybook, *Burt Dow, Deep Water Man* (McCloskey, 1963). Material for Lamar's stories, especially new kinds of characters, also came from the class study of the ocean. All manner of fish swallowing all manner of creatures, including children, will figure into the stories to come.

Lamar's Drawing. Early in the school year, Lamar's explorations of drawn lines and swirls of colors were surrounded by, but had no observable role in, the interactional rhythms of Lamar's oral story making — the joint constructions and rounds of performances. By the winter months, those rhythms were shaping, and being shaped by, his drawing, which had become a new medium for collaborative story making. In this collaboration, however, the evolving story was filtered through each participant's separate paper; in effect, the story was enacted through individual strands of interdependent story composing.

That is, Lamar and his peers functioned as collaborators, using their speaking turns to build on each other's story contributions. Their turns were marked both by the repetitions and pronouns that linked participants' utterances during joint constructions and by the playful one-upmanship of story presentation rounds. But their "collaborations" fueled their separate stories, as in the following example.

> The children are working on their *I am* books, in which children are
> to draw themselves doing many different kinds of activities. Lamar
> and James have each decided to illustrate themselves being swim-
> mers. Both boys tell and, sometimes, perform a story as they draw.
>
> JAMES: (chants) I'm swimming in the lake, I'm swimming in the
>   lake. I won't come in and eat my cake. This gonna be the
>   waves. (drawing waves) This gonna be the waves.
>
>   . . .
>
> LAMAR: Do you know what these lines are? (pointing to his own
>   drawing [see Figure 7.1]) They're the waves. They're push-
>   ing me this way.

FIGURE 7.1.   Lamar's Adventure in the Water

JAMES: Look at these waves (pointing to his own drawing).
LAMAR: And then the water gets higher (drawing his waves
              higher). (Note that "and then" links Lamar's turn with his
              own prior turn, not with James's.)
JAMES: Mine's gonna get higher too. My water's higher than you.
              (Note the use of pronouns ["Mine's"] and repetition
              ["gonna get higher too"].)
LAMAR: Shoot. Mine is higher than yours.

              Mine is over my head. Told you mine's higher than yours.
              Mine got deeper. Deeper.

              (to Tyler) Ain't this deep – ain't this deeper than James's?

TYLER: (nods) It's pretty deep.

          . . .

JAMES: Look at me diving in the water. Lamar, look at me diving in the water. Look at me diving in the water, Anthony.

          . . .

LAMAR: And then a shark was coming. Then a shark was coming. (The "and then" links back to Lamar's previous story lines.)

          . . .

JAMES: If they had a shark in the water, we'd get ready to get out of the water.

LAMAR: I'm getting ready to get out of the water 'cause the shark. (Lamar takes James's idea and incorporates it into his own story.)

          . . .

          (chanting) I'm deep in the water. The shark's gonna kill me.

JAMES: But oh:! There's a shark in the water. (Now James incorporates Lamar's idea into his own story. The "But oh:!" refers to a development in James's own piece.)

LAMAR: Look it. I got a big shark.

JAMES: (laughs) I got a baby shark in the water.

LAMAR: I got a daddy, I got a daddy shark. (Note how Lamar's comment builds on James's but also leads to new developments in his own piece.)

          I'm gonna make the blood coming out 'cause the shark bit the octopus. I'm gonna make the blood in the water. (adds red by octopus)

          . . .

ANTHONY: He's gonna eat you.

LAMAR: He up there but I'm down here. I'm afraid he's gonna eat me but he's not. He thinks — my mom thinks there's two sharks in the water because this part [a fin] is pointing and this part [tail] is pointing.

          . . .

          But they're not. She's just afraid of the picture.

Lamar's drawing was deliberate, controlled, as he sought to make his waves "higher than yours," adding one wave after another. Drawing was not an exploration of color and line, about which a story could be invented, as it had been for Lamar — and for James, Anthony, and Tyler — at the beginning of the year. Rather, drawing was a way of giving graphic voice to his intentions; it was, in Vygotsky's (1978) words, a kind of "graphic speech" (p. 112) that foreshadowed the use of orthographic speech — written language — to compose stories. The nature of Lamar's graphic voice was shaped by his social work with James.[2] The boys functioned as collaborators — playfully competitive collaborators.

When Lamar shared his "I am" page with the class, he explained the adventure that evolved through peer play; that is, he told about the shark attacking the octopus, about his own presence in the water, and about his mother's worry. He changed his stance from a playful, collaborative peer to a presentational author; and, when Eugenie asked him how he made his octopus, Lamar presented his procedures in a communicative style (e.g., "See, first I made a triangle, and then I made these little balls on the side . . . and then I made two long arms"). On the official classroom stage, Lamar's story also became part of the general class reflection on texts that were mainly factual and those that were mainly fiction. Lamar's unofficial social work fed into an official forum in positive ways.

Lamar's official and unofficial agendas did not completely overlap (e.g., Louise did not "assign" Lamar to talk with James), but they did not overtly conflict (e.g., Louise's open-ended composing and allowance for quiet peer talk allowed space for Lamar's social work — as long as he did his official work, that is, his story).

Lamar's Writing.   By the winter months, Lamar was not only a more sophisticated drawer, but he was also more sophisticated about, as well as intensely curious about, print. During teacher-led literacy activities, Lamar displayed knowledge of all uppercase alphabet letters and about half of the lowercase letters. He also had a clear grasp of sound/symbol connections and the orthographic nature of written language.

> LOUISE: Anthony, what does *truck* start with?
> ANTHONY: C.
> LAMAR: That'd be *kuk*.

During dictation, he frequently asked questions and offered comments about letters and words (e.g., "My name starts with *L* and my mommy's name starts with *L!*"); he no longer simply remembered his dictated texts but worked hard to match voice and text when rereading.

Lamar was, then, intellectually and socially engaged in the literacy tasks in his classroom and, in April, he began to orchestrate his written language knowledge — to mobilize it — to add short texts to his drawn and dramatized adventures, that is, to write his own stories, just like the first graders did. After drawing, Lamar added words to his ocean scenes and dramas. He copied them from displayed study unit word lists or, with Louise's encouragement, at least partially "sounded 'em out." Texts like "The GFISH [Goosefish]" and "CATfish GOT SWALLO," however brief, were undergirded by stories enacted through another kind of graphic speech — drawing — and fueled by his social talk with friends. Writing was not yet an integral part of his imaginative and social life; still Lamar was beginning to write.

On the last day of my June observations, however, Lamar received an example of the social — the mediational — power literacy can potentially exert, for good or ill. Sitting by James, Lamar had drawn and dramatized another story in which two boys are by the ocean; they fall in, and a shark eats them. James had co-constructed this adventure with him and had a similar picture. Lamar then wrote a much reduced version of his story, one without the compelling dialogue he performed and the dramatic images he drew. (See Figure 7.2)

To Bys Wt
N TE WD
A SRK
(Translation: Two boys went in the water. A shark.)

FIGURE 7.2. Lamar's Story: "Two boys went in the water. A shark."

James was intrigued by Lamar's efforts. Less knowledgeable about print than his good friend, James asked Lamar how to write "Once there was a boy and Jaws come." Lamar responded.

LAMAR: Man, you should write this. (pointing to his own text)
JAMES: Why?
LAMAR: 'Cause (reading) "Boys go in the water."

James asks again, and Lamar reiterates that he should write what he has written. He knows that what he has written is not what James has asked for, but he also seems to know that (a) James has no way of knowing that and (b) he would find it very difficult to write James's request. So Lamar tells James to copy his letters, "So the boy can go in the water." And when James asks him about writing that Jaws came, Lamar tells him to copy SRK and then grins sheepishly at me.

LAMAR: I tricked him. I can read. I didn't know I could do that. I didn't know I could do nothing but sit here all day. (See Figure 7.3 for James's story.)

In the midst of interacting with James, Lamar had an unexpected sense of his own literacy and its potential social power.

When Louise came by, Lamar asked if she wanted "me to read it to you," the first such spontaneous performance. Louise asked him a question, seemingly to help Lamar elaborate on *a srk*. Having adopted a presentational stance, however, Lamar did not interpret Louise's question as "help."

LAMAR: (reading) Two boys went in the water, and shark.
LOUISE: And shark (expectant pause), did what?
LAMAR: (explaining) Shark is already in the water.
LOUISE: Uh huh.
LAMAR: And they (pointing to the drawn boys) want to come in the water.

In sum, throughout Lamar's kindergarten year, his stories, like Jameel's early first-grade texts, could draw on a complex of cultural materials, with popular, folk, and school literary roots. Lamar, however, was particularly attentive to — and could meet — his perceptions of Louise's task demands. In the last half of the school year, Lamar drew and dramatized exciting adventures, supported by collaborative play; he enjoyed presenting those multimedia efforts on the classroom stage. By the end of the year, Lamar could independently write brief written stories, stories that were, nonetheless, undergirded by his social work and intellectual engagement in both official and unofficial worlds.

FIGURE 7.3. James's Story: "Once there was a boy, and Jaws come."

Eugenie: An Involved Learner and a Collegial Peer

Eugenie and Vera are sitting side-by-side as they compose, helping each other with spellings. Finally, Eugenie asks, "I don't know my words. Do you, Vera?" Vera is too busy trying to figure out a spelling word to answer.

Like Lamar, Eugenie worked to establish collegial relationships with others. In unofficial worlds, Eugenie and her friends talked about their social lives, evaluating the qualities of varied peer characters, much as they did the fictional ones during official reading times. And, although spelling *was* a struggle, drawing was a satisfying social mediator in unofficial worlds and also a means for visual performances in the official one. While Eugenie seldom asked to present her writing per se to the class, she did want to show a picture, *if* she was pleased with it.

Moreover, Eugenie was very interested in other children's writing and drawing. Just as she remembered the names of children's parents, she remembered favorite topics of children with consistent themes. Hannah's would be, "oh yeah, about the kittens." And Brett's would certainly be about space ships. The rug time sharing provided positive interactions, mediated by graphic products, with children with whom, like Hannah and Brett, she had little contact outside official activities.

In the next sections, I offer closer examinations of the complex social work Eugenie accomplished through drawing and writing. As will be seen, while the generic stuff of Eugenie's written texts did not play a substantive role in her social work, the fact of writing itself did, particularly learning to spell.

Eugenie's Drawing.   During drawing, Eugenie, unlike Jameel and Lamar, focused primarily on her own actions (e.g., "I'm gonna make . . . "), rather than on the actions of the figures and events in her represented world (e.g., "And then a shark was coming . . . ").[3] This stylistic approach to drawing lent itself to collegial talk undergirded by themes of social connection and individual competence, as illustrated both in Chapter 4 and in the following brief excerpt.

> Vera and Eugenie are drawing ocean scenes.
>
> EUGENIE: You have to make something like—I'm gonna make a bird fly.
> VERA: Well, I'm gonna make—this is a sea gull. (drawing) I'm gonna make about four birds. One more.
> EUGENIE: See? Look at my bird.
> VERA: That's not how I do 'em.
> EUGENIE: See, I usually don't make my bird like this. See mine don't look pretty, huh?
> VERA: Oh.
> EUGENIE: See. (Eugenie seems to be trying to get an appreciative comment from Vera, which will be forthcoming, but not immediately.)
> VERA: All you have to do is make a beak like um—
> EUGENIE: I love beak. I'm gonna make a beak.
> VERA: Those are the wings?
> EUGENIE: Yeah. See?
> VERA: Uh huh.
> EUGENIE: You don't like mine, huh?
> VERA: Yes I do. I always like your pictures.

In the above excerpt, Eugenie and Vera, like their younger classmates Lamar and James, collaboratively drew their pictures, building off of each other's drawing actions. Their pictures, though, were graphic mediators of scenes, not narratives, and the children talked about the adequacy of those scenes. In addition to talk about pictures, Eugenie and her friends talked a great deal about spelling. Before examining that talk, however, I briefly consider the nature of Eugenie's written "sense."

Eugenie's Texts. Eugenie's early written stories reflected the visual scenes she constructed while drawing. During the winter months, her texts changed from present tense art notes ("I like this house") to past tense descriptions ("The dog was outside") and even elaborations of those descriptions that sometimes hinted at narrative lines ("And he was in trouble"). For example, the following texts accompanied pictures of "outside" scenes, including houses, children, and/or animals; the spelling becomes more conventional as the pieces span the months from January to March (to illustrate the increasing conventionality, the spelling of *outside* is italicized).

iT Wus drc *aT SiT*	[It was dark outside
and SMOG wi cM *at Sid*	and smoke was coming outside.
Mi Fis Wi *iT sit*	My friends went outside.]

it was sne *itsit*	[It was sunny outside
and Me and Mi fes	and me and my friends
Plat	played.
i Plat WT Ariella	I played with Ariella.] (Eugenie said this was
	not true; Ariella had moved from the area at
	the beginning of school. This text accompanied
	the drawing shown in Figure 7.4.)

THE DOG

it was Nit *aWt Sit*	[It was night outside
and The Dog WuS	and the dog was
outsiete late	outside late.
he WuS in chbow	He was in trouble.]

Despite the dominance of pictorial meaning or "sense," Eugenie did use genres that depended more exclusively on discursive (written language)

FIGURE 7.4.   Ariella Outside

meaning. She occasionally wrote love letters to Shawnda (e.g., "Dear Shawnda You r Mie friend I LiKe You Love Eugenie"; Shawnda did not reply, but Eugenie wrote herself a letter, "Dear Eugenie I LiKe Me Eugenie you r The best").

And, near the end of the year, Eugenie even wrote four texts in a "Jameel-style," as Louise put it. Similar to his narratives (and those of other young children [Dyson, 1989a]), Eugenie explored dialogue and, in so doing, moved through narrative time (i.e., one voice speaks and then the other). In fact, three of her texts were rhythmic tales about cats and hats, similar to Jameel's.

> The cat sat on the hat.
> Cat, don't sit on the hat!
> (punctuation added to reflect her own reading)

And one, her last, was a version of a class genre introduced by Jameel, the "love story," in which at least two people talk about love.

> I love me.
> Do you love me?
> Yes I do love you.
> So do you love me?
> I do love you.
> (And so on . . .)

Eugenie had been absent—due to ear surgery—when Jameel introduced song writing, or perhaps she would have made the latter a love song instead of a love story. (When she returned to school, though, children generally were talking about Jameel's "good writing," especially Shawnda and Monique, and this may have influenced her writing decisions.)

These "Jameel-style" texts, though, appeared late in the year and, also, after Jameel had already made them a part of the official school world. Jameel's consistent use of language's music and of unconventional (in school) genres could lead to conflict in the official arena, as could his performative stance. In contrast, Eugenie drew minimally on narrative or performative traditions when she wrote. There was no reason to question Eugenie's sense, just her spelling.

Eugenie's Spelling. As readers may recall from Chapter 4, early in the school year Eugenie used self-critical comments to gain spelling support from adults, but *not* from peers. As the year continued, Eugenie's tearful displays stopped, at least in part because she became a much better speller. Moreover, while the generic material of her stories did not form the basis for peer inroads (just as it did not become a curricular claim), the act of spelling became a sort of inroad, a part of the common ground undergirding unofficial and collegial social work. Eugenie would exchange spelling help with a peer — as long as the help went both ways. Collegial relationships, after all, can be threatened if one is treated not as a colleague, but as a needy other.[4] The intensity of Eugenie's interest in spelling, and her desire for public competence (not public one-up-manship), are illustrated in the following exchange.

> Monique and Eugenie are writing together at a table. Louise has asked the independent writers to circle the words whose spellings they don't think are right. As they work, Louise comes by to see how they are doing.
>
> LOUISE: Eugenie, you're right. (Eugenie smiles.) You need help with *special*. Special is one of the strangest spellings. You will be so surprised when I show you how they spell *special*. S-P-E-C-I-A-L.
>
> As Eugenie puts *special* in her home-made dictionary, Louise helps Monique spell *more*. Eugenie listens and then spells the word aloud herself, as though rehearsing it. Louise returns to Eugenie's piece.
>
> LOUISE: Do you remember how to spell *makes*? How do you spell *makes*?
>
> EUGENIE: /m/ /a:kes/ No, don't tell me. M-A-K-E.
>
> LOUISE: That's right!
>
> . . .
>
> OK. I'll bet you remember *going*. Don't use your dictionary. Think for a minute. *Go*.

EUGENIE: G-O.
  LOUISE: What do you do about *ing?*
EUGENIE: I-N-G?
  LOUISE: You got it. Do you need to put that in your dictionary?
EUGENIE: NO!
  LOUISE: I didn't think you did.
Monique now asks for *went*, and Eugenie pipes up with help.
EUGENIE: W-E-T.
  LOUISE: That would be *wet*. She needs *went*.
EUGENIE: No! Oh! W-E-N-T. That was one of our spelling words.

Despite Eugenie's spelling growth, she still found encoding hard, and,
with a trusted colleague, she might express her worries (e.g., "I don't
know my words, do you?"). Nonetheless, Eugenie now presented herself
as a competent student in all official circles (all activities governed by
Louise); Louise supported not only her spelling, but her desire to be competent. "Eugenie, you're right," said Louise, but she didn't add "because
that word *is* spelled wrong."

Eugenie's declaration of her own competence (e.g., her spelling loudly
at every opportunity in official circles) was irritating to Shawnda, who
wondered why Eugenie "always hafta open [her] mouth." Indeed, from
the opening months of school, the issue of competence had been a tender
point between Eugenie and Shawnda (see Chapter 4). As writing and
reading became important activities that friends did together, those activities became increasingly caught up in Eugenie's and Shawnda's wavering
relationship.

Shawnda sometimes complimented Eugenie on her writing (e.g., "You
guys [Monique and Eugenie] got a lot of words!") and commiserated with
her on the frustrations of writing (the pages that rip when you erase, the
recopying of the wrong line when making a final draft for display). On the
other hand, Shawnda sometimes subtly questioned Eugenie's competence,
which was not lost on Eugenie.

Eugenie and Monique have been writing together. As they write, Eugenie looks up periodically to make a face at Shawnda, who is on the
other side of the room. She explains her irritation to Monique.
EUGENIE: Shawnda over there mad 'cause I rolling my eyes at her.
            She say, "I'm doing my spelling test," and then she gonna
            cover up her words and she gonna act like I don't know my
            spelling words! (Shawnda is going to act as if Eugenie
            might copy her test.)

MONIQUE: Who?

EUGENIE: Shawnda.

Eugenie begins erasing and re-spacing her words, which Louise had said were too close together.

EUGENIE: Oh, I'm tired of doing this over and over and over! Ain't
           you?

At the end of the year, when the children were looking over the work they had done throughout the year, Eugenie came upon a love letter she had written to Shawnda. She commented to Vera, "Oh look. I definitely — I want this about Shawnda. So I can take it home and tear it up."

In sum, Eugenie worked to weave a comfortable web of relationships throughout her official and unofficial worlds. The composing activity took place amidst this social work. Eugenie established a collegial, at times collaborative, approach to this activity. She and her friends talked about their struggles to spell, about what "we" have to do in "our" work, and exchanged compliments. While Eugenie had a rich repertoire of performative and communicative language styles not yet tapped by writing, she, like Lamar and Jameel, had made a good beginning, in my judgment and in that of Louise.[5]

YEAR 2:
COMPOSING ON CURRICULAR SIDE ROADS

Martha Wilson's room was filled from one corner to another, from floor to ceiling, with evidence of children working — charts, posters, child-made books and store-bought ones, file boxes for work-in-progress, piles of work completed, cans of crayons and pencils, and on and on. Martha, a European-American woman in her thirties, had a reputation among teachers and parent visitors as a hard-working teacher who engaged students in serious study through fun projects. Martha believed in an integrated curriculum. Reading and writing activities were woven throughout study units; these units culminated in varied products, including child-made books. Martha, called Mrs. Wilson by the children, aimed to foster in children the discipline to work responsibly on and complete such products. During the months I visited her room, the children studied, among other topics, ancient Egypt, the Civil War, and the civil rights movement.

The children sat at assigned desks, pushed together in groups of five or six to form *teams* (a term from cooperative learning approaches; see Slavin, 1988), and they were encouraged to help other children on their team if a member was having trouble with her or his work. Among the 25 children forming these teams were Lamar, now a first grader, and Eugenie, a second grader; their friends James, Tyler, Anthony, Vera, Monique, and Shawnda were all in different classrooms. Table 7.1 details the grade, sex, and ethnicity of Martha's class; in Appendix C, I list the grade, sex, and ethnicity of all the 1/2 children who figure significantly in this chapter.

When I first observed the two children in their new class, I felt some invisible narrator had scripted their opening moves. Eugenie's first words to me, besides "Hi, Anne," were a message to give Louise "when you see her." She told me to say that her grandfather had "passed away" and that she was sorry that Louise could not come to the funeral. This was sad news, but its delivery, though a collegial, grown-up message for her former teacher, was consistent with my understanding of Eugenie, and the kind of social connections that mattered to her.

TABLE 7.1. Grade, Sex, and Ethnicity of 1/2 Children

	1st			2nd			Total
Sex							
Female (F)	5			3			8
Male (M)	11			6			17
Ethnicity							
Af. Am.	7	(1F,	6M)	6	(3F,	3M)	13
Asian Am.	3	(1F,	2M)	0			3
Eur. Am.	2	(1F,	1M)	2	(0F,	2M)	4
Latino	1	(1F,	0M)	0			1
Mid Eastern	1	(1F,	0M)	0			1
Af. Am./Eur. Am.	1	(0F,	1M)	1	(0F,	1M)	2
Af. Am./Asian Am.	1	(0F,	1M)	0			1
Total	16			9			25

Note: Officially school began with 28 students. One (Jameel) moved the first week of class. Two children spent the bulk of the day in Special Education and are not included in this table.

Also consistent was her collegial chat with two new friends, Vanessa and LaToya, although that chat now included discussions of clothes and dances and rap recitations, none of which I had heard from Eugenie the previous year. Although the three friends were assigned to separate teams, they still managed to keep in collegial contact throughout the school day, as I will illustrate.

Lamar, for his part, showed me the large "killer whale" on his brand-new black t-shirt. His first composed adventure, however, did not have to do with whales but with "army men" who shoot "bad guys" and, "accidentally," each other. The situation in the Mideast and the Gulf War occupied the imagination of many children that school year, including Lamar, whose father had been in the army. Assigned a seat between Lynn and LaToya, neither of whom drew adventurous scenes themselves, Lamar whispered loudly to the only team member with a similar composing style, Matthew; indeed, he became so involved in performing his story for Matthew that he got up out of his seat (an action against class rules) to move closer to his attentive peer.

Eventually, Lamar returned to his seat and erased that drawn and dramatized adventure, which was part of an assigned self-portrait for the cover of his *ME* book, an ongoing class project. Lamar had drawn himself watching the army drama on a TV show. He, however, wasn't supposed to be doing "stories," he knew, and especially not army stories. ("[Mrs. Wilson] doesn't like this stuff, all this blood and stuff.")

That erasing, and that worry about whether he was doing the right thing, was not an uncommon experience for Lamar, as will be illustrated. Indeed, Lamar and Eugenie were both having a difficult school year. Martha felt the children were more into their own agendas than into their schoolwork, perhaps in part because they were having a difficult time at home. Martha felt Eugenie's mother was very caring but too overwhelmed this year to attend sufficiently to Eugenie and her school progress, what with her father's death and the new baby, whose father was in prison. Lamar's parents also were very caring, but perhaps their recent divorce was somehow interfering with Lamar's attention to his work. (At the end of the school year, in fact, Lamar was recommended for retention primarily because of his difficulties with literacy activities; his parents elected to send him to another public school, which agreed to promote him.)

The child behaviors that worried Martha have already been evident in the brief vignettes presented above. And, indeed, as a former classroom teacher myself, I admired the patience and good humor with which Martha responded to Eugenie and Lamar and, indeed, to all her children. Still, as researcher, I wanted to understand the negotiation between the children's social work and their academic work, especially their composing. For, within the interpretive framework I was developing, children are always negotiating among multiple social worlds, among their social agendas as "students," "peers," "friends," "sons" and "daughters."[6]

In the sections to come, I focus on the interplay between the children's social work and their oral and written composing. But, as a backdrop for the children's actions, I first describe those aspects of the 1/2 curriculum that Lamar's and Eugenie's experiences seemed to highlight, curricular features that seemed to contribute to a less permeable boundary between the children's official and unofficial worlds. These features are not at all exclusive to Martha's classroom but, in fact, are reflective of common elementary school practices.

Composing on the Main Road in the Official World

One simple and very common classroom rule for staying within the boundaries of the official school world, but a rule often violated by Eugenie and Lamar, was staying in one's proper seat. In the K/1, the children sat in many places throughout the school day. Indeed, kindergarten classrooms in the school were set up for such movement. For example, the children worked at tables, not desks, storing their belongings in "cubbies" or small storage compartments. And while children were sometimes assigned a work table for an activity, they typically exercised control over where they sat at that table. The children were often assigned to work together for varied reasons (e.g., to be reading partners), but, during composing, friends could manage to sit together most of the time if they chose to. Indeed, making decisions to sit with friends or to sit alone was a topic of class discussion.

In the 1/2, as in many elementary classrooms, the children sat at desks arranged in clusters or teams; each desk had a storage compartment. The teams were balanced for ethnicity and sex of child, as the K/1 work groups often had been. But teams were constant throughout the school day. Moreover, friends were sometimes strategically separated. Finding colleagues and collaborators could mean moving off the curricular main road and, quite literally, getting out of one's seat.

Another official requirement was to follow teacher directions for composing tasks. As in the K/1, composing activities were sometimes follow-up activities to the reading of a picture book or to study unit lessons. However, there were relatively more specific guidelines for composing content and organization. For example, after the whole class activity, the children often wrote about what they had learned. Sometimes Martha put sample sentences on the board; the children could copy the sentences and then compose their own. On other occasions the children folded their papers into eight "boxes," unfolded them, and then drew and wrote in each "box"; later these papers could be made into small books about project topics.

The many steps of composing tasks presented, not only much guidance as to teacher expectations, but also many opportunities to fail to meet those expectations, to make mistakes. The children had to remember to copy or not copy, fold or not fold, number boxes or count lines, or not do so, and so on, all nongenre-related questions and all dependent on the teacher's directions, not their own decisions.

Another and related official requirement was to orient oneself to the teacher as addressee, not to peers. Martha typically met with individual children about their writing, making sure their texts were complete, given the directions, and sensible. As was usually the case in the K/1, composing was conceived of as an individual task, rather than a collaborative one (as in Daiute, 1989). However, in the 1/2, in contrast to the K/1, there was no regular forum in the official classroom community for oral presentation of child texts (although private performances in the unofficial world occurred, as children went off the "main road").

These curricular features were not problematic for all children; each child's academic skill, unique personality, and sociocultural resources figured into their ways of responding to the official world (and the official world's way of responding to them). Moreover, Martha's classroom was rich in many ways, particularly in its emphasis on curricular content that highlighted the histories, experiences, and contributions of people of color in the United States and in her valuing of children's involvement in projects. However, the typicalness of the cited features (Goodlad, 1984) and of the concerns about Eugenie's and Lamar's school involvement made it an invaluable setting for examining children's social work in ways that might be helpful to educators.

Lamar's and Eugenie's lives in their unofficial social worlds were no less active than they had been in the K/1. But their social work more often took place outside the official school world or, at best, down curricular side roads, as I will illustrate in the three events excerpted in the sections to follow.

The Recipe: Curricular Abandonment

The recipe activity was inspired by *Stone Soup* (Brown, 1947), a story in which a juicy stone is the first ingredient of a wonderful soup recipe. The children as a class dictated the first five steps of their own stone soup recipe, which Martha wrote on the board.

1. Use a big pot. Put it on the stove.
2. Fill the pot 1/2 way full with hot water.
3. Find a great big juicy stone. Wash the stone well and put it in the pot.
4. Turn on the flame.
5. Clean and cut carrots. Put slices in the pot.

Now the children were to number their paper from 1 to 10, copy the first five steps from the board, and then add five more steps of their own. (Later the children would copy each direction onto a separate page of a construction-paper book and illustrate the directions.)

Both Lamar and Eugenie got right to work. Lamar glanced sideways at the board, wrote a few letters, and then looked up and to the side again to find the next letters on the chalkboard—head down and then up, twist to the side, head down and then up, twist to the side, and so on. Children, like Eugenie, who could read the steps listed on the board could repeat the words over and over to themselves as they wrote, and thereby avoid the head twisting (which was why Eugenie's and, indeed, many children's texts were spelled wrong, despite the accurate writing on the board). Lamar, as he explained to me, did not remember what the lines said; he engaged in a slow, painstaking process that was, in essence, a mechanical copying of each letter.[7]

In the midst of this work, Marcus started a conversation with Matthew about Teenage Mutant Ninja Turtles. Lamar listened for a while, and then joined in on the joint reconstruction. "Remember when . . . " started line after line, as the turtles' deeds and words were recalled. Lamar especially enjoyed recounting the good lines (e.g., "Never pay full price for late pizza").

"Remember when you did your work?" said Justin to the boys, to no avail. Lamar was taking a break, which children, like adults, regularly do. But Lamar repeatedly took breaks from his copying, and he engaged in no talk about the recipe. He seemed to be applying his discourse skills to social work in unofficial worlds, while intermittently completing what was, for him, a mechanical task.

The talk about Ninja Turtle movies spread throughout the class, recruiting child after child. Eugenie, however, had no interest in this conversation. She was concentrating hard. She had numbered her paper from 1 to 10, quickly filled her first five lines with material from the board, and now was writing directions with her own ingredients: noodles, salt, celery, eggplant, peas, and, as a final touch, bay leaf. Vanessa had been working beside her, but her presence in the wrong seat had been noticed, and she was sent back to her own team.

As Eugenie worked, she did not interact with Austin, sitting across from her, or with Ricky, sitting beside her. Rather, she looked up repeatedly, glancing at Vanessa and LaToya. If her behavior today followed her usual rhythms, the girls would meet at one of their desks to talk about their work, after a careful look at Martha's position (usually in a corner conferring with a child).

As soon as Eugenie had finished her tenth step, she announced to Mrs. Walker, Mrs. Wilson's teaching assistant,[8] that she was done. Unfortunately, noted Mrs. Walker, Eugenie had filled the first *five lines* on her paper with board material, but she had not copied fully the *five steps*; she had added her own ingredients too soon. Eugenie stared glumly at her paper. Mrs. Walker offered encouragement: Eugenie could copy the missing steps on the back of her paper, without mass erasing. But she would have to copy the board.

Mrs. Walker left. Eugenie made a border of stars around her paper. Across the aisle, on another team, Dwayne was claiming to weigh 150 pounds. (Dwayne's approach to the task was similar to Lamar's, as was Ricky's.) Eugenie joined in, "I'm gonna ask Meryl when she comes today. I'm gonna say, 'Meryl, do your son Dwayne weigh a hundred and fifty pounds?'" After the discussion of weight, Eugenie initiated a lengthy joint reconstruction of the high points of a recent movie. The talk continued until LaToya came by with her recipe.

"Eugenie, look at my pages," she said, presenting her work to her friend. LaToya had finished her recipe. It was a long one, two pages.

"So?" said Eugenie. She accused her friend of lying about her recipe, saying it was longer than it was.

"No, I'm not lying," retorted LaToya. "You shouldn't be doing that [making stars]. You should be trying to do that [the recipe]." Moreover, "you shouldn't tell nobody that they lying 'cause you gonna tell the wrong person that . . . you're gonna say 'Oh, I'm sorry' and they say, 'You li::ar!' and you're gonna say, 'I told you to get back please. Get back.' . . . " The story continued for many minutes.

And Eugenie had no retort to her friend's story. "I'm mad because I have to start over on this stupid crap," she said. And soon the period was over.

Eugenie's frustrated abandonment of her work, which happened repeatedly, cannot be attributed simply to having made mistakes, nor could the brief tension with LaToya be attributed simply to the latter child's success with the task. Indeed, in the K/1, Eugenie had often redone her written work; and Monique, a frequent work companion, had spelled and read much more easily than she had. But rewriting texts after "editing" (when work was to be displayed) had been part of an official and recurring cultural activity, one that was regularly talked about. Children had been expected to discuss their decisions about crafting texts and to report their plans. The necessity and appropriateness of draft corrections could be protested; indeed, Jameel had often done so. But correcting had been something "we first graders" all did—and something "we" all could be quite miserable about. Readers may recall how Eugenie had commiserated with her friends over rewriting drafts ("I know how you feel, gir::ll!"). She had emphasized the collaborative doing of activities and collegial, mutually responsive helping, and she had worked to avoid being singled out as needy.

In the case of the recipe, as in other first- /second-grade composing activities, the children were individuals who completed "their work" correctly or did not. And neither Eugenie nor Lamar did. Moreover, both had engaged in a great deal of peer social work. But that social work per se did not seem to cause their difficulty. Rather, it seemed as if, in the negotiation among multiple social worlds, these young children's official and unofficial worlds did not intersect in socially or intellectually satisfying ways.

Facts and Fiction: Curricular Side Roads

At times, the children did engage in extended collaborative and collegial talk about their composing, given activities that engaged their language resources and opportunities to support their writing with other symbolic tools (e.g., drawing). However, the social work fueling that talk often seemed to lead children down curricular side roads: The children's unofficial language resources did not enter the official world in a publicly acceptable way where they could be named, connected with, or redirected. To illustrate, I turn to two events, one involving an historical figure, the other a picture book. The former features Eugenie, the latter, Lamar, since each child's behavior in the respective events was typical of that child's dominant social and language work.

Historical Facts—or Fiction.   The historical literacy event was a follow-up to Martha's lesson about Abraham Lincoln, "the anti-slavery president." While Martha stressed Lincoln's role in ending slavery, she ended her presentation with his death in the theater. Now the children were to fold a paper into eight boxes, number each box, and then draw and write in each something important about Lincoln.

Eugenie prepared her paper and set to work. As she did so, she talked collegially with Dwayne, on the other side of the aisle. Lincoln "always wear a hat," said Eugenie.

"A big hat," said Dwayne, and both children drew Lincoln wearing a tall hat.

Eugenie's drawing was interrupted by a loud whisper from her friend Vanessa, who was holding up her picture. Vanessa was hard to hear, but she clearly had drawn Abraham Lincoln getting shot at a theater. Eugenie quickly wrote "He was nice" under her first picture and began work on her own theater picture. She drew a girl with long blond hair — Lincoln's child, she said, or maybe "a friend of his." (She wasn't sure if Lincoln had any kids or not.) Nonetheless, Eugenie had a dramatic scene in mind, one centered on what might have happened before that fateful trip to the theater.

> EUGENIE: (presenting her work to me) She's [the blond-haired girl] saying, "I love you." Because before he got ready to go to the theater, she said, "Even if you get killed, I still love you." (said with great feeling)

Eugenie wrote "I Love You" in a bubble coming out of the girl's mouth. Then, with a glance at Mrs. Wilson (in the corner with a child), she moved over to Vanessa's desk. LaToya soon followed.

Vanessa presented her completed paper to her two friends. (See Figure 7.5.) She had not focused on Lincoln's political life, the emphasis of the lesson, but on his personal life. While lacking in precise details, she had drawn Lincoln as a little boy by a house, Lincoln as a man by yet another house, Lincoln's girl friend, Lincoln getting married (complete with wedding vows), and the house where Lincoln and his wife lived. Interspersed with Vanessa's presentation of her work, the children discussed their own views on boy friends (they currently did not have them), growing up (much anticipated), and babies (they all wanted them).[9]

Mrs. Walker, who had just entered the room from another classroom, sent the girls back to their seats. Down on the team again, Eugenie drew Lincoln's houses, his wife, and his wedding day (complete with vows). (See Figure 7.6; final three pictures completed at another time.)

Eventually, Vanessa and LaToya came to her desk. Eugenie now presented her work to her friends, dramatically reading the lines "I love you" and explaining their import. LaToya then motioned her friends into the classroom library; she had a dance step to show them. Martha saw the dancing and sent them back to their seats.

As in the recipe event, Eugenie's dominant stance was a collegial, at times collaborative, one. She discussed her decisions and content with her friends. Moreover, Eugenie's written voice was influenced by the social work she engaged in with her friends; her piece on Lincoln reflected the

FIGURE 7.5. Vanessa's Important Facts About Lincoln

FIGURE 7.6. Eugenie's Important Facts About Lincoln

themes and dramatic style of the girls' talk, especially their "talking about somebody" stories. Eugenie had, in effect, composed a piece that fulfilled an official assignment and also furthered important but unofficial social work. However, the text did *not* function as a kind of crossroad.

First, there was no public forum for Eugenie to present her work in the official world, to bring out her performative language, the dramatized event she had imagined, the family life the girls had constructed when drawing. There was also no official way to discuss the work (for example, the decision to imagine details), to compare it with other classmates' contrasting decisions, or to connect it with varied kinds of genres in the larger world (e.g., cartoons, historical fiction). Her unofficial social and language work could not become part of the official classroom culture. It would be checked for completion according to the required assignment— paper folded in eight boxes, eight pictures, and eight sentences about Lincoln's life.

Second, Eugenie was also not transforming material from an official exposition, using it as a kind of common ground, a possible inroad, for social work in unofficial worlds. She, like Vanessa and LaToya, simply was attuning to the Lincoln picture book project, assuming the generic material she drew upon was perfectly suited for her task.

Thus, unlike in the recipe event, Eugenie's official and unofficial school worlds did seem to intersect, but the social and language resources thereby tapped did not enter into the larger classroom community, nor did the language of the larger community seem to enter into Eugenie's composing. Eugenie was not making decisions about potential kinds of literacy dialogues ("This is not fact. This is fiction"). Her text was neither a claim on the official world, nor a deliberate transformation of official material into the unofficial realm. Eugenie had composed along a curricular side road, one with limited possibilities.

Picture Book Reproduction—or Invention?   Lamar's products also were frequently crafted on curricular side roads, on excursions into his "own agenda." Consider, for example, his incomplete variation on *Cloudy with a Chance of Meatballs* (Barrett, 1982). After reading the children the book, Martha asked them to write their own versions of the tale. To prepare, she and her students brainstormed the varied sorts of delicious food that might rain from the sky, just as food did in the picture book.

Lamar participated with enthusiasm in the brainstorming activity; he had many suggestions for Martha and many unofficial comments for his teammates. He remarked on the foods he liked and those he disliked, sometimes telling narratives of experience about one food or the other (e.g., "My mom cooked some snails before . . . "). At one point, he even turned the official topic ["good food"] into a language play, a kind of inroad (and a pretty good pun), for his classmate Marcus.

LAMAR: (to Marcus) You look good.
MARCUS: (smiles) I got new shoes.
LAMAR: You look good.
MARCUS: Thank you.
LAMAR: I mean delicious. Goody gum drops.
MARCUS: You mean to eat? (bemused)
LAMAR: I can picture you in a cherry pie. (licks lips and rubs stomach) And I'm not just gonna swallow you whole. I'm gonna swallow you half. (A threat that echoes back to *Burt Dow*, and one that makes Marcus laugh.)

Eventually Martha asked the children to fold their papers into eight boxes, number their boxes, and write; there were, she said, copies of the book available to consult, but no two children should end up with identical stories. Among the children themselves, questions immediately arose as to whether they were *to copy* or *make up* the pictures? What about the words? As quiet controversies began, Mrs. Walker walked in. Martha sent Terence, Lamar, Evan, Eugenie, and Vanessa to work with her assistant at a semicircular back table, an atypical move during my observations. Someone should, Martha said, read the book to Mrs. Walker, because she was not familiar with the story.

Papers and pencils in hand, the children arrived at the table. Eugenie immediately began reading the picture book to Mrs. Walker — and telling the other children to listen. Eugenie, Vanessa, Terence, and Mrs. Walker became engrossed in the book, making many collegial comments about the silliness of each page and their own experience with food relative to those of the book's townspeople (e.g., Mrs. Walker commented, "I make pancakes but I don't flip them quite so high." Eugenie followed with "My grandfather he flip 'em slowly," and Terence said, "My father, his go high and he catch 'em with his hands").[10]

Meanwhile, on the other end of the table, Lamar and Evan began copying an illustration from the book, as best they could, since the book was surrounded by children. They chose a picture in which fried eggs and toast fall from the air, to the delight of people, squirrels, and birds. Lamar added pancakes, peas, birds catching peas, and then he followed Evan's lead into an elaborate drama, which was, in fact, collaboratively constructed via strands of story making. In this drama, the falling egg shells contained, not sunny-side eggs, ready to eat, but whole chicks. Once on the ground, those chicks looked for worms. Soon the boys added worm caves, creating a ground below as complex as the sky above.

The boys, who did not sit by each other normally, did not interact with
the seamless turn-taking of Lamar and James, but they did build on each
other's comments and each other's pictures. They continually called each
other's attention to their work, and Lamar in particular referred to what
"we" were doing together.

EVAN: Lamar, look. This is the other half of the worm.
LAMAR: Ah. You should draw the hole [where the worms live].
EVAN: There go the house [where the worms live].
LAMAR: Oh, where's the [baby worm] eggs?
EVAN: It gonna be right here.
LAMAR: The worm goes shoo::. You should erase that line right there.
EVAN: Where?
LAMAR: Right there. So the worm goes like that and goes mm: boop
           [and bumps himself]! Cause worms don't have eyes. They can
           feel. They can go "Em:: OW! I hit my nose!"
EVAN: (laughs)

Lamar now adds a cave "home" too. (Lamar's is more realistic than
Evan's slant-roofed version; Lamar, as readers may recall, knows,
and enjoys knowing, a lot about animals.)

LAMAR: This cave is gonna be much, much bigger. The house is
           gonna be much, much bigger [than yours]!
EVAN: Lamar. Lamar, this is a secret passage door.

                                    .   .   .

LAMAR: Should we draw some snakes eating one chick or the snake
           eating this chick?
EVAN: No.
LAMAR: Why? It make you cry?
EVAN: I don't want them (the chicks) to cry.

                                    .   .   .

LAMAR: Here comes the snake.
EVAN: But it's [the chick] not getting eaten up.
LAMAR: I know. But the snake's in his underground hole. Snakes live
           in underground holes.
EVAN: I know.

                                    .   .   .

LAMAR: (gasps) We're not supposed to be drawing this.
EVAN: What?
LAMAR: This.
EVAN: This what?
LAMAR: This.

                                    .   .   .

           This picture.

EVAN: Why?
LAMAR: Mrs. Wilson won't like it.
EVAN: Yes she will.
LAMAR: Oh, I should put more peas [falling from the sky].

· · ·

Ricky walks by the table.
RICKY: You're making up those stories! (accusing)
LAMAR: No we're not. (defensive)
EVAN: Of course [we are making up stories].

Like Eugenie's Abe Lincoln text, Lamar's piece was influenced by peer social work; his story was collaboratively constructed, its generic material reflecting a familiar theme (creatures threatening other creatures, although, in this case, the drama was underground, not underwater). But, also like Eugenie's text, Lamar's piece did not function as a kind of crossroad. His collaboratively constructed story would not work its way into an official forum, where someone might say, "I love to hear it," when he is done. The ideas and language had no life beyond a potentially displayed completed product.

However, unlike Eugenie, Lamar worried that he was not doing the right thing ("We're not supposed to be drawing this"). While his official and unofficial worlds seemed, at times, to overlap for him, he also seemed to catch himself outside official boundaries, not meeting task expectations. While Eugenie and her two close friends made resistant comments at times (like "the stupid crap" remark), Lamar never did. Indeed, he regularly told me how glad he was to be in Mrs. Wilson's room (and how happy he was not to have Tyler's first-grade teacher, whom he had seen yelling at children and considered "mean"). He seemed to worry that he himself had done something Mrs. Wilson would not like, something wrong. In contrast to the previous year, he did not seem to trust his own decision-making power, his own interpretive sense. And, indeed, his own sense could lead him outside the bounds of the carefully structured composing tasks, down curricular side roads.

As it just had. Lamar had drawn an elaborate picture, sprawling over many "boxes," started an additional picture (copied from the book), and written no text. (See Figure 7.7; Lamar had started to copy one page of the book but crossed it out when Mohammed said he was only supposed to copy a picture, not words.) Lamar would soon stuff his incomplete product into his desk, with all the other incomplete products. It would be finished on a "catch up" day, when the children would stay in from recess and try to get their work done.

FIGURE 7.7. Lamar's Food-Filled Sky and Worm-Filled Ground

On the Question of Writing Progress

The curricular changes from K/1 to 1/2 made problematic any judgment about developmental changes in the children's use of crafted texts to mediate their social lives. During my observations, Lamar independently wrote no stories; his observed collaborative story making and his performative language plays were in unofficial worlds or on curricular side roads. Moreover, he tended to copy whatever models Martha provided; when he did write a sentence or two on his own, it was clear he had not lost the orthographic knowledge he had acquired in kindergarten (i.e., he could still invent spellings). But he no longer proclaimed his own knowledge about literacy, nor did he adopt a directive or helpful stance toward his peers about *writing* (or, indeed, reading) per se.

Nor did I observe Eugenie adopt such a role in her 1/2 classroom (but see note 10). She did seem to be using the drawing aspect of composing differently than she had in the K/1. Her talk focused not only on her own drawing actions but also on her imagined scenes, which could encompass both drawing and writing (as in the "I love you" event). Like Lamar, she did not seem to have lost any orthographic skill, but she also did not produce extended stories.

Certainly oral story composing continued in the 1/2, as did the children's efforts to establish and maintain satisfying relationships with other children. However, the social work that seemed to energize both Eugenie and Lamar's composing seemed to lead them down curricular side roads.

ON CROSSROADS, SIDE ROADS, AND UNPREDICTABLE STORIES

In describing the beginnings of writing in Eugenie's and Lamar's K/1, I continued an interpretive story begun many chapters ago. In this story, children's social work energizes their composing growth, providing social purposes and interactive partners — collaborators, sympathetic colleagues, responsive audience members; moreover, the generic material the children use to accomplish that social work (its themes, styles, and structures) potentially becomes material for action and reflection in the official world.

In the 1/2, I continued to focus on the interplay between children's official and unofficial worlds, but that exploration led me off the curricular main road. And, in fact, such deviations are well-worn paths in the professional and popular literature about schooling.

For example, the cover of *Newsweek*'s (1990) special issue on education displays the cartoon character Bart Simpson and his classmates busy with all manner of illicit activities, among them, shooting slingshots, flying paper airplanes, and making funny drawings. Moreover, educational ethnographers themselves tend to portray children's social worlds as oppositional to the academic world, a sort of child response to authoritarian classrooms (Erickson, 1987; McDermott, 1977).

And yet, as D'Amato (1987, 1988) argues, young children from all sociocultural backgrounds in our society engage in peer social work, *whatever* the classroom organization structure. The visibility and intensity of that work may be influenced by societal structures, including the children's perception of the ultimate use of school (Ogbu, 1987). Still, peer social work does *not* have to be in contention with the school world.

Indeed, "good reasons for accepting school appear to be no more and no less important than the risks, dramas, and sheer fun available to [children] through participation in instructional games consistent with their own games of identity" (D'Amato, 1988, p. 543). Based on his research with young Hawaiian children, D'Amato suggests that such "games" avoid explicit comparative evaluations and allow for collaborative and collegial approaches to academic work—characteristics valued by many children and, in fact, found in recent conceptions of ideal schooling (e.g., Gardner, 1991).

The concern of the current project, though, is not only that young children's social work peacefully coexist with official requirements but that children's social and language resources not be sidetracked, that they *substantively affect the official curriculum*. Tightly structured tasks and interactive spaces do not ensure tightly focused children—but they may make substantive interplay between social worlds problematic.

To use Geertz's (1983) words, learning to manipulate written signs and symbols in particular ways involves entering into the "life of a society, or some part of a society, which, in fact, gives them [the symbols] their life" (p. 119). Moreover, texts that can serve as crossroads between different social arenas in that "society"—texts with intertexts that reverberate among social worlds—cannot exist unless those texts, with their multimedia roots, can enter and influence the official world, the seat of societal power, as it were.

I do not know, of course, what would have happened if Lamar and Eugenie had been in a more permeable curriculum.[11] However, in Erickson's (1986) words, "the core issues in teacher and student effectiveness concern meaningfulness—the grounds for legitimacy and mutual assent—rather than causation in any mechanical sense" (p. 139). By examining the social grounds on which Lamar and Eugenie seemed to lose legitimacy as responsible students, I aim to offer one interpretive perspective for envisioning classroom possibilities.

What if, for example, historical (or even animal) fact and fiction, dramatic reproductions and inventions, jokes, cartoons, and even popular songs and dances had found some connection to the official community? Such phenomena, as readers will see, did happen in the third grade, and while they did not make for a classroom utopia, they did make possible curricular claims and textual crossroads.

In a brief commentary on anthropology and education, D'Amato (1987) suggests that the aim of research is to clarify "story lines and [help] the collectivity to change and to accommodate change in the way that it constructs [its] history" (p. 360). By highlighting the interplay between young children's social and academic work, I hope to contribute to our collective efforts to reconstruct all too familiar story lines, in which eager and competent children become disconnected from the official school world. Given that a key cause for school concern is not intellectual capacity but academic involvement, we might at least ask if finding ways of channeling children's "unseemly and unlawful communication" (Ashton-Warner, 1963, p. 103) might not help us imagine new possibilities for the children we teach.

CHAPTER 8

AYESHA AND WILLIAM
The Politics of Composing in the Third Grade

*The word does not exist in a neutral and impersonal language (It is not,
after all, out of a dictionary that the speaker gets his words!), but rather
it exists in other people's mouths, in other people's contexts, serving other
people's intentions: it is from there that one must take the word, and
make it one's own. . . . With each literary-verbal performance, con-
sciousness must actively orient itself amidst heteroglossia, it must move in
and occupy a position for itself within it, it chooses, in other words, a
"language." Only by remaining in a closed environment, one without
writing or thought, completely off the maps of socioideological becoming, could a man [sic] fail to sense this activity of selecting a language.*
— Bakhtin, *The Dialogic Imagination*, 1981, pp. 294–295

In this chapter, Louise's third graders take the stage, children who indeed
were not in "a closed environment" but in the complex sociocultural environment of their urban school. And as might be expected, these older
children were more politically and culturally conscious than their younger
peers, more aware of how ways of using language reflected group identity
and power. William, one of the focal third graders, illustrates well the
children's greater sensitivity to the boundaries between the official and
the unofficial worlds and, moreover, the links between those boundaries
and the ways in which the children expressed themselves.

Louise has asked her students to compose "About the Author" pages
for their new classroom-published books. The class will present these
books at the upcoming publisher's party. William, Ayesha, and Rashanda, all friends, are meeting with Louise to discuss what kinds of
information might be in such a section. None of them want to write
about information that is, in Rashanda's words, "personal business."
William proposes to write, "I love to get in fights." Louise is a bit

189

taken aback and asks him to think about his audience — parents,
teachers, and other classroom visitors who will be coming to the
party. William does not relent. "That's too bad they don't like it," he
says, "I'm gonna express myself."

William and the other children return to their seats to work for a
while. Then William returns to Louise and solemnly hands her his
"About the Author" page . . . and they both start to laugh. William
has written that when somebody tries to "mess" with him, he "just
walks away." He turned his tough guy pose into one perfectly attuned to the audience — a rhetorical twist that both teacher and student find clever.

In literacy education, we do value, as William seemed to know, child
"voice" or "self-expression," and child "ownership" of text. But individuals, including children, do not have but one voice, nor do they, as solitary
selves, "own" their texts. Moreover, as Bakhtin (1981) discussed, the social
interaction between composer and audience itself takes place against a
landscape of social and power relations. Thus composers "must actively
orient" (p. 295) themselves as members of certain social groups with particular values, authority structures, and language norms. Thus William
threatened to "express" himself in a way that might alienate an audience
of visiting adults and impress an audience of peers, who sometimes admire
such boldness.

In the following pages, I introduce Louise's third-grade class and the
children who were my major informants on classroom life, Ayesha, William, and each child's circle of friends. In so doing, I emphasize the children's sensitivity to the social boundaries of institutional authority and
sociocultural background. I then illustrate how the children's social work
in unofficial worlds — their efforts to establish social linkages, criticize others or defend their honor, and take the interactional stage — influenced
their actions in the official composing curriculum.

As will be evident, the children's social work mediated their texts in
more substantive ways than did that of the younger children. This greater
role of generic substance — of theme, style, and structure — had both positive and negative consequences for the official world. The third graders
staked claims and made inroads, using social processes Jameel introduced
in Chapters 5 and 6, and Louise once again established a permeable curriculum that made possible such child initiations. At the same time, however, the children's unofficial social work did not necessarily lead to curricular engagement; in fact, it could lead to curricular "take-overs," in which
unofficial worlds did not simply intersect with but, rather, overwhelmed
the official world.

LOUISE'S THIRD-GRADE CLASS

Louise had a small class of 20 children, 13 girls and 7 boys (a boy/girl ratio that bothered William); 12 of the children were African-American, 5 European-American, 1 was Chinese-American, 1 Korean-American, and 1 biracial (African-American and European-American). (See Table 8.1 for further details; Appendix D provides the grade, sex, and ethnicity of all third graders who figure significantly in this chapter.)

Upon her entry into the class, Louise initiated a writing program, as she had in the K/1. The children wrote drafts and conferred about text sense, spelling, and punctuation with Louise and with peer partners. Relative to the K/1 children, Louise found the third graders to be more fluent writers. While the younger children told and drew much more than they wrote, the older ones could easily and happily write for 30 minutes or more; and they were often rather quiet as they did so—no loud sound effects or dramatic, audible dialogue as stories unfolded.

During meetings on the classroom rug, Louise taught lessons about specific aspects of composing, among them, brainstorming, paragraphing, revising, editing, and the structure of varied genres; more so than in the K/1, she stressed elaboration and organization of ideas and consideration of audience. As in the K/1, children also used rug-time meetings to present or perform their work. Although Louise encouraged her students to make comments that might help the presenting writer, negative comments during rug time were rare. Such comments occurred only when the children presented work for which Louise had given specific directions; in those cases, the criticisms were about not following those directions.

TABLE 8.1. Sex and Ethnicity of 3rd Grade Children

Ethnicity	Male	Female	Total
Af. Am.	5	7	12
Af. Am./Eur. Am.		1	1
Asian Am.	1	1	2
Eur. Am.	1	4	5
Total	7	13	20

Reflection and Action in the Official World

As teacher, Louise continued to stress child reflection and decision making across the curriculum. Indeed, even seating arrangements were matters of such reasoned choice. While the third grade, unlike the K/1, was furnished with individual desks, Louise asked the children to decide whom they would enjoy sitting and working by and also whom they would not enjoy and/or could not work by; on the basis of their input, Louise assigned seats in the two curving lines of child desks. The children, though, could change seating for partner reading, collaborative writing, and sharing texts, among other reasons, as long as they made progress in their work.

Consistent with her teaching approach, Louise discussed with her class the social world that existed outside the school walls. However, the third graders initiated many more political and social topics than had the K/1 children; among such topics were AIDS, drugs, war, racism, apartheid, consumer boycotts, rap, varied popular movies, and popular songs.

Some of these topics specifically involved language. For example, Louise and the children discussed the difference between "noticing" differences, which was "OK," and "teasing," which was not. And they talked about how we all have "accents" but some people's accents are unfamiliar, a discussion motivated by the children's student teacher from India. Mona summarized that discussion as follows:

Because [the student teacher] speaks another language. And it's probably hard for her and for us — and for her to talk English because she talks Indian and it's probably hard for us to know — it's probably hard for us to listen and to know what she's saying.

Reflection and Action in the Unofficial World

As the list of discussed topics might suggest, the third graders were warier about school and the world in general than the younger children had been. A number had been retained, and the children worried about "flunking" and being older and larger than everyone else, not to mention disappointing their parents. The little children all automatically signed thank you letters to school personnel and visitors with "Love" and their name; the third graders dispensed a written "love" much more carefully. Indeed, love and marriage themselves were no longer discussed by the girls with the straightforward longing of their younger counterparts.

AYESHA: (commenting to Mona and Lena, who are sitting beside her)
           I ain't getting married.
MONA: I'm gonna get married and have me a baby.
AYESHA: Man, she is <u>dumb</u>.
LENA: <u>If</u> you have a husband.
AYESHA: <u>Y</u>ou is so stupid.

                            .   .   .

           When you take the pain, you just don't know how the pain
           gonna hurt.
LENA: And I said <u>if</u> you get married, <u>if</u> you have a husband. (Lena
           means here, I infer, that Mona might have a baby but not
           have a husband, a topic of other conversations among the
           girls.)

More broadly, peer group symbols of the "in" and the "not in" were much
stronger in the third grade — kinds of music, ways of talking and of dressing, even certain products could have social and symbolic meaning. During class music study, for example, the younger children had taken to
symphony music as if it were an adventure in raw emotion — eyes widen-
ing with crescendos, anticipating something grand, and then crinkling
with their giggles when the musical climax arrived; the third graders
of varied sociocultural backgrounds made it clear that such music was
"boring" — they preferred rap (and, in the cases of Ayesha and William,
soul music as well).

Efforts on the part of children to define their own social worlds as peers
are common in our society and, indeed, may be inherent to the institution
of schooling, where the imposition of authority seems to give rise to a
counterforce, some kind of resistance, visible or not, on the part of children (D'Amato, 1987; Roberts, 1970). Tensions between adults and children, however, may be more visible when adults and children differ in
cultural and social circumstance, when children have experienced school
failure, and, moreover, when children are members of a minority group
that has experienced racism in its historical, social, and economic forms
(Ogbu, 1987).

And, indeed, for Ayesha, William, and their close friends, who were
also African-American, race was explicitly discussed as an important part
of their social world. For example, Ayesha, William, and their friends
considered Coke "a White man's drink," because its sponsors "don't support [Black] South Africa." Both Ayesha and William were reluctant to
write a written response to a book on George Washington because they
didn't like this president who had owned slaves. Ayesha in fact reported

that no one in her family liked George Washington; they did like Abraham Lincoln: "He was White, but he wasn't prejudiced." To further illustrate, Ayesha and her girl friends discussed the race of their dolls. While Lena had only White dolls, Ayesha and her friend Crystal had only Black dolls, except for one that Crystal maintained was "mixed."

In the next section, I more formally introduce William, Ayesha, and their friends; in doing so, I stress the children's sensitivity to both sociocultural background and institutional authority. I thereby lay the groundwork for the chapter's subsequent focus on the interplay between the children's official and unofficial worlds during classroom composing.

WILLIAM AND AYESHA

Social Connections in Unofficial Worlds

William.   A few of William's peers provide their own commentary on his social life in the following excerpt.

Charles, Crystal, and Bianca are sitting around a table writing.
Charles has written about his best friends, with a bit of help from his friends at the table.
CRYSTAL: Dag! That's your best friends? That's all your best friends?
CHARLES: No, not — ain't all my best friends. I got lotsa' more best friends. They just all my best best, especially William. You should know, William is my best, best, best friend.
CRYSTAL: I like William. William used to make me scared at first grade.
BIANCA: He was big!
CRYSTAL: He was like — he came up to me and I was like, "MO:::MY:::!"

As Crystal's comments suggest, William was tall and large-boned. He was older than the average third grader, having been retained in first grade, which embarrassed him. Once he inadvertently let slip his age (almost 10) to his friend Darren, and when Darren expressed surprise, William immediately said, "I'm turning 9. I wish I was turning 10." In the K/1, I had heard children discussing "big William," and perhaps this notoriety for his physique contributed to his tendency to slump in his chair — and his utter dislike for sitting on the rug, where he never did seem to get quite comfortable.

William's large size and his vocal resistance to unappealing directions (like sitting on the rug) could be misleading. He was a socially sensitive child, who paid attention to his friends, who included boys, like Darren, Charles, and Paul,[1] and girls, like Crystal and Ayesha; he knew their favorite rap groups and games, their parents and cousins, their after-school schedules and weekend plans.

He himself was into cars, sports, going hunting, rap music, and drawing. He usually had a picture he was working on just inside his desk, ready for any available free moment. William was aware of the border symbolized by what's hidden just inside the desk and what's placed for display on the desk—the border between the official and unofficial classroom worlds. He sometimes deliberately played with that border, taking the interactional spotlight for an unofficial performance. While writing a polite thank you to a classroom helper, he might recite a quite rude one, thereby using official school language as an inroad for peer group enjoyment, or he might repeat Louise's Standard English phrases in nonstandard English under his breath, as in the following example.

> The children are on the rug, sharing their writing. Louise has suggested they ask each reader two questions about his or her text. It is Darren's turn to read. William is perturbed because he has to wait until next-to-last to read his piece (because he was next-to-last on the rug). He listens to the proceedings glumly, finally speaking up to object to Charles's question to Darren. (Such a public objection to a peer's response is not typical of William.)
>
> CHARLES: (to Darren, who has just read about his grandparents' farm in Louisiana) Your pig got a dill nose?
>
> WILLIAM: That is not a question. <u>That</u> is not a question.
>
> CRYSTAL: Yes it is. <u>DOES</u> your pig have a dill nose?
>
> WILLIAM: Oh yeah.
>
> LOUISE: Thank you. If you start it with "Does."
>
> WILLIAM: (under his breath but loud enough for Crystal to hear) Do.
>
> William may be trying to reestablish social cohesion with Crystal. And, in fact, Crystal picks up the cue. She now says under her breath, "Do your pig have a dill nose?" When Darren unexpectedly calls on him for a question, William works to get "do" into his query.
>
> WILLIAM: Do, um, how about did—do um, do your, do um, do your grandma have all kinds of grains?
>
> DARREN: On her farm she do.

Such play with language was common in William's case. Like children the world over (Opie & Opie, 1959), William very much enjoyed turning the school world on its head. However, the fact that this turning, as it were, sometimes involved the vernacular language of his community gave William's behavior a political or power dimension beyond that of the official school world versus the peer world; it also involved home versus school.[2]

On the other hand, when helping his friend Charles write or collaborating on a story with Darren, he typically corrected nonstandard forms. "You been forgetting your [ending] *s*'s," he cautioned Darren, and, rereading a sentence, "All the cars was extinct — <u>are</u> extinct." Given a role of authority in the official world, his language use reflected his different position in the social world and, also, his sociocultural breadth — his sensitivity to social situation and language use.

Ayesha.   Like William, Ayesha, who had turned 8 in October of the school year, also had a lively social life beyond the official school boundary, where snack foods were distributed, holiday stickers exchanged, and after-school activities planned. A slender child with an enthusiastic smile that suggested barely contained energy, her closest friends were Rashanda, Lena, and Crystal; she typically included Mona, Jackie, and Bianca in public declarations of friends (e.g., in essays about friends) and, sometimes, William, Darren, and Charles. Ayesha and her girl friends enjoyed rap music and dance but not sports. When the third-grade math teacher gave them basketball cards as rewards for good behavior, they traded "the cute Black guys" but professed no knowledge of who was a good player and who was not.

Also like William, Ayesha displayed a strong sense of identity with her home community. While William sometimes deliberately played with potential boundaries between home, peer, and school worlds, Ayesha seemed less deliberate than William, more spontaneous in her actions — and more surprised when she found her voice out-of-tune with others. For example, in one event, Ayesha's strong religious convictions, shared with community friends, led to potential tension with her peer Manrissa.

> Manrissa, who immigrated from China when she was 5, is sitting between Ayesha and Mona. Mona reprimands Ayesha for "using God's name in vain," and Ayesha defends herself, pointing out that she had not put his name "with a cuss word." At this point Manrissa, who is very curious about people, their roots, and their beliefs, speaks up.
> MANRISSA: (to Ayesha) Do you like him?
> AYESHA: Yes I like Him. (exasperated but amused) I love Him. He's in heaven.
> MANRISSA: Is he real?
> AYESHA: Yes, He's real. What else questions you wanta ask?

Mona laughs. Manrissa shrugs and goes back to her work.

AYESHA: Dag! She asking if God was real. (turns to Manrissa) Did you know He made you? He made you outa sand and dirt.

Louise has heard this last bit of talk and intervenes.

LOUISE: You know and I know that different people have different beliefs about that.

Louise leaves and Ayesha's stance immediately changes from critical to politely inquisitive.

AYESHA: (sweetly) Do you believe in God, Manrissa?

Manrissa shrugs.

MONA: No, because she don't go to church.

AYESHA: You don't know that! (irritated and critical toward Mona).

. . .

I don't go to church, but that don't mean I still don't believe in God. I have church in my own house. So?

MONA: You live in an apartment, Ayesha.

AYESHA: I know I live in an apartment. I have it in my apartment.

Despite her amused exasperation with Manrissa, Ayesha found Manrissa as interesting as Manrissa found her. In fact, like her peer, Ayesha was very interested in the histories and cultures of people she regarded as different. She consistently asked questions about unfamiliar countries that Louise mentioned: Did people from there have wars? Did they fight with the United States in the Gulf War? Did they ever immigrate to this country? What kind of names do they have? What kind of food do they eat? Moreover, she was exceedingly interested in the history and heroes of African-American people.

Indeed, as earlier discussed, Ayesha, William, and their friends all explicitly acknowledged race as an important part of their shared world. This importance was vividly illustrated during class visits to the library, in which the children called each other's attention to books or magazines containing references to or pictures of African-American people. Relevant books were limited in number and generally quite old, though, so the children passed the same books among themselves repeatedly. Indeed, one day Darren told Ayesha, who claimed that she was going to keep reading a book about Martin Luther King until she died, "You ain't gonna go to this school that long. You gotta send your kids here and let them bring it home. And then their kids. . . . " Ayesha and her girl friends even spent a number of recesses planning a play on Martin Luther King, an idea all their own. (The play faltered, in part because no one wanted to play the White bus driver who tells Rosa Parks to move and because they could not agree on what "cute boy" should get to play Martin Luther King.)

In sum, William, Ayesha, and their friends were more culturally and politically aware than the younger children had been. They acted more deliberately as members of a particular sociocultural community—their roots and cultural symbols (e.g., music, language) were important to them in very explicit ways. At the same time, they were interested in the information and materials made available in the official world—although they felt vulnerable in that world.

Vulnerability in the Official World

Ayesha and William both viewed doing well in school as important for making their families proud of them and also for meeting their career goals—Ayesha to be a lawyer or a preacher, William to be an artist. But they also each viewed their success in school as potentially problematic. Of most concern was the possibility that Louise might flunk them. Although she reassured them that she would not do this and that they would learn, the children did not seem convinced of this.

As readers might recall, this concern about flunking was evident even in the K/1. The younger children did not dismiss or resist school, but they did view school, particularly high school, as a place where teachers keep kicking "you" out and "you" keep having to try to get back in.

JAMES: They [the school] just throw you out so you have to jump on the ground, huh?

· · ·

LAMAR: And then you can't go in school no more.

JAMES: And then you have to go to another high school. Like, like if you was 13 and and and—you—and all the time you have to get—all the time you have to get D's, they would have to kick you outa school, huh?

LAMAR: Yep. Every single school!

JAMES: And then—then you have to go to a new high school.

Similarly, the older children seemed to see themselves as vulnerable to the school's power to push them down if not out. Ayesha's friend Lena, for example, was especially worried about flunking, since she had already been flunked once. Moreover, she had a 13-year-old cousin who was flunked so often she was still in the fifth grade. Luckily, said Lena, her cousin was small. One day Lena became distraught during a timed math quiz. Ayesha wrote her own narrative account of the emotional experience.

Today my best friend Lena was crying and I said, "whats the matter?"
She said, "I got My time table wrong." I said, "don't worry." She think
she's going to flunk. I said you are not going to flunk. You are a
smart girl. You don't have to cry you are going to make me cry Mona
said you are going to make me cry to. Crystal said me to so Lena
stop crying and did her work.

Ayesha had had a history of school success, but she also saw herself as
vulnerable to school failure. "My mom said I had a good report card," she
wrote. "It look like I was going to the 4th grade. . . . When I was in 1st
grade I was the smartest kid in my hole class. I had to teach people how
to read but now that I'm in the 3rd grade I hope I pass. . . . "

As Lena first told me, William did have a history of school failure.
Unlike Lena, however, William did not want to acknowledge that failure
in any way. When Louise asked the children to write a piece about report
cards, William resisted. He drew two small punk figures on the bottom of
his paper. "I don't like this topic," said one; "me either," said the other
(see Figure 8.1). Further, William was very sensitive to public displays of
any errors. (However, just as he enjoyed taking the spotlight in the unofficial world, William also could enjoy taking the spotlight in the official
one, as will be illustrated.)

Despite — or perhaps because of — the children's concerns about flunking, they were consistently supportive of friends with academic problems,
as seen not only in Ayesha's support of Lena, but also in the children's
friendship with Charles, the child with the most serious academic difficulties. During composing, the other children helped him spell, and by the
end of the school year they helped him read when he took center stage
during rug-time sharing. Sometimes a child would help him with nearly
every word, but he seemed enormously pleased to be reading; no one
displayed any impatience with the slowness of his efforts. Moreover, William in particular took every opportunity to praise him. One day in the
midst of a discussion of vocabulary words from a story, Louise asked for a
sentence with "beachcomber" in it.

"The beachcomber saw a beautiful shell," said Charles.

Louise was pleased, and William said loudly, "That's the best thing he
ever did, that I ever heard anyway."

Louise herself was straightforward and supportive of Charles. However,
while Louise could model acceptance and ways of guiding, and while she
could encourage mutual helping, she could not mandate friendship, and
Charles was included in the children's circle of friends.

In brief, William, Ayesha, and their friends did not accept or reject
others on the basis of academic competence — although they, like the

FIGURE 8.1. William's Commentary on the Topic of Report Cards

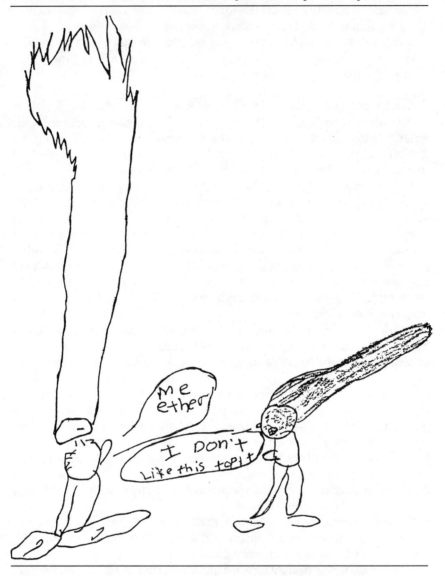

younger children, brooked no bragging. Moreover, they were united in their wariness about the school's view of their own academic worth, and they supported each other.[3] The complexity and intensity of the children's relationships with each other were visible on the social stage provided by the daily composing time, as discussed in the section to follow.

NEGOTIATING CLASSROOM WORLDS
THROUGH COMPOSING

Louise has called the children to the classroom rug to distribute new folders to keep their homework in. Because the school does not furnish folders, she has bought them herself. She first allows the children who turned in their homework to pick a new folder (Carl, April, Janene, Charles, April, Melissa, Mona, Paul, and Kate). Then the others get a turn. Darren takes red, Crystal picks light blue, and then Ayesha takes light blue, as do Lena and Bianca. Rashanda frowns; now that it's her turn, light blue is gone. She takes dark blue. William takes red, like Darren. The children's fussiness about the color of their folders frustrates Louise, who points out that each one cost the same, 50 cents. And "$10" for all, points out Ayesha, sitting happily with her light blue.

Just as Louise's folders assumed complex meanings within the children's worlds, so too did the daily composing time. The children's social work—especially their efforts to proclaim their connectedness and to put forward their own smartness, as it were—energized their writing and led to complex negotiations among multiple social worlds. After all, composing was the time when children, in William's words, were supposed to "express themselves."

Below, I illustrate key ways in which the children negotiated among their social worlds. The illustrative events include William, Ayesha, and their peers, but I highlight William, whose case study most dramatically revealed how composing could bring at least some children's official and unofficial worlds together in satisfying and powerful ways.

Curricular Coexistence and Potential Take-Overs

Both Ayesha and William seemed to enjoy the daily writing time, although William in particular was not interested, initially, in its procedures of editing and revising. Eventually, with prodding, he would circle potential misspelled words, consult with an adult and/or dictionary, and enter his work on the classroom computer for final drafts. Early in the project, he sometimes shared his texts during class meetings after writing time, but sometimes he did not.

For William and Ayesha and, in fact, for many children in the class, a major purpose of writing was to establish social cohesion—to declare themselves as competent kids who were members of important social groups (like "the guys"). Indeed, for the opening two months of the project, this seemed to be *the* purpose of William's composing. Although he had difficulty spelling—his texts were sometimes hard to decipher, William regularly wrote essays or expressive pieces of 75 words or so about his "best friends," his enjoyment of football, sports cars, drawing, jokes, and his supposed disliking of girls (a public show).

Most of William's time and energy went into the drawing of detailed portraits of vehicles, sports heroes, and friends. In his texts, he was one of the guys, so to speak, who teased girls, told jokes, and played sports. (See Figure 8.2 for a picture of "the guys.") William wrote in a conversational style, collegially addressing the *you's* of his peers, as in the following example:

> I like jokes. Do you know why? Because they are fun to do and you
> can make girls and boys and women and men laugh and a lots of
> kids.

Writing about friends and about likes and dislikes was appealing to the children, and it was also useful for Louise. Beyond getting her children writing, such texts allowed her a means for learning about her children's

FIGURE 8.2.   William's Drawing of "the guys"

social lives and personal interests. And yet, the children's personal essays and narratives did not necessarily serve as textual crossroads, supporting the children's efforts in multiple social worlds. The texts did not introduce unexpected generic material from unofficial worlds, nor did they typically serve as sites for child engagement with official material. The children's unofficial social agenda often seemed to simply coexist with the official one.

To elaborate, through such texts the children did not in any obvious way stake a claim on the official world; Louise, after all, invited and welcomed the children's personal narratives and essays. However, the children did not wholeheartedly engage in the official world either. As first discussed in Chapter 1, the imaginative universe of process writing assumes a participation structure in which individual children communicate to an audience of teachers and peers; moreover, it assumes as well that children will want to revise and edit ("publish") important communications—to make them clear, as it were—for public display.

However, Ayesha and, especially, William wrote regularly, not to communicate information to others, but to establish and manipulate social relationships. For these ends, the children sometimes engaged in joint constructions, in which composers collaboratively built a story or essay. Most often, though, the children's collaborative talk was filtered through a child's individual text. During rug-time sharing, the child could use the text to reach out to many children in the class; if successful, the text would be met with affirmative nods or verbal acknowledgments ("Yeah, Me too!"). There was no need to revise or edit such a text for clear communication—the piece had already done its work.

For example, one day Ayesha was having some trouble coming up with a writing topic. Louise suggested she write about somebody she knew. Ayesha thought she could write about her sister Rochelle—maybe even a poem about Rochelle, as long as she was careful not to include her sister's "personal business" (a concern Rashanda, Ayesha, and William voiced in the opening anecdote). When Ayesha wrote the following two lines, however, the interest of the children around her heightened considerably:

Her best is rappers.
She like B. B. D.   M. C. Hammer   Bobby Brown

Lena, Darren, Rashanda, and Crystal all began to contribute the names of rap stars they had seen on the Grammy Awards show the preceding night. The enthusiasm of her collaborating peers seemed to excite Ayesha; her list of rappers grew, and she abandoned the plan to write a poem about Rochelle. Later, she read the piece with pleasure to her peers, anticipating their confirming responses: "M. C. Hammer, yes. Bobby Brown, yes."

Ayesha's text suggests the promise and the potential problems that could occur as composing activities became more firmly embedded in the children's social lives. Ayesha's social agenda coexisted with the official one; it was neither suppressed nor diverted to side roads. And the involvement of her collaborating peers did heighten Ayesha's interest in the writing activity per se. But, from the standpoint of Louise's goals, it did not necessarily tap the richness of her language resources or composing skill.

To further illustrate, consider William's essay about girls.

> We have too much girls in our class, and I don't like girls at all. Just my mom. Do you know why I hate girls? Because they hate football. So I hate girls. Now do you see? I'm sorry, but I do. I wish girls liked football. (William added the last sentence after talking with Louise; spelling and punctuation corrected for ease of reading)

William's piece might seem like an ideal text for critical reflection, particularly about images of girls. And, indeed, Louise did talk to William about his text. Was the point that he really didn't like *girls*? Some girls, she pointed out, like football. The point, William agreed, was that he really liked football and that he wished girls in their class did. While William did add the last sentence, his piece was not written for clear communication (or for artful performance, for that matter). Rather the essay served both to declare William's social cohesion with the boys *and* to manipulate—criticize or, more playfully, tease—the girls (Crystal in particular).

The essay actually evolved in the midst of ongoing teasing between William and Crystal, who, in fact, liked each other. Crystal, sitting across from William as he wrote, giggled at his texts and wrote her own.

> Sometimes I wish that my Dad did not like football because they always watch football, baseball, and basketball. Because me and my mom never get to watch any T.V. with my brother. My brother is only 7 months and he is very cute to me.
>
> All boys are bad because it's just a nerve in their head. I don't know [why] every boy has the same thing in their mind.

Indeed, for Crystal, such unofficial social purposes as teasing others could lead to curriculum take-overs. That is, Crystal sometimes exploited the public stage provided by the official world in ways that threatened peace in the classroom community. For example, she sometimes couched her teases in fictional stories; she then used the daily sharing time for classroom manipulation on a grand (and, from my point of view) rather bold scale. Breaking the classroom rule about checking with children before writing about them, she would read stories naming certain classmates as her friends or sisters, designating certain others as their "boy friends" and, once, still others as "wimps." (Crystal's "wimps" were April and Manrissa, two children with different social backgrounds from Crystal's and different senses of humor as well. April in particular complained, and complained loudly, about the insulting designation.)

While William and Ayesha wrote no such stories, their texts were similar in social purpose: They used their texts to declare and manipulate their social relationships in peer worlds. While using friends as characters is a potentially helpful strategy for text development, many children in the class literally stuffed as many peers' names as possible into their pieces. The goal was direct manipulation, not subtle exploration. William's texts in particular did not seem to capture the humor and the social insight (the play with social boundaries) that was so visible just under the surface of the official curriculum.

And it was, in fact, drawing more fully upon those language resources just under the surface of the official curriculum that seemed to lead to the children's most sophisticated writing *and* their most intensive participation in the official curriculum itself, as I explain in the next section.

Performative Claims and Textual Crossroads

The children introduced into the official curriculum a variety of genres that were reflective of their home community traditions, including folk rhymes and true stories, and overlapping popular ones, like rap. As she did with Jameel's popular songs, games, and cartoons, Louise made interactive space for these genres. Indeed, she led a class study unit on raps and even invited a rap artist to the class (which completely surprised Ayesha: "I would have never guessed"). Louise also brought in many kinds of literary texts, including the popular anthology *Talk That Talk: An Anthology of African-American Storytelling* (Goss & Barnes, 1989).

In assuming positions as artful performers for a classroom audience, the children required participation structures that were, in fact, compatible with the official ones Louise offered—that is, they required opportunities to present their work as distinctive individuals to an audience of appreciative, involved others. Moreover, the desire to perform also made relevant the crafting processes Louise fostered and the reflective talk she encouraged (although both Ayesha and William, like Jameel, resisted critical feedback given publicly). In effect, the role of a performer made unofficial resources available, and it also made official possibilities sensible.

From the very beginning of my observations on this project, Ayesha brought her performative powers to bear on the official curriculum. Her poetic texts about African-American heroes brought her official and unofficial admiration, and, in fact, they also earned the out-of-school appreciation of her mother. Ayesha told me repeatedly what historical figures or modern-day political happenings her mother liked or didn't like. One hero was Martin Luther King (see Figure 8.3 for accompanying drawing).

> Martin Luther King was a preacher.
> He really knew how to talk.
> In August he led a peace march.
> He walked and walked and walked.
> One day they threw a bomb at his house.
> It was bigger than a mouse.
> The KKK was very bad.
> They made the people very mad, and also made them sad.
> He was a serious man,
>   and taught peace on the land.

Like her Martin Luther King poem, 7 of the 19 products collected during the project were about African-American historical figures, and most were written in rhythmic prose and, often, crafted explicitly as poems. Her most admired heroes were M. L. King and Harriet Tubman.

FIGURE 8.3. Ayesha's Peace March

Appropriately, given her own appreciation of language, part of what she admired most was the ability of these individuals to use talk. Indeed when she grew up, wrote Ayesha:

I would like to Be a Lawer or a prcher
like Dr. Martin Luther King
talk for peace and freedom
and do thing like Harrit tuBmen
Be a prcher
prch for god
talk the truth
(spacing arranged to accentuate the piece's poetic structure)

Of all the third graders, though, it was William whose stories illustrated most dramatically the power that texts rooted in children's unofficial resources had for engaging them in the official curriculum. And this was true precisely because William had been so unengaged in the composing processes of editing, revising, and even sharing.

William on Stage.   William's writing initially showed no evidence of his performative powers; indeed, during January and February, all 13 of his collected products were relatively short personal essays written in a conversational style. But, in March, William's writing changed suddenly; performative and, most often, narrative writing dominated during the last three and a half months of school.

William referred to his performative stories as "true stories," the kind "my mom likes." "True stories," as readers may recall, was the label also used by the observed K/1 children. "This is a true story," a child might say, and then tell a story that could not be true, an exaggerated, humorous, and performative tale that often revealed the cleverness of the teller.

William, however, did not *tell* his true stories. He wrote them — and they were long, from 200 to 300 words. The first such piece was motivated by the arrival in the classroom of two pet birds. The birds reminded William, he had said, of his uncle's "cussing bird," a phrase that got the whole class laughing. Perhaps it was that laughing, that appreciation from the classroom community as a whole, that led William to write the first of three interconnected stories about his uncle and his pets. William seemed to anticipate his peers' giggles, as he quickly and with great concentration wrote about his uncle (whom he displayed as not too bright) and himself (a disparaged but eventually respected character in his own tale).

William spent quite a bit of time with his uncle, who cared for him when his mother's work schedule kept her away long hours. His uncle, he felt, could be awfully bossy, and William took no small delight in a story of the teasing uncle who, in the end, was put in his place.

MY UNCLE AND THE CUSSING BIRD

OK this how it started. My uncle wanted a bird so bad, he tried to get one out of the sky. Now that's dumb. So one day he was hoping that he can get a bird free. And I said to my Uncle Glen, "How are you going to do that?" And he said, "I don't know." So two months later a box came, and it said bird. And my uncle started screaming and teasing me. He was saying, "Oh yes. I have a bird. Ha, ha, ha ha, ha. I have a bird. Ha, ha, ha ha, ha." And he opened it, and the bird was dead. And he started to cry. The whole couch was wet with tears. I tried onions but he started to cry more. Then, he started to cry more. The next week, more and more boxes, and he kept saying, "Ha, ha, ha ha, ha." And one day a box came—Yes yes yes! The bird said "I'm polly-want-a cracker." [And] he said, "F_____ [sic] you big mouth." And my uncle never wanted a bird again. Do you know what he wanted? A fish. (piece given conventional spelling and punctuation for ease of reading)

Through this story, William aimed to perform, to entertain others artfully, or so suggested both his performative language and his eagerness to take the classroom stage with his work. To elaborate, William's story was more crafted than any of his earlier pieces. There was an opening orientation to his uncle and the situation ("My uncle wanted a bird so bad, he tried to get one out of the sky"). William not only carefully sequenced a series of events, he captured the affective quality of the experience. He used evaluative comments ("Now that's dumb"), extended, expressive dialogue, and even a well-placed interruption of the story's rhythm ("Yes yes yes!").

Moreover, the two stories that followed were carefully scripted to match the initial story of the cussing bird. First came the biting fish, which began right where the last one ended ("Do you know what he wanted? A fish").

In the last story, the cursing bird liked to cuss. Let's see what happens in this story. It was 1990 and my uncle wanted a fish. So one day me and my uncle went fishing and my uncle caught a fish.

In this story, the tension between the uncle and William assumes a more dominant role. Moreover, new performative features were evident that served to highlight this tension. For example, William shifted verb tenses, which contrasted the reported teasing of his uncle and the characteristic it typified.

> He took it [the fish] home. He started to tease me. But that was nothing big. He does it all the time.

He also incorporated voices from popular media and folk sayings, which enlivened his tale in expressive ways. When William taunts his teasing uncle, the uncle chases after him. His uncle catches him when he falls over a big rock. William yells out:

> "Well people all over the world. I'm going to die. If you want to see me before I die come see me at 2829 or call me at 754-9295." I got out and said, "I'm not going to die." And I started to say, "I'm a free man oh yeah." Then I broke out saying and started to sing, "If it wasn't for bad luck I wouldn't have no luck at all."

The "biting fish" also introduced a slapstick sort of humor, which may be why William started calling them "comedy stories." This sort of humor increased in the last of the stories, set up in the concluding lines of the "biting fish." Since a package came containing a fish — which jumped up and bit his hand — his uncle decided he didn't want a fish anymore.

> And do you know what he wanted? He wanted a dog.

In the last story in the series, "The Bad Dog," William plays numerous tricks on his uncle at a party — a party to which his uncle had, in no uncertain terms, not invited him. In that story, William reveals, in true, "true story" fashion, that he himself has been the clever person behind the obnoxious pets. It is William's turn to laugh.

> "Remember when you was laughing at me? Now ha ha ha. And remember all those pets? Here they are."

The fish jumps up and bites his uncle, the bird curses at him, and, then, a box arrives for his uncle. Yes. It is a dog that comes out and bites him. William gloats:

> "Do you want a dog now? Do you know why all that stuff happened to you? Why? Because I set you up that's why." Do you know what he wanted? Nothing. The end.

All three stories were huge classroom hits. Indeed, William anticipated that they would be. He finished his "cussing bird" piece right as the class was leaving for its weekly library period. William was enormously disappointed: "That's why I want to read it on the rug, so everybody can hear it. But she said we have to go the library. Maybe she'll let us read them when we come back."

He did read the piece after the class came back from the library—and many times after that, at his classmates' own request. This anticipation—and desire for—success on the official classroom stage may have supported a change in the quality of William's participation in, as well as the products resulting from, the daily composing time.

William was drawing on language from unofficial worlds—the language of popular media and of folk traditions—but he also was entering into the official activities of composing, including planning, drafting, reflecting, and performing. Moreover, his stories became part of the official culture of the classroom, even as they drew on unofficial sources; the stories were talked about by other children, requested as stories to hear again, and even imitated by his classmate Paul.

William's increased investment in the official world, and his reflectiveness about his texts and their social meaning, were in fact displayed at the very publishing party whose guests William had seemingly disregarded. At the party William read his "cussing bird" piece to the invited guests, with enormous pleasure. However, he made a key adjustment for the audience, as he explained to Louise and his classmates as they chatted after the party guests had left.

WILLIAM: I had, like, to put something different in the cussing bird story. When I had the F word, I had to say something different. I was gonna say, "He said the F word." But I said, "never mind." (William had read that "he said a bad word.")

LOUISE: That was smart. You have to consider your audience.

When he turned toward his classmates, however, he emphasized the tough talk and slapstick; indeed he deliberately planned to do just that. When William finished his first story about the cussing bird, he immediately commented on the next tale.

WILLIAM: That's gonna be the next one I'm writing about—a fish. This is a true story. . . . A true story about a fish. It's gonna be re::al rad. A lot of cussing and a lot of biting.

And it was, real rad, that is.

This cussing and biting highlights the role of William's stories as kinds of crossroads — as texts that were supported by, and supporting, William's action in multiple social worlds. As the complex intertext of his stories suggests, such crossroads are themselves built by crossing textual, social, and cultural boundaries.

VERBAL PERFORMANCE IN THE DIALOGIC CURRICULUM

As illustrated throughout this book, children's self-expression in the classroom is also their social expression, their voicing of how they are situated within the complex worlds of the classroom. Amidst the breadth of possible relationships, children's voices articulate who each thinks she or he is relative to particular others in particular historical moments. William dramatically illustrated such sociocultural intelligence as he re-voiced Louise's words in vernacular English for an unofficial language play and also as he re-voiced a friend's vernacular for an official classroom essay.

Of all the genres or types of speech communication, it was the performative story that seemed to allow individual children to express most fully the complexity of their worlds. Child authors, like adult ones, intermingle voices that, in theme, style, or structure, are linked for them and for their readers to specific situations and to the values and authority structures of those situations. Thus, like all authors, they not only manipulate the boundary between the real world and the fictional one, they also manipulate cultural boundaries, those of age, status, sex, class, race, ethnicity, and on and on. Artful stories do not smooth out or hide tensions, nor do they directly manipulate them — they craft them for display. And they do so by intermingling voices drenched in cultural meaning. Curses and pleas, television come-ons and playground put-downs, literary allusions and rap song rhythms — all can coexist in the story. It is this that gives them their sociocultural depth — their capacity to reflect the sociocultural complexity of a child's world.

This depth was first seen in Jameel's texts, as he intermingled voices from diverse social spheres. The third graders were more experienced writers and students. William, for example, did not innocently assume that his storytelling powers would be appropriate for the classroom stage. But emboldened perhaps by the camradery of Louise and his peers — their laughter at his oral jokes — or perhaps by the diversity of cultural traditions accepted in the class, or maybe simply by the irresistible appeal of a stage, William brought unofficial language resources into the official classroom world.

Social and cultural boundaries, however, are crossed not only within children's stories but also in the very fact that those stories exist within the official classroom world. An opposition of vernacular and/or peer ways with words to school ways is often assumed (e.g., Labov, 1982; Ogbu, 1987), and indeed William himself seemed to assume such an opposition in his unofficial language play. But stories are vehicles for bringing diverse voices into the classroom itself. Thus William brought into the official classroom world "true stories" that were linked to his identity in unofficial worlds. Indeed, the importance of a composing link to families and home communities and to cultural identity was evident in other children's experiences as well. For example, Ayesha's rhythmic writing and story poems about African-American heroes earned her classroom appreciation—and also her mother's; Manrissa regularly referred to Chinese cultural figures and symbols in her own stories, which intrigued the class as well.

In their pleasure and involvement in all these texts, the children themselves came together, which is the last and most important social and cultural boundary I note. That is, not only were social and cultural boundaries crossed, first, within the children's texts and, second, in the existence of those texts within the official classroom community, but they also were crossed in the very coming together of teacher and all class members to enjoy the texts. William's stories especially may have been classroom favorites at least in part because their sharing in a classroom forum touched common chords in the children. For the diverse details of the children's lives, when crafted, can reveal their connections.

They were all, at the very least, children in an adult-governed world. And in that world, where politeness and kindness are the ostensible values, William pushed hushed emotions beyond the point of embarrassing self-revelation ("personal business," in Rashanda's terms); his bold voices were crafted, in fact, with language tools valued in the official school world. This delight in tough talk in polite places (this legitimate way to "express myself") is common, in fact, in childhood. Teasing the adult world through language is a cross-cultural if not universal pleasure of childhood (Opie & Opie, 1959).

Further, the children all enjoyed the music of language itself—its rhythm and rhyme—an enjoyment that is also a near universal in childhood. Many children took pleasure in rhyming their talk as much as possible, an interest that may have been strengthened by the popularity of rap. In fact, William's and Ayesha's own pleasure in a story poem April presented was particularly poignant, because both children had expressed explicitly to Louise a desire not to sit by that child. And yet, when April shared the following text, William and Ayesha were the most vocal of all in their calls for her to "read it again." (The piece is not only carefully crafted, it is also rather slapstick in its humor, and, perhaps, a child's version of a Robert Louis Stevenson classic.)

MY SHADOW

I saw my shadow sneaking
over to my bedroom door
I spied on him, then quickly
I walked over with my sore.

I wrestled with my shadow.
I kicked him half to death.
I called him names like "Pinocchio,"
and "Little Beth de Seth."

I gave him all my socks
they say
Well maybe one or two.
But when my shadow walked out the
door with me,
I hit him with my shoe.

Such discoveries of commonality are not automatic — and they inevitably come mixed with the classroom tensions (for teacher and children) suggested by the description herein of curricular coexistence and takeovers. Children constantly renegotiate their classroom selves; in a world of differences, children's roles in diverse social worlds can conflict. But this potential conflict only highlights the value of those moments when children and teachers are all wrapped up together inside a crafted tale, those moments when children see themselves as interconnected people in the classroom community.

In closing, I return to the chapter's opening quote and to Bakhtin's notion of socially conscious people who, in a sense, choose a language. In the official world, the observed children seemed most deliberately manipulative of *language* when composing artful texts, choosing words with care for their musical as well as their literal sense.[4] The social work of performative stories was, after all, well-understood by their younger sisters, brothers, cousins, and classmates in the kindergarten. And, perhaps, to use Vygotskian themes, being so firmly rooted in the "spontaneous" or everyday experiences of their lives, such texts were prime material for deliberate reflection, for the "scientific" language of crafting that Louise fostered (Vygotsky, 1962). Moreover, such texts drew in powerful ways on their social and language resources as child members of their home community. That is, the texts had sociocultural depth — they resonated in the children's lives beyond the official curriculum. And, finally, for children feeling vulnerable in the official world, the texts allowed a sense of control, an opportunity to display their own smartness and to make others listen, laugh, and appreciate.

William and Ayesha and their peers did not engage in all kinds of writing with the enthusiasm with which they engaged in performative genres. Writing summaries or personal responses to read books, for example, held no interest for William; he did such tasks as quickly as possible, rarely failing to ask, "How many sentences do we have to write?" The minimum was the maximum. Without underestimating the power of the children's artful genres, we must also engage children in a range of literacy dialogues. And powerful resources for that engagement exist, in fact, in the very sociocultural intelligence the children displayed. That is, resources can be tapped by helping children understand the kind of social work — the relationship to other people and to the world — implicit in varied literacy dialogues and by supporting their efforts to connect the complex of worlds within which they live. In the final chapter of this book, I consider how the experiences of Louise and her children might inform all our efforts as educators to help children compose fulfilling and meaningful places for themselves in the classroom and beyond.

CHAPTER 9

COMPOSING THE
CLASSROOM NEIGHBORHOOD

School is the meeting place of the private and the public, the individual and the group, of the children and the adult. The open [permeable] classroom not only welcomes the children and their own ways of thinking and feeling, but it also creates a life of its own . . . a delicate web of relationships . . . which is as complicated as that in any home. As complicated but different, for it creates new possibilities, new speculations, new styles.

— Rosen & Rosen, *The Language of Primary
School Children*, 1973, pp. 31–32

This book began with Lamar's row of child houses, his imagined neighborhood of classmates and friends. Lamar was engaging in social work, using his verbal resources to compose a shared (if "fake") life. In this chapter, I focus on how teachers themselves might construct a particular sort of shared life with their students, one with permeable boundaries, open to a breadth of social dialogues, a depth of cultural reverberations and connections. And I highlight the role of child composing in the formation of such a "delicate web of relationships."

The instructional considerations I offer are based on the study of a small group of children of one sociocultural group in one school. However, my research concern was not behavior specific to any one group of children, but rather the dynamics of, or the interplay between, children's social work and the institutional setting of school and how that interplay figured into learning to write. Similar dynamics might well occur in other school settings involving socioculturally different children, especially given a teacher who values self-expression and a sense of community (Erickson, 1986; McDermott & Hood, 1982).

As illustrated throughout this book, a sense of classroom community, of neighborhood, is not easily achieved, because the classroom itself is not a

215

homogenous world. Children negotiate membership in overlapping, sometimes contradictory worlds governed by "imaginative universes" — cultures, as it were, or shared ways of infusing objects and actions with tz, 1973). Against the backdrop of these diverse worlds, al themselves, not as exemplars of cultural categories, but xtured selves (Williams, 1991).

Indeed, the acknowledgment of such complexity seems to be a critical first step in respectful relationships between teachers and students and in the building of a shared life. As teachers we have access to only parts of children's selves. Describing Ms. Powell, a first-grade teacher, Sarah tfoot (1978) writes, she "is aware of the constraints and social context, and she recognizes that her vision of the stic but a partial one that is situationally defined" (p. 213).

Respect for the diversity of children's worlds, for the partiality of our own visions, keeps us from putting children into neat "sociological categories of race, social class, ethnicity and family structure [which then] become the primary factors of differentiating among children" (Lightfoot, 1978, p. 211). And, more specifically, it allows us to avoid overly neat categorizations of children's language as well (e.g., as "oral" or "literate," "communicative" or "performative"). As all the observed children illustrated, child language users do not have only one composing style, nor do they have only one end goal. As people of breadth, the child writers each drew upon different genres, different discourse traditions, as they reached out to different others, including teachers, peers, and neighborhood friends.

Respect for the diversity of children's worlds also fuels our respectful curiosity about children's lives, our desire as teachers to understand all the factors that contribute to a child's wholeness, to his or her individuality. Teachers with such curiosity, and Louise was one such teacher, invite children to share responsibility for negotiating the language life — the valued texts — of classroom life (Genishi, 1992). In such a way the intertextual universe of the classroom itself attains sociocultural depth, as diverse genres, diverse cultural traditions, mingle on the classroom stage, giving rise to "new possibilities, new speculations, new styles."

The kind of cultural negotiation required is more complex than Bruner (1986) seems to suggest, when he speaks of learning as a "communal activity, a sharing of *the* culture [emphasis added]" (p. 127). To be viable, a singular classroom culture will need to be formed through a kind of alchemy, through creating an official classroom world that intersects among many. And to spark such alchemy, teachers must do more than "scaffold" children's entry into the valued ways of the society as a whole (Bruner, 1975). Rather, they must themselves be "active, interactive, and vulnerable," in the words of the sociolinguist Eleanor Ochs (1988, pp. 244–245). She hypothesizes that adults' own understanding of the world is transformed through the questions and responses of children.

Such negotiation, such openness, is not easy if curricular mainroads have rigid boundaries within which children must respond. In such a curriculum, the "sense" of each task may be to please the teacher, a kind of sense that is differentially meaningful to children. In contrast, a permeable curriculum assumes and, indeed, exploits children's susceptibility to the appeal of meaningful activity and their sensitivity to situational context. Further, it acknowledges the complexity of children's social worlds and cultural materials. And it attempts not only to create bridges between worlds, but to support children's own naming and manipulating of the dynamic relationships among worlds.

In the following sections, I consider in more detail the nature of the permeable curriculum, particularly the situated vision of literacy that informs it and the ways in which it allows for the sociocultural dimensions of child writing, that is, for breadth and depth.

DEFINING DISCOURSE BOUNDARIES: RIGIDITY VS. PERMEABILITY

When children enter school, they encounter, perhaps for the first time, a world in which written language itself is foregrounded. The observed children all had a strong sense of the importance of learning to write and read, especially "to make your family happy," to use Lamar's words. In Louise's room, the children were allowed marking materials, many examples of t   ipate in writing and reading. The children   free to write   ever and however they chose.

In ac   , however,   of   ildren or adults, are ever "free to write." Writing, like all language use, is always a situated response, an addressing of another in a particular time and place, a motivated making of words for some end. The written words are only mediators—and, for young children especially, only partial mediators—of social action. This understanding—that writing isn't free, that it is inextricably tied to social activity and cultural meaning—undergirds teachers' efforts to evaluate the permeability of classroom boundaries. Permeability will depend, in part, on classroom social structures that make sensible diverse kinds of social action and text sense. But to achieve such an understanding teachers must actively work against contrary assumptions that pervade the discussion of childhood literacy.

To elaborate, a diversity of social goals for literacy use—and the diverse kinds of texts they require—has long characterized U.S. society, existing prior to the availability of universal schooling (Cook-Gumperz, 1986; Heath, 1981). People from a broad spectrum of American life have used writing to entertain, correspond with, and inform others, among other purposes. And yet schooling itself may have contributed to a narrow and rigid definition of literacy, one that "changed forever the relationship of the majority of the population to their own talents for learning and for literacy" (Cook-Gumperz, 1986, p. 27). In schools, literacy, this grand social mediator, has been conceptualized as something apart from social dialogue; it has become defined as a "decontextualized knowledge validated through text performances" (p. 41).

This definition of literacy—and its confounding with a particular kind of analytic reasoning—potentially makes problematic children's diverse ways of entering school literacy. As suggested in Chapter 1, the imaginative universe undergirding the literature on child writing seems founded, in large part, on this narrow definition. Individual expression and explicitness of information are valued, as are requests for clarity from responsive audience members—whatever the genre, whatever the child's social purpose. Within such an imaginative universe, only certain kinds of child social work—and only some kinds of texts—may make "sense."

Moreover a narrow definition of literacy encourages our tendency as humans to assume "mutually exclusive categorization" (Williams, 1991, p. 10). Thus, educators who value children's performative powers and, more particularly, their stories, songs, and rhymes, may be evaluated as not valuing less performative school genres or, even more dangerous, as implying that children themselves do not value and indeed should not (and do not) learn varied ways with words.

This tendency is clearly seen in the literature on young school children's storytelling, where generalizations about children's language use often are made on the basis of data gathered on only one social stage (e.g., Gee, 1989). Children are invited to tell a story, as it were, which is then discussed as though their way of telling stories was a pervasive language "style," not a response to a situation. And then this documented style becomes a new reason for school failure, a "difference" to be respected and bridged perhaps, but not situated and incorporated (McDermott, 1987). Ultimately, the rigidity of school boundaries is not challenged.[1]

Seeing each child's behavior as a situated response in a moment in time allows us to create classroom contexts in which we can value a diversity of language and social powers—and the diversity of any one child. Jameel's performative stories and songs, Lamar's collaboratively constructed tales, Eugenie's collegial expressions of affection—and even her melodramatic historical fiction—all seem valid ways of entering the ongoing literacy life of the classroom. None seems less legitimate than the typical forms of early writing reported in the professional literature — the labels, captions, and brief statements about a topic. Moreover, a situated vision of literacy also allows us to consider how we might create social situations that support children's entry into new ways of using language.

ACKNOWLEDGING AND SUPPORTING SOCIOCULTURAL BREADTH

Composing in oral or written language involves entering into a dialogue with another, using words to construct a social place, in a sense, where self and other are connected. The observed children responded to the interactive spaces Louise offered with a diversity of kinds of social work. And that diversity infused words like *audience*, *response*, and *sense* with sociocultural meaning. In so doing, it allowed insight into the kinds of social places children may require if they are to make use of the breadth of their language resources.

For example, the children made visible joint constructions in which the child composer aimed to cue shared knowledge and contribute to a collaborative story, and thereby build social cohesion. Work toward social cohesion also occurred when children wrote individually about topics they knew would elicit "oh yeah's" or other kinds of acknowledgment from peers. Thus, Lamar's and James's stories of sharks and endangered little boys, Ayesha's listing of rap singers at the Grammy Awards, and William's pieces about liking football — and not liking girls — all seemed to reinforce in very straightforward ways the children's membership in certain friendship or peer groups with particular values.

Individual children also aimed to take the interactive spotlight, another kind of social work, and thereby gain an appreciative, admiring audience. It was, in fact, while composing performative pieces that the children both drew most clearly on their oral folk resources *and* manipulated their texts most explicitly; for example, they tried to make words rhyme, phrases rhythmic, dialogue fast-paced, and images funny. That is, the children "deliberately structured the web of meaning" and reflected on their compositional choices, to use Vygotsky's (1962, p. 100) description of the writing act. Rethinking text (i.e., revising) seemed to come most readily during preparation for a performance, as long as no help was provided by a perceived audience member. Thus, children were most apt to stake claims for unofficial genres (e.g., true stories, popular songs, raps, rhythmic verses) *and* to be intensely involved with official purposes when given a stage — an opportunity to show their stuff.

A third kind of social work was to establish collegial relationships with others. Children responded to each other as sympathetic peers, as people in the same boat, as it were. Together they could commiserate about the trials and tribulations of learning to write, including spelling and spacing, doing it over and trying to read it. "I, KNOW, HOW, YOU, FEEL, GIRL!" said Eugenie to the determined but irritated Shawnda, and, indeed, she did. All of the observed children valued informal, mutual helping, and all took pleasure in making inroads by turning the official material on its head (e.g., the peace march in heaven, the rude — but only recited — thank you letters, and my personal favorite, not previously noted, Crystal's and Lena's gospel-style "partner singing" [rather than partner reading] of a basal reader selection).

Fourth, the children enjoyed helping. From kindergarten on, explicit naming and comparing went on in the context of helping needy others who, of course, might not see themselves as needy. Still, the hoped-for response seemed to be "thanks." The children took pride in providing an unknowing other with a needed label or explanation, illustrated best, perhaps, by brave Anthony (brave from my point of view); as a kindergartner, he would tell even the first graders a thing or two. Indeed, passing on needed information to those of higher status was particularly appealing to all the children.

In another episode not earlier noted, William talked at great length in class, uncharacteristically so for him, explaining to an inquisitive, seemingly unknowing Louise about the relationship between *bunt, punt, putt*, and *extra kick* — and eagerly taking to a dictionary to find support for his own definitions when classmates disagreed. Moreover, the children welcomed my own rather passive but curious stance. Jameel especially enjoyed lecturing me about barnacles and birds, "toons" and picture books, all topics about which I seemed, and most often was, ill-informed.[2]

Finally, all of the children could work to be dutiful students, providing information to a *knowing* other in anticipation of a "very good," rather than a "thank you." This kind of work could lead to pleasure — and to feelings of vulnerability, of being exposed as not smart.

This breadth of social work, with its shifting participation structures and social roles, suggests the importance of articulating the specifics of instructional contexts for writing (see also Gutierrez, 1992). And so doing — making distinctions among helpers, audience members, and collaborators, for example — might allow us as teachers new ways of observing children's participation in writing activities *and* new ways of planning writing activities with children.

Informed by an understanding of composing as social work, we as *child observers* might pay attention not only to what children literally are *saying*

(Clay, 1975; Paley, 1986) but also to what children are *doing*. For what children are doing is part of their message, part of the declaration of a social self. "I am in control," says the individual performer; "we share a common world," says the joint constructor.

As *instructional planners*, we might also make space for what they are doing: Colleagues must be free to consult and commiserate, to admire and admonish — and to find a space apart for private shaping and reflection; similarly, collaborators require partners, performers need an audience, "teachers" must have "students," or they cannot enact their roles, display their skills, accomplish the ends that make their lives satisfying. Interactive space can be provided informally, which necessitates a more specific definition of "time off task" (than the time-worn rhetoric of "If you're talking you're not working" [see Dyson, 1987, for an elaboration]). But the diversity of children's social work also can be explicitly and officially acknowledged. For example, Louise talked with her children about their preferred ways of composing, making explicit the variation and offering choices. Did they wish to write alone? with a partner? in a quiet corner? at a table with other composers? Further, teachers can specifically provide for certain kinds of social work. For example, Daiute (1989) has collaborated with teachers who themselves provide for collaborative peer writing, giving all children potential opportunities to experience the fun of jointly exploring and playfully manipulating language.

Expanding the Conversation

While children need interactive space to compose relationships with others — mediated by texts — that make sense from their own points of view, they also need guidance so that they can enter new kinds of conversations, new sorts of dialogues with the world. And for this to happen some kind of social engineering, as it were, may be needed. That is, educators may need to create occasions for guided writing beyond open-ended composing periods, when diverse purposes and audiences can be socially negotiated and made socially sensible for and with children (Gray, 1987; Heath & Mangiola, 1991; Moll & Greenberg, 1990).

Louise's K/1 careers unit provided an illustration of the potential power of such social arranging (see Chapter 2). As readers might recall, Louise invited the children's parents and other community members to visit and discuss their jobs. Louise and the children made an interview guide, with four questions that they asked each visitor; the visitor's responses were recorded on a sheet of chart paper and hung in the room. After each visit, Louise led a discussion in which the chart answers were compared. By the fourth visit, the children themselves spontaneously made comparisons:

"Everybody said. . . . No, not everybody 'cause. . . . She said . . . but
he said. . . . "

Guided by Louise, the children were jointly analyzing an experience
they all had had; moreover, their analysis was mediated, at least in part,
by recorded experience, that is, by the lists of interview responses. And
the result was the oral and collective enactment of another kind of text —
one meant to analyze and summarize information for one's own edifica-
tion and that of others. Such oral and collective enactment foreshadows
individual children's ability to compose such texts to regulate their own
thinking and that of others (Vygotsky, 1978). To use the words of the
Australian educator Gray (1987), who writes about social constructivist
approaches to teaching, the children were "concentrating on and making
choices in order to construct meaning. They [were] not involved in imita-
tion or rote learning of form" (p. 17). But they *were* involved in a social
activity, mediated by text, that engaged their intellectual, social, and
affective energies.

It was this engagement of the children's energies — this sense of the kind
of social work involved — that seemed to be absent for some of the children
in expository writing tasks. Writing for the interactional spotlight was a
kind of social work that made sense. But writing "about what we did at
the aquarium" or "to summarize your story" or "to explain" a science
experiment — these were not engaging.

The children's intense discussions of social studies and science topics, of
new words from official or unofficial activities (e.g., words about sports or
popular music), all suggest the difficulty was not necessarily the children's
engagement in disciplinary topics or interest in explicit discussions of
words and ideas, but, at least in part, the meaningfulness of the kind of
social and intellectual work involved in writing "about things you already
know about because you was here" (or there, as it were), to use Jameel's
words.[3]

When I shared Jameel's lectures on science topics with Louise, she commented on the importance of children having opportunities to teach those
legitimately needing help. Louise noted that many of her children were
enormously engaged by teaching and, in so doing, would adopt features
of her own discourse. Teaching was a kind of social work that made sense
to them. As Louise suggested, simply having children study different topics
and, from the very beginning, couching that study in the context of responsibility to teach — to explain things to others, in part through their
writing — would seem helpful.

More broadly, if children engaged in diverse literacy practices over the
school years, perhaps coordinated across school grades, over time children's intellectual and social work would come to be mediated increas-

ingly by the composing act itself (rather than by, for example, guided interaction with a teacher-scribe) (Vygotsky, 1978). In such ways, children's understanding of varied sorts of official ways with words (the so-called code of the "culture of power" [Delpit, 1988]) would be grounded in the experiences of the children themselves, who have brought to bear on texts their powers to name and to analyze. And they would have done so to engage in social work that made sense to them, including to explore collegially, to construct collaboratively, and to teach.

Moreover, in a permeable curriculum, teacher and child visions of powerful discourse would themselves undergo modification. Educators concerned with teaching children the so-called discourses of power sometimes articulate the social and discursive practices children must learn to be successful by school standards. But attention only to socializing children into such ways with words does not challenge the too-neat boundaries drawn between children, language, and cultures — that is, between "home" and "school," "popular" and "literary," "mainstream" and "nonmainstream"; nor does such a unidirectional curricular vision reveal the individual child, situated amidst diverse social worlds, working to construct a coherent place for herself or himself at school.

ACKNOWLEDGING AND SUPPORTING SOCIOCULTURAL DEPTH

From a Bakhtinian perspective, a situated view of literacy — indeed, of child language users — demands more than attention to the dimension of breadth, to the horizontal relationship between composer and addressee. In entering a conversation mediated by writing, children are guided by the history of past conversations they have had. And those past conversations, linked to their experiences with family, friends, and community, root the child's present moment in the broader world; that is, they provide sociocultural depth, the vertical relationship between inner meanings and outer signs (already used words).

Childhood may well be a time when we more freely exploit the cultural material around us, having not yet fully discovered the fences societies may erect between the "high" or "proper" cultural stuff and the "low" (Jenkins, 1988; Levine, 1988). Indeed, the focal children attuned with ease to the language of the literary books Louise chose; there was no indication that that language was uncomfortable, even for children whom Louise judged (on the basis of school performance and parent discussion) as having had little preschool exposure to books. And, indeed, the observed children were all familiar with the use of language in artful, musical ways; in fact, children's literature itself is constructed in large part with the stylistic tools of oral storytellers (Kushkin, 1980).

Given a permeable curriculum, children's propensity to cross cultural boundaries may make possible potentially powerful learning in at least three interrelated ways: (1) it allows children rich resources for entering school literacy; (2) it makes possible the beginnings of children's critical awareness of how language situates them in the social and political world; and (3) it contributes to children's increasingly deliberate manipulation of symbolic worlds of words.

Entering the Conversation

The observed children illustrated how oral folk traditions and popular culture may serve as child resources for school literacy. The children were interested in how people spoke in cartoons and picture books, in poetry and speeches. The world is filled with lessons about texts and how they work (Meek, 1988). But whether or not children have opportunities to "recite" their lessons, to make use of their knowledge and know-how in school, is another matter altogether.

Children's diverse resources may more readily support their entry into school literacy if the classroom teacher has a dialogic—rather than a dichotomous—vision of cultural traditions, as did Louise. In fact, it was the very nature of the dialogic life Louise established with her children that set the stage for the beginnings of critical awareness for herself, her children, and me. In Louise's classroom, children were encouraged to have their say—to ask questions, offer their own opinions, suggest alternative ways of accomplishing classroom activities. She and her children talked about "throwing away" the sexist language that appeared in their books (e.g., "mailman," "policeman"), explored people's willingness to break unfair laws (e.g., the civil rights movement), and wrote letters of protest about varied matters.

It was in such a classroom that the children staked claims on the official curriculum, introducing cartoons, true stories, pop songs, and, less dramatically, humorous thematic and stylistic language. Louise, in turn, downplayed the source of greatest resistance—the public advice during rug-time sharing; and she worked with children to name their efforts, to place their work in the social landscape of discourse. In classroom sharing times, she not only allowed each child appreciation—public visibility and respect—but also listened for connections among children, connections of theme, of style, and of structure.

Louise did this, in part, by providing all children's texts with the dignity of a name (e.g., fiction, nonfiction, descriptions, plays, songs, games, poems, jokes), and she worked to establish connections between their efforts and those of the wider world of discourse: "That sounds like a Shel Silverstein poem. . . . Your story has a pattern, just like *The Cat in the Hat*, doesn't it?" Thus, her children, too, named their own work (e.g., cartoon stories, true stories, comedy stories) and found these connections.

Moreover, Louise responded to her children's diversity by incorporating into her own official repertoire the richness of our intertwined folk, popular, and literary heritages. The children studied the symphony and rap music; they read folktales of varied peoples and children's books in which diverse vernaculars of American English can be heard. The enacted curriculum in Louise's classroom included a diversity of texts, of kinds of sense, of possible dialogic responses to children's oral and written words. Each child's own composed text thus entered into an intertextual universe — a school culture — that was not some kind of anemic world, where words are disembedded from social contexts (cf. Donaldson, 1978); it was one where words reverberated with the diverse rhythms and sounds of human voices. And, of course, one to which the children contributed.

Reflecting on the Conversation

Placing children's texts in the social landscape of discourse seems central to a language arts curriculum that is concerned not simply with individual sensemaking, but with the dialogic process of figuring out how diverse kinds of discourse function in school and beyond. While Louise did not specifically ask the children to become "ethnographers," so to speak, that is, to study the different kinds of discourse used in their communities (Heath, 1983), they certainly brought varied discourse into the classroom.

Moreover, in their own worlds, the children did adopt a reflective, sometimes critical stance toward the content of unofficial discourse, particularly popular culture. For example, the youngest children discussed whether Batman was really a superhero or actually "soft." They considered whether Michael Jackson was real or not real, dead or alive, old or young. (He was a particularly appealing but confusing character.) In their playful talk, they revealed their knowledge about the talk of TV announcers, cartoon characters, and pop culture figures. Similar kinds of conversations have been observed among young children in our society from diverse social and cultural backgrounds (e.g., Dyson, 1989a; Paley, 1980). Further, the older, more school-wise third graders displayed an explicit knowledge of linguistic variation (i.e., dialects, slang) and its connection to racial and cultural identity.

It seems a short step from the everyday naming and critiquing that children engage in to the more formal considerations teachers may lead of how people talk — and how talk is displayed — in comics and picture books, rap songs and poetry. Older children might study different ways people tell and write stories; the kinds of dialects and languages represented in cartoons, newspapers, and literature; the varied ways people organize persuasive discourse in letters of complaint to the principal or to the local newspaper editor. Such talk about text seems important not only for bringing diverse kinds of discourse knowledge into the classroom, but also for increasing children's critical awareness of the connections among language, context, and power. (For discussions of the kinds of issues children might discuss about diverse forms of discourse, see Clark, Fairclough, Ivanic, & Martin-Jones, 1991.)

The third graders' peer play highlighted the critical importance of such a permeable curriculum. For, in their play, the children sometimes enacted an oppositional, rather than a dialogic, vision of vernacular and standard ways with words. An oppositional view of not only dialects, but discourse themes, styles, and even whole genres is furthered by our societal tendency to define narrowly the "literate," "the cultured," "the proper." If such a tendency is not counterbalanced in school, children may not bring their language and experiences into the official curriculum but, at best, display them on side roads or use them primarily to overwhelm (even undermine) the official world. Indeed, many educational anthropologists have argued that it is precisely rigidly compartmentalized worlds that set up difficult choices for some children among home, peer, and school worlds (e.g., Au, 1979; Fine, 1987; Jacob & Jordan, 1987; Labov, 1987).

Playing with Boundaries

The discourse of those who themselves discuss critical language awareness and pedagogy sometimes seems drenched in the oppressive, academic jargon of those on a mission to save the world from itself. Very rarely do the voices and worldviews of young children appear within such discussions. And perhaps that is alright. I am interested not in saving children from themselves or from the world, but in preserving and furthering children's willingness to engage with the world and to reconstruct sociocultural boundaries with increasing reflectiveness and deliberateness. And those occasions when children engage in such reconstruction may be marked by playfulness, not somberness. Indeed, Bakhtin (1981) himself used such genres as parodies, jokes, and songs to illustrate how mindful language users avoid domination by the surrounding discourse, how they dialogize the authoritarian demands of those in power.

It was Jameel who first and most dramatically displayed the fun and sense of control gained through crossing boundaries. He wrote songs about science topics and dramatized TV quiz games with me during recess, testing my own ignorance about scientific matters; he even made science jokes for his peers.

Edward G. says he is writing a story about space.
EUGENIE: And Edward G. loves space.
JAMEEL: You know what, you know who he gonna marry?
EUGENIE: Who?
JAMEEL: One of the planets. (Eugenie chuckles.)

Stories, songs, games, expositions, and language teases — all were articulations of Jameel's complex relationships with others.

And so it was with all the children. Further, this ability to play with official material in unofficial realms, to use unofficial genres and styles in the official one, allowed children's texts to become a kind of crossroads. Such texts drew from, and allowed children to take action in, diverse worlds. In this way, both official and unofficial worlds became enriched, interconnected. Worlds did not dissolve into each other — such a situation not only would have been impossible, given the pervasiveness of differences, but it also would have silenced the dialogue.

Crafting Amidst Boundaries.   The most powerful genre for crossing cultural boundaries was the performative story. Certainly child storytellers are not free agents, so to speak, as critical pedagogists have pointed out (e.g., Gilbert, in press). Their own texts are built from the stuff, the words, of the larger cultural story of what it means to be a person of a certain gender, race, class, region, and on and on. But, as already noted, children do not necessarily politely fall in with the dominant text, as they can be playful, irreverent, even resistant. Moreover, stories untold are stories that have no possibility of being dialogized, rendered an option among alternative stories.

Most of the children were interested in *crafting* stories, not in simply expressing themselves or telling mundane narratives about their daily lives. And they all crafted important stories by literally taking others' voices and putting them on paper. Readers may readily recall Jameel's cartoon talk, Eugenie's melodramatic child, William's cussing bird, or Ayesha's verses about those who "knew how to talk." It was Anthony, however, who provided perhaps the best example. His first school attempt at writing a message was motivated by the class study of the speeches of Martin Luther King. Like many of the children, Anthony was captivated by King's speaking style. He drew King with mouth wide open, letters coming out — and, in another corner of the page, he drew himself, mouth wide open, letters coming out.[4]

In varying ways, all of the children constructed worlds in which they controlled voices on paper, voices otherwise separated in space and time, power and status, in their very realness. And, having done so, they declared their authority, their authorship, on the public stage of the classroom. This sharing of textual worlds "peopled by characters who take on life and breath" (Tannen, 1988, p. 92) contributed, indirectly but powerfully, to the building of a shared classroom life (see also Dyson & Genishi, in press). Story images and rhythms reverberate in the memories of audience members, who reconstruct the story with the stuff of their own thoughts and feelings.

Through story composing, then, children take steps to find both self and others in a shared place, a kind of neighborhood. But to avoid neat conclusions, simplistic links between stories and community, I circle back again, here in the closing pages of this book, to the opening pages of Chapter 1 and the story of Jameel, Mollie, the Cat, and his friend Hat. As that story revealed, each child's text can be read only in the context of the larger imaginative universe that governs both composer and audience. Jameel and Mollie, like all of us, needed help in understanding where the other was coming from, so to speak, and what each was aiming for.

THE SOCIAL WORK OF TEACHING

Building relationships with diverse individuals, being sensitive to their social agendas and cultural resources, is not, of course, easy to do. Teachers, working with children from many different sociocultural and familial backgrounds, are bound to recognize the intelligence — the sense — of some children more easily than of others, potentially to be unfair in judgments and in actions. Certainly there is a need to talk with parents and other teachers who share individual children's backgrounds and, thereby, critical insight into their cultural resources (Lightfoot, 1978; Delpit, 1988). Beyond this, however, the most critical requirement for a curriculum that neither denies nor dissolves differences, that allows for the distinctiveness of the individual and of diverse cultural resources, is a teacher who conveys a respect for children and their communities, a respect that is actualized by observing and by actively working to make curricular space for all students.

If we as educators do not work to "widen the boundaries of possible discourse" in school (Rosen & Rosen, 1973, p. 1), we risk setting up unnecessary choices among home, peer, and school ways with words. Thus, we must work to explicitly acknowledge sociocultural breadth, that is, to acknowledge the different decisions any one individual makes in his or her ways of writing, as well as in ways of talking, in order to lessen rigid associations children may make between ways of using language and gender, ethnic, and social class identification (Heath, 1983; Labov, 1987).

And we must work, too, to emphasize sociocultural depth, that is, the thematic, stylistic, and structural connections among different ways of using language, including the fluid and dialogic relationships among what is considered folk, popular, and literary discourse. For example, we can do a better job of explicitly acknowledging the usefulness of playful language, of metaphor, and of narrative imagination across the official curriculum (Ball, 1992; Daiute, 1989; Redd, 1992; Scott, 1990; Smitherman, 1986, in press).

Just as important, we might not work, but play. That is, we might let ourselves enjoy collaborative and playful talk with our students. Such moments are not planned; they arise from a sensitivity to the happy mix of childhood and language, and, given that they contribute to classroom cohesiveness and comfort, they are generative of more such moments.

And, finally, we might consider with renewed appreciation the power of stories — and of a public stage on which to share and perform them.

These implications for teaching are not separate items in a list, but interconnected actions: attention to children's social work, to the cultural materials they bring from homes and communities, to the kinds of official texts — visions of the possible — that teachers provide, to children's and teachers' analytic reflection on — and play with — texts, and to public stages for the sharing of stories — all these actions are necessary for weaving together texts. And in weaving texts, we weave lives, thereby composing a classroom neighborhood, filled with the distinctive sounds of child voices.

IN CLOSING:
ON COMPOSING TEXTS AND COMPOSING SELVES

The key theme of this book has been the link between composing a text and composing a place for oneself in the social world, a theme inspired by Bakhtin.

What the self is answerable to is the social environment; what the self is answerable for is the authorship of its responses. Self creates itself in crafting an architectonic relation between the unique locus of life activity which the individual human organism constitutes and the constantly changing natural and cultural environment which surrounds it. This is the meaning of Bakhtin's dictum that the self is an act of grace, a gift of the other. (Clark & Holquist, 1984, p. 68)

Within our classrooms, children respond to each other and to us as teachers within a complex and "constantly changing natural and cultural environment." In addressing others, children compose texts that declare their existence in the world, but that existence is acknowledged, momentarily completed, only by the response of the other. All of us come to know ourselves as we take responsibility for responding to the other; our fates are bound together in dialogue.

When children enter school, they come with complex histories as family and community members. And this history is reflected in the used words, the signs, with which they respond to the interactive spaces we as teachers create. And in our response to the children, we help shape their understanding of what it means to be an educated person in our society. If our classrooms are not places of sociocultural breadth and depth, we risk sending messages of alienation, messages that say that educated people are not rooted in their own histories, in strong relationships with people that matter.

Moreover, we deny them, and ourselves, the scholarly benefit — and the good fun — possible when language and experiences are shared. For, in answering the children, we are also composing ourselves. In their plurality, in their diversity, our children offer us the opportunity to widen our own worldview, to see aspects of experience that might otherwise remain invisible to us, to understand better ourselves as situated in a complex world of multiple perspectives.

And so it was for me, and I hope for my readers. The children offered lessons about the potential power of the artistic performer, the vulnerability of the academic one, the possibilities engendered by permeable boundaries, the failures promoted by rigid ones. Most important, they taught again the lesson I first learned as a small child trying to divide the world into the Catholics and the Publics.

As human beings we seem to be driven to categorizing aspects of the world into neat boxes — the popular, the literary, the folk, the oral, and the literate — developmental lines and sociocultural boxes. But these neat boxes keep all of us, children and adults, trapped. Within such linguistic and social containers, it is hard to imagine singing scientists, literary comedians, storytelling biologists and historians, and preaching lawyers. A vision of plurality, a cultural embracing of diversity, is a gift we can only give each other. Thus, in working to create permeable curricula, we further the development of young people with complex visions of themselves, whose varied and varying voices will enrich the cultural conversations of us all.

APPENDICES

APPENDIX A.   Grade, Sex, and Ethnicity of K/1 Children

	Grade	Sex	Ethnicity
Angie	1st	F	European-American
Anita	K	F	Latina
Anthony	K	M	African-American
Austin	1st	M	European-American
Berto	1st	M	Latino
Brad	1st	M	European-American
Brett	1st	M	European-American
Calvin	K	M	African-American
Celia	K	F	Latina
Daisy	1st	F	European-American
Edward G.	1st	M	European-American
Edward J.	1st	M	African-American
Ervin	K	M	African-American
Eugenie	1st	F	African-American
Hannah	1st	F	European-American
Jameel	1st	M	African-American
James	K	M	African-American
Jesse	K	M	European-American
John	K	M	Hungarian
Lamar	K	M	African-American
Mollie	1st	F	European-American
Monique	1st	F	African-American
Shawnda	1st	F	African-American
Sonya	K	F	European-American
Tyler	K	M	African-American
Vera	1st	F	African-American

APPENDIX B.   Data Analysis Categories for Event Components

COMPONENT
Category: Category Description

STANCE TOWARD OTHERS (characterized primarily by interactional control; quotations are intended to characterize the substance of the stance, but they are not exact child quotes; categories are not necessarily mutually exclusive)

presentational: "Let me tell you about this"; child is clearly seeking attention and interactional control

appreciative: "I like that"; child expresses admiration of another's presentation; child is participating as an audience member for another

cooperative/collegial: "I'll go along with that," deemed "cooperative" with teacher, "collegial" with peers; child is participating in the give and take necessary for interaction to proceed peacefully and is thus sharing control

collaborative: "We'll do this together"; child is working with others on a shared product; he or she is sharing control during the activity although he or she may assume control (i.e., present the product) at another time

protestant: "You've got no right"; child feels others have overstepped their social bounds and are seeking control in inappropriate ways

oppositional: "I won't"; child is refusing to cooperate and thereby not allowing others control

helpful: "I can help"; child is offering services to someone perceived as needing help; he or she is offering to take control in some way

directive: "Do this"; child is seeking to control another in ways the other has not solicited

critical: "I think you're wrong"; child analyzes another's work, typically to point out a weakness; he or she is assuming control over another

needy: "I need you"; child is soliciting another's help so that he or she can accomplish some task, and thereby is asking the other to take some control

inquisitive: "I want you to tell me"; child is seeking information about how the world works from another (information that he or she does not have); while child is acknowledging that the other has desired information, that information is not necessary for his or her own ongoing composing task (i.e., child is in no way asking others to assume some control of the task)

coexistent: "I am into my own business"; child is not interacting with others and is completely involved with controlling his or her own business, as it were

MOOD (includes only categories most relevant to analysis)

serious: "This is the way it is"; child is not exaggerating or in any way manipulating the referential truth value of messages

playful: "I can transform the way it is"; child is in some way manipulating the referential truth value of own or other's message *angry*: "This is not the way it is supposed to be"; child's talk and behavior are emotionally charged, and he or she is reacting to the stance or truth value of another's (verbal or nonverbal) message

PRODUCTS (quotations marks indicate word used by at least one focal child)

captions: texts composed of labels or single statements describing affection for a drawn object

"cartoons": texts composed primarily of dialogue based on television cartoon shows

chants: texts composed of repeated words or phrases

expositions: texts composed of statements about the way the world works; when oral, may be interspersed with questions to elicit audience involvement

expressives: texts composed of statements expressing personal feelings

"jokes": texts, typically composed of question and answer pairs, intended to be funny

"joke stories": texts composed of ludicrous statements about cartoon or cartoon-like figures

language play: texts composed of patterned statements that vary in some systematic way (e.g., patterns of rhymes or opposites)

"letters": texts addressed to a specified person, typically framed with "Dear [addressee's name]" and "Love [author's name]"; most often contain expressions of affection

"love stories": texts composed of questions and statements about classmates' special friends of the opposite sex

narratives: texts composed of at least two chronologically related propositions (not necessarily in linear order) that refer to a specific (rather than a general) event, real or imagined; there were many kinds of narratives:

> *narratives of anticipated experience* (ANT): texts that present event(s) child anticipates experiencing

> *narratives of experience* (EXP): texts that present event(s) child has personally experienced or witnessed

> *narratives of narratives* (NN): texts that present child's recollections of experienced narratives (e.g., movies, books, a child's told story; may be interspersed with textual analyses)

> *hypothetical narratives* (HYP): texts that present event(s) that would take place given other circumstances

> *"story" narratives* (STR): texts that present fictional states or actions

> *"true story" narratives* (TSTR): exaggerated stories with elements of truth in them (for discussions of the role of such stories in African-American culture, see Smitherman, 1986, and Heath, 1983, who uses the same emic term).

> *"talking about somebody"* (TA): texts that are evaluative in nature and about a particular peer; "talking about somebody" texts may be of varied types, including:

TA/ANT: texts that present event(s) child anticipates experiencing with child being talked about

TA/EXP: texts that present event(s) child witnessed or experienced involving peer being talked about

TA/NN: texts that present child's recollection of narrative told about (i.e., what someone said about) child of interest

TA/HYP: texts that present event(s) child anticipates would happen if child being talked about was in a certain situation

TA/ATT (attributed ongoing narratives): texts that present child's best guess about what child being talked about is currently saying or doing

TA/ROU (routines): texts composed of statements specifying a typical sequence of talked-about child's actions; texts are not narratives in that they are not about a specific event; nonetheless routines are common in TA conversational exchanges

confronting somebody (CA): texts that are evaluative in nature and about a particular peer who is also an interlocutor in the ongoing conversation; confronting somebody texts may include all types of texts included under TA ("talking about somebody") category above

pattern books: variants of shared published books composed of repeated interactional rounds (e.g., "Brown Bear Brown Bear what do you see? I see a giraffe looking at me.")

personal essays: texts composed primarily of statements about the nature of persons or events in child's life as family member or friend

raps: texts composed of rhyming statements recited to a particular syncopated beat

routines: related to the concept of "scripts" (Nelson, 1978; Schank & Abelson, 1977), texts composed of statements specifying a typical sequence of action; they could occur as part of an exposition or as background information for a narrative

"songs": words set to or meant to be set to tunes

*"stories"** : texts composed of fictional states or events (when stories are enacted in spontaneous peer play they are referred to as *dramas*; when stories are formally dramatized from a text they are referred to as *plays*)

playful "teasing": put downs or insults not to be taken literally; "tough teasing" involves threats to another's physical welfare (for a discussion of the role of teasing in African-American culture, see Smitherman, 1986)

textual analyses: texts composed of analytic (evaluative, explanatory, comparative) statements about particular (oral or written) texts; related to Vasquez's (1991) concept of "extensions"

---

*"Stories" are typically narratives. However, in the case of written stories, the observer may need to listen to the child's talk while drawing and writing as well as read the text in order to appreciate that a narrative was intended. That is, the written statements may not be temporally related, but the child's composed story (of which the text is only a part) may reveal the narrative.

APPENDIX C. Grade, Sex, and Ethnicity of 1/2 Children

	Grade	Sex	Ethnicity
Dwayne	1st	M	African-American
Eugenie	2nd	F	African-American
Evan	1st	M	African-American/ Asian-American
Justin	1st	M	African-American
Lamar	1st	M	African-American
LaToya	2nd	F	African-American
Marcus	1st	M	African-American
Mathew	2nd	M	European-American
Mohammed	1st	M	African-American
Ricky	1st	M	African-American
Terence	1st	M	African-American
Vanessa	2nd	F	African-American

APPENDIX D. Sex and Ethnicity of 3rd Grade Children

	Sex	Ethnicity
April	F	European-American
Ayesha	F	African-American
Bianca	F	African-American
Carl	M	European-American
Charles	M	African-American
Crystal	F	African-American
Darren	M	African-American
Kate	F	European-American
Lena	F	African-American
Manrissa	F	Chinese-American
Melissa	F	European-American
Mona	F	African-American
Paul	M	Korean-American
Rashanda	F	African-American
William	M	African-American

NOTES

Chapter 1

1. In order to make needed analytic distinctions in the children's social and language worlds, I am using the word *folk* to refer only to oral performance traditions particular to the children's home community. Certainly there are phenomena that are part of the folklore of children, handed down from child to child and found in many areas of the globe; among such language phenomena are playground games and teasing songs (Opie & Opie, 1959). In this project, however, such genres are considered part of *popular* traditions, along with the genres of contemporary media (e.g., television, films, songs), because they are known generally in the peer world.

2. Hymes (1980) commented similarly on Bernstein's widely used terms *elaborated* and *restricted* code, which are identified with the British middle and working classes, respectively: There is "a longstanding tendency to dichotomize kinds of meaning and communication, and to consider kinds primarily in terms of a cognitive ideal, whereas the actual fabric of relationships among kinds of meaning, communicative style, and social consequences is intricate" (p. 42). In other words, such classification schemes attend to language form but not to the particular person putting forth a specific message in some time and place and anticipating some response from particular others.

3. Vasquez (1991), in a study of literacy practices in Mexican immigrant homes, reported that there were few examples of talk about *written texts*, but there was much talk about texts per se, given an expanded concept of texts that could include either "oral or visual representations of knowledge" (p. 14), such as photographs or media events.

4. The percentage of *children* who were Black was higher than the percentage of adults. For example, 28% of all 5- and 6-year-olds in the city were Black, compared with 18.2% of the total population. Of all 5- and 6-year-olds, 55% were White (including those of Hispanic ethnicity), compared with 66.7% of the total population. (The available census data did not provide figures in which children of Hispanic heritage were distinguished from those of non-Hispanic White.)

5. I am European-American and in my forties. When I was the children's age, I lived in a rural village with my mother, brother, and sisters; we had limited economic means (and lots of good humor).

6. Paula is Italian-American and in her forties.

Chapter 2

1. Among the researchers who have discussed the importance of the evaluator role in classroom interaction are Heath (1978), Cazden (1988), and Lemke (1990).

2. Thus, while the preceding section's emphasis on diversity involved issues of equity or fairness, here the emphasis is on cultural diversity, particularly differences in ways of crafting stories and poems, of "imaginative universes." The ways societies acknowledge (or fail to acknowledge) cultural diversity is one aspect of equity and fairness issues.

3. During the last half of the school year, as individual kindergartners responded in more sophisticated ways to books (i.e., attended to the graphic information in them), they participated in formal reading groups too.

4. The first graders' reading groups were heterogeneous in terms of student ability and varied in membership. The small group size allowed discussions in which more children participated and opportunities for more children to receive individual help. The instructional focus was on the evolving story, and extended discussions of story meaning regularly occurred. Louise offered varied decoding help, but emphasis was on student self-correction by using multiple (context and graphic) cues. This is in contrast to classroom studies of reading ability groups, in which "low-group" children, who may include a disproportionate number of low-income and minority children, receive instruction emphasizing correction of student decoding and word pronunciation, and behavioral management, and "high-group" children receive instruction emphasizing comprehension (Allington, 1980; Collins, 1986; Eder, 1982; McDermott, 1977).

5. For a thorough review and critical discussion of the concept of school literacy, see Cook-Gumperz, 1986.

Chapter 3

1. Narratives refer herein to texts composed of at least two chronologically related propositions (not necessarily in linear order) that refer to a specific (rather than a general) event, real or imagined; there were many kinds of narratives, as detailed in Appendix B.

2. In order to examine the social use of narratives in the children's worlds, I selected for close examination key events that, as a set, included (a) all K/1 focal children and the peers with whom they regularly interacted, and (b) a rich display of narrative episodes. Nine events were thus selected. These nine events yielded 71 episodes in which a particular narrative ($T = 64$) or routine ($T = 7$) was socially enacted. (I did not include in this set any narrative talk that served exclusively *intra*personal functions, that is, talk that served to guide and control the child's own actions, particularly during drawing.) Information about the functions, experiential sources, and themes of the children's narratives is based on analysis of this data set, although all resulting findings were validated by comparing them with project data as a whole.

3. My analysis was influenced by the work of Goodwin (1990). She studied how African-American preadolescents used talk as a tool for social organization,

while they played in the streets of their urban neighborhood. To analyze the children's talk, she adapted the basic sociolinguistic concept of "participant structure," which refers to the assumptions interlocutors share about their rights and obligations to talk in a language activity or event, like a conversation, a debate, or a lesson (Philips, 1972; see also Hymes, 1972). Guided by conversational analysts (Sacks, Schegloff, & Jefferson, 1974) and fellow sociologists (especially Goffman, 1974), Goodwin defined "participa*tion* structures" as dynamic, as the result of individuals' social actions.

4. Analysis of each episode in the described data set revealed four major experiential sources. Those sources and the percentages (rounded) of total episodes drawing primarily on each source were:

Experiences at school (48%)
>   Experiences in unofficial school worlds (e.g., narratives about what one child did or said to another; included narratives about eluding or facing teacher authority as it entered children's social world) (85%)
>
>   Experiences in official world (e.g., narratives about what a child did as a part of an official classroom event; included oral narration of story being written for the official world) (15%)

Experiences at home (e.g., narratives of experiences with one's pet or siblings) (22%)

Vicarious experiences through the popular media (e.g., retelling parts or all of a TV show or movie) (21%)

Experiences in city (e.g., narratives of going to the doctor, attending church) (10%)

5. A substantial body of psychological research has focused generally on so-called disadvantaged children raised in poverty. This research has examined low-income children's lack of explicit language in school-like situations (e.g., Feagans & Farran, 1982).

6. In her research on Australian Aboriginal children's school experiences, Malin (1991) observed that comradery may happen only between a teacher and students who share her or his own social background; the teacher may feel most comfortable, most at ease, with them. However, this was not the case with Louise; such comradery and playfulness were often present in whole class and small group discussions.

7. Similar child talk has been studied by Goodwin (1990) and by Parker and Gottman (1989), the latter of whom studied middle-class children.

8. Jesse's phrase "hecka, really, really big" is interesting because "hecka" was a phrase used almost exclusively by African-American children. Jesse, who was European-American, seemed to be working to gain control over the word, pairing it with the redundant "really, really big," just as Anthony, who used "hecka" with ease, worked to gain control over "huge": "big ol', the big huge, the huge ol' fish."

In the midst of this collegial conversation, Jesse's talk conveys a sense of social connection or cohesion.

Chapter 4

1. The occurrence, and the nature, of such symbol-weaving is shaped not only by the child, but by the instructional setting and cultural context, which may or may not allow children access to, and deem appropriate, the use of diverse media.

2. Gumperz (1981) reports a similar strategy used by lower-class African-American children to gain adult company regardless of whether the children actually needed help. While this may have been true on some occasions for Eugenie, it is also true that Eugenie *was* clearly confused and also that she benefited from the provided help.

3. Eugenie worked to gain appreciative comments from me as well. Because I was a rather passive observer, Eugenie had to offer me explicit guidance.

EUGENIE: (drawing beds) I can't make my bed good. (Eugenie directs this comment to me. I write it down. After a pause, Eugenie cues me:) You can say they look pretty. (with irritation)

DYSON: They do look pretty. (with sincerity)

Chapter 5

1. Heath (1983) discusses how children in the working-class African-American community she studied engaged early and often in analogic reasoning, relating situations configurationally and, in school, seeing parallels teachers did not intend. My point here is that Jameel (and other focal children, especially Anthony, Lamar, and William) was particularly sensitive to humor and could abstract the essential absurdity and recreate it in other situations, without necessarily being able to verbally analyze what he was doing.

2. Keats's *Whistle for Willie* is an example of a "melting pot book," as Rudine Sims Bishop (Sims, 1982) uses the term. The book's illustrations reveal the lead character Peter's ethnicity, but the text itself suggests that Peter could be "any" child. Consistent with books supposedly about "any" child, the ways Peter's family relate to each other (e.g., the roles of mother, father, child) and their ways of talking (i.e., Standard English) suggest a middle-class, mainstream child.

3. A substantial body of psychological research has focused generally on so-called disadvantaged children raised in poverty. This research has examined low-income children's lack of explicit or decontextualized language in school-like situations (for discussion of such research, see Feagans & Farran, 1982). More recent research on young children's stories is sensitive to the cultural value of diverse narrative styles. Yet a general implication (or perhaps a truism) of some of this work is that young children can be described as having an "oral" style *or* a "literate" style (e.g., Gee, 1989; Michaels & Collins, 1984; Olson, 1977).

4. I wish to thank Judi Garcia, an early childhood teacher, and her four children, whose insights guided me into the world of cartoons.

Chapter 6

1. Edward may have wanted to engage in a kind of vernacular or folk play that Jameel could not or would not do. To elaborate, insults are described as preparing boys from African-American communities for more linguistically playful verbal insults (Goodwin & Goodwin, 1987; Heath, 1983). Jameel in fact *could* already engage in ritualistic insulting, playfully manipulating people's words and exaggerating their characteristics in ways documented among older Black preadolescent and adolescent males (Abrahams, 1970; Labov, 1972; Simons, 1990; Smitherman, 1986). It was direct insults to his work that angered him.

2. Ramsey (1991) provides a thorough review of literature documenting how cultural differences influence the social organization of and interaction within young children's peer groups. She includes in her discussion Rizzo and Corsaro's (1991) research, which documented differences in the degree of teasing and oppositional talk between Headstart children of African-American and Hispanic heritages, on the one hand, and white middle-class children on the other.

3. For a close analysis of teacher discourse strategies that seem to support social equity and responsibility in the classroom, see Maria Paz Echeverriarza (1992), who conducted her study in a second-grade classroom at this same school site.

Chapter 7

1. Agar (1982), Brodkey (1987), and Glesne and Peshkin (1992) all discuss, in varying ways, how ethnographic research is shaped by the interplay of the values, experiences, and goals of the researcher, the researched, and the intended audience. In Agar's (1982) words, "ethnography is neither 'subjective' nor 'objective.' It is interpretive, mediating two worlds through a third" (p. 783).

2. Just as verbal prompts in laboratory situations may result in more differentiated and more organized drawings by young children (Golomb, 1992), so too in classroom situations, children's dramatic, often social play can support children's efforts to control their unruly lines (Dyson, in press).

3. There are individual difference in young children's ways of using speech during drawing; Eugenie's style of language use is a common one among young children, as is Lamar's and Jameel's more narrative style (Dyson, 1989a; Gardner, Wolf, & Smith, 1982).

4. Rizzo (1989) studied friendship development in a first-grade classroom in a small town midwestern school; he documented how reading ability group membership influenced children's perceptions of each other's ability and, therefore, friendship choices. (Children in the same reading groups perceived each other as more similar, which supported a sense of solidarity, an aspect of friendship.) In this project, the observed children did not make friendship choices on the basis of academic ability, a point to be emphasized in Chapter 8. However, appreciation

or criticism of academic work could figure into ongoing interactions between children, as it did between Shawnda and Eugenie.

5. Both Lamar and Eugenie composed in ways that are very similar to those observed in a previous study of primary-grade children's composing (Dyson, 1989a), in which kindergarten and first-grade children also relied primarily on drawing and talking during composing, rather than writing itself.

6. I am not discounting the potential impact of children's home lives on their school lives. In this project, however, the focus is on children's lives at school and on offering teachers new perspectives for understanding and supporting children in the spaces that educators control.

7. For extended examinations of the varying features of composing activities, including copying, see Dyson (1984), Florio and Clark (1982), and Edelsky (1991).

8. Mrs. Walker was a middle-aged African-American woman.

9. The girls' writing was very typical of preschool and elementary-age girls in our society (see, for example, Graves, 1975; Nicolopoulou, Scales, & Weintraub, in press).

10. Eugenie's collegial stance during reading, illustrated here, was very similar to that she displayed in the K/1. In fact, Eugenie attended a "Chapter 1" (federally supported) reading class, as did other second- and third-grade children; her reading teacher had a teaching style similar to Louise's in that a great deal of collegial as well as analytic talk about text occurred. (Consistent with her teaching approach, Martha not only had children engage in the literacy activities integrated in the study units, she also heard children read *individually* to her from basal readers that she called "Challenge Books," which allowed her to assess children's reading progress.) Eugenie's social stance in the Chapter 1 reading class was just as it had been the year before in Louise's room; Eugenie made evaluative comments about story characters and, as often as possible, piped up to help other children stuck on words. Eugenie's favorite books from her reading class were those James Marshall has written about two hippos, George and Martha, although she thought "they should get married once in a while, 'cause they best friends."

11. It seems important to note that Anthony did make substantive progress in a first-grade writing program similar to Louise's. As a kindergartner, Anthony had primarily written in a nonalphabetic way (i.e., by writing letters seemingly randomly). During the months of follow-up observation, Anthony wrote (via invented spellings) a rap, a poem, and a number of extended stories (picture book transformations and personal narratives), all amidst collegial and performative talk. His most extended writing—a two-page poem—was in response to Eloise Greenfield's (1978) poem "Honey, I Love," which fit Anthony's own "story line," given the poem's rich vernacular rhythms and Anthony's own performative powers.

Chapter 8

1. Paul was Korean-American. He and William were not neighborhood friends but became friends in school. They shared an interest in many aspects of popular culture—they traded baseball cards, talked about all kinds of sports, and enjoyed

helping each other draw figures from the popular media (the cartoon figure Bart Simpson was a favorite). Like William, Paul explicitly discussed his cultural roots — he even gave William and Darren Korean money; Paul, though, felt his friends were confused about his race: "My friends think I'm brown and white."

2. In Ferdman's (1990) words, "At the individual level, cultural identity has to do with the person's sense of [and feelings about] what constitutes membership in an ethnic group to which he or she belongs" (p. 192). William's sense of himself as a cultural being informed his manipulation of the official language. He did not, for example, play with Louise's intonation or with the content of her talk, both common ways in which school children color — or, as Bakhtin might say, infuse *their* own intonation into — the reported speech (Volosinov, 1973). Rather, he played with a linguistic feature of her talk, substituting a feature used in the vernacular shared exclusively by children from his home community. Thus, his cultural identity as an African-American seemed to inform his social action here.

3. The observed children's response to school differs from that described in most discussions of nonmainstream children's trust or belief in school. In the dominant view, when a complex of historical and situational factors leads to children's distrust of school, children may develop an oppositional culture in which they collectively "resist" the learning demands of school. (For a discussion of resistance theory, see Erickson, 1987.) While the children did sometimes resist specific assignments or directives, and while they were distrustful of the school's authority over them, the observed third graders did not have a general opposition to school. On the contrary, they were united in their desire to be "smart children" in their classroom.

4. Support for this connection between students' deliberate and skilled manipulation of language and the use of performative tools is found in recent research on older students. For example, based on analysis of 17-year-olds' written texts for the National Assessment of Educational Progress, Smitherman (in press) reports that students' writing scores in informative, persuasive, and, especially, narrative modes were positively correlated with their use of features of the African-American verbal tradition. (See also Redd, 1992.)

Chapter 9

1. Critical evaluations of the concept of "cultural style" are provided by Au (1979), Ladson-Billings (1992), McCarty and colleagues (1991), and Moll and Diaz (1987). In a particularly powerful critique, McCarty and colleagues challenge findings that Native American children have a pervasive nonverbal learning style; there are, they note, *situations* in which children respond with silence. In classrooms where teachers talk with children, clearly seeking and valuing their ideas, where children's daily experiences are included in curricular content, and where children's linguistic and cultural resources are exploited, students generally *are* verbal and eager to analyze their experiences.

2. Researchers have consistently documented that students' intellectual, emotional, and social engagement is most evident in situations in which they have

some control over an activity's content and procedures. For example, Sleeter and Grant (1991) studied junior high school students' perceptions of school knowledge. The students, multi-ethnic and working class, viewed such knowledge as a set of tasks to accomplish, tasks that were outside their control; they devoted the bulk of their school efforts to concerns of the peer social world. (As per Note 1, teachers can counter such alienation by allowing students some control.)

3. The asking and answering of known-answer questions (questions adults ask to test children's knowledge) is a kind of discourse exchange that is not a cultural universal. Moreover, children of lower socioeconomic class than their teachers may be particularly reluctant to answer such questions, which are potentially threatening (e.g., an answer must be given immediately, typically only one answer is correct). For discussions, see Cazden (1970 [an older but still very helpful discussion]), Heath (1983), and McCarty and colleagues (1991).

4. Dialogue was also an important narrative tool for children observed in a previous project (Dyson, 1989a). Through dialogue, even children whose texts were closely tied to drawings (which present a moment *in* time) could move *through* time to tell a story.

REFERENCES

Abrahams, R. D. (1970). *Deep down in the jungle . . . ; Negro narrative folklore from the streets of Philadelphia*. Chicago: Aldine.

Abrahams, R. D. (1972). Joking: The training of the man of words in talking broad. In T. Kochman (Ed.), *Rappin' and stylin' out* (pp. 215–240). Urbana: University of Illinois Press.

Abrahams, R. D. (1976). *Talking Black*. Rowley, MA: Newbury House.

Agar, M. (1982). Toward an ethnographic language. *American Anthropologist, 84*, 779–795.

Allington, R. L. (1980). Teacher interruption behaviors during primary grade oral reading. *Journal of Educational Psychology, 72*(3), 371–377.

Anderson, R., Hiebert, E., Scott, J., & Wilkinson, I. (1985). *Becoming a nation of readers* (Report of the Commission on Reading). Washington, DC: National Institute of Education.

Applebee, A. N. (1978). *The child's concept of story: Ages two to seventeen*. Chicago: University of Chicago Press.

Ashton-Warner, S. (1963). *Teacher*. New York: Simon and Schuster.

Au, K. H. (1979). Participation structures in a reading lesson with Hawaiian children: Analysis of a culturally appropriate instructional event. *Anthropology and Education Quarterly, 11*, 91–114.

Bakhtin, M. (1981). Discourse in the novel. In M. Holquist (Ed.), *The dialogic imagination: Four essays by M. Bakhtin* (pp. 259–422). Austin: University of Texas Press.

Bakhtin, M. (1986). *Speech genres and other late essays*. Austin: University of Texas Press.

Bakhtin, M. (1990). Art and answerability. In M. Holquist & V. Liapunov (Eds.), *Art and answerability: Early philosophical essays by M. Bakhtin* (pp. 1–3). Austin: University of Texas Press.

Ball, A. (1992). Cultural preference and the expository writing of African-American adolescents. *Written Communication, 9*, 501–532.

Barrett, J. (1982). *Cloudy with a chance of meatballs*. New York: Macmillan.

Bauman, R. (1977). *Verbal art as performance*. Rowley, MA: Newbury House.

Bauman, R. (1986). *Story, performance and event*. Rowley, MA: Newbury House.

Britton, J. (1992). *Language and learning* (2nd ed.). Harmondsworth, Middlesex, UK: Penguin.

Brodkey, L. (1987). Writing ethnographic narrative. *Written Communication, 4*, 25–50.

Brown, M. (1947). *Stone soup*. New York: Scribner.

Bruner, J. (1975). The ontogenesis of speech acts. *Journal of Child Language, 2*, 1–40.

Bruner, J. (1986). *Actual minds, possible worlds*. Cambridge, MA: Harvard University Press.

Bruner, J. (1990). *Acts of meaning*. Cambridge, MA: Harvard University Press.

Burningham, J. (1977). *Come out of the water, Shirley*. New York: Crowell.

Calkins, L. (1986). *The art of teaching writing*. Portsmouth, NH: Heinemann.

Cazden, C. (1970). The neglected situation in child language research and education. In F. Williams (Ed.), *Language and poverty* (pp. 81–101). New York: Markham.

Cazden, C. (1988). *Classroom discourse: The language of teaching and learning*. Portsmouth, NH: Heinemann.

Chafe, W. (1982). Integration and involvement in speaking, writing, and oral literature. In D. Tannen (Ed.), *Spoken and written language* (pp. 35–54). Norwood, NJ: Ablex.

Clark, K., & Holquist, M. (1984). *Mikhail Bakhtin*. Cambridge, MA: Harvard University Press.

Clark, R., Fairclough, N., Ivanic, R., & Martin-Jones, M. (1991). Critical language awareness, Part II: Towards critical alternatives. *Language and Education, 5*, 41–54.

Clay, M. (1975). *What did I write?* Auckland: Heinemann.

Clay, M. (1979). *Reading: The patterning of complex behavior*. Auckland: Heinemann.

Clay, M. (1991). *Becoming literate: The construction of inner control*. Portsmouth, NH: Heinemann.

Collins, J. (1982). Discourse style, classroom interaction, and differential treatment. *Journal of Reading Behavior, 14*, 429–437.

Collins, J. (1986). Differential instruction in reading. In J. Cook-Gumperz (Ed.), *The social construction of literacy* (pp. 117–137). Cambridge: Cambridge University Press.

Committee on Policy for Racial Justice. (1989). *Visions of a better way: A Black appraisal of public schooling*. Washington, DC: Joint Center for Political Studies Press.

Cook-Gumperz, J. (1981). Persuasive talk: The social organization of children's talk. In J. Green & C. Wallat (Eds.), *Ethnography and language in educational settings* (pp. 25–50). Norwood, NJ: Ablex.

Cook-Gumperz, J. (Ed.). (1986). *The social construction of literacy*. Cambridge: Cambridge University Press.

Corsaro, W. (1981). Entering the child's world: Research strategies for field entry and data collection in a preschool setting. In J. Green & C. Wallat (Eds.), *Ethnography and language in educational settings* (pp. 117–146). Norwood, NJ: Ablex.

Corsaro, W. (1985). *Friendship and peer culture in the early years*. Norwood, NJ: Ablex.

Cross, T. (1978). Mother's speech adjustments: Contributions of selected child listener variables. In C. Snow & C. Ferguson (Eds.), *Talking to children: Language input and acquisition* (pp. 151–188). Cambridge, Cambridge University Press.

Curry, N. E., & Johnson, C. N. (1990). *Beyond self-esteem: Developing a genuine sense of human value* (Research Monograph, Vol. 4). Washington, DC: National Association for the Education of Young Children.

Daiute, C. (1989). Play as thought: Thinking strategies of young writers. *Harvard Educational Review, 59*, 1–23.

D'Amato, J. D. (1987). The belly of the beast: On cultural difference, castelike status, and the politics of school. *Anthropology & Educational Quarterly, 18*, 357–360.

D'Amato, J. D. (1988). "Acting": Hawaiian children's resistance to teachers. *The Elementary School Journal, 88*, 529–544.

Delpit, L. (1988). The silenced dialogue: Power and pedagogy in educating other people's children. *Harvard Educational Review, 58*, 280–298.

Diaz, S., Moll, L., & Mehan, H. (1986). Sociocultural resources in instruction: A context-specific approach. In California State Department Bilingual Education Office (Ed.), *Beyond language: Social and cultural factors in schooling language minority students* (pp. 187–230). Los Angeles: Evaluation, Dissemination and Assessment Center.

Donaldson, M. (1978). *Children's minds.* New York: Norton.

Dunn, J. (1988). *The beginnings of social understandings.* Cambridge, MA: Harvard University Press.

Dyson, A. H. (1984). Learning to write/Learning to do school: Emergent writers' interpretations of school literacy tasks. *Research in the Teaching of English, 18*, 233–264.

Dyson, A. H. (1986). Transitions and tensions: Interrelationships between the drawing, talking, and dictation of young children. *Research in the Teaching of English, 20*, 370–409.

Dyson, A. H. (1987). The value of "time off task": Young children's spontaneous talk and deliberate text. *Harvard Educational Review, 57*, 396–420.

Dyson, A. H. (1989a). *Multiple worlds of child writers: Friends learning to write.* New York: Teachers College Press.

Dyson, A. H. (1989b). "Once upon a time" reconsidered: The developmental dialectic between function and form. *Written Communication, 6*, 436–462.

Dyson, A. H. (1991). The word and the world: Reconceptualizing written language development, or, Do rainbows mean a lot to little girls? *Research in the Teaching of English, 25*, 97–123.

Dyson, A. H. (in press). From prop to mediator: The changing role of written language in children's symbolic repertoires. In B. Spodek & O. Saracho (Eds.), *Early childhood language and literacy.* New York: Teachers College Press.

Dyson, A. H., & Genishi, C. (Eds.). (in press). *The need for story: Cultural diversity in classroom and community.* Urbana, IL: National Council of Teachers of English.

Echeverriarza, M. P. (1992). *Choosing equality: An analysis of the social roles of the teacher in an ethnically diverse classroom.* Unpublished doctoral dissertation, University of California, Berkeley.

Edelsky, C. (1991). *With literacy and justice for all: Rethinking the social in language and education.* London: Falmer Press.

Eder, D. (1982). Differences in communicative styles across ability groups. In L. C. Wilkinson (Ed.), *Communicating in the classroom* (pp. 245–264). New York: Academic Press.

Eder, D. (1988). Building cohesion through collaborative narration. *Social Problems Quarterly, 51,* 225–235.

Einsel, W. (1980). *Did you ever see?* New York: Scholastic Publications.

Erickson, F. (1986). Qualitative methods in research on teaching. In M. C. Wittrock (Ed.), *Handbook of research on teaching* (pp. 119–161). New York: Macmillan.

Erickson, F. (1987). Transformation and school success: The politics and culture of educational achievement. *Anthropology & Education Quarterly, 18,* 335–356.

Ervin-Tripp, S., & Mitchell-Kernan, C. (Eds.). (1977). *Child discourse.* New York: Academic Press.

Feagans, L., & Farran, D. C. (Eds.). (1982). *The language of children reared in poverty.* New York: Academic Press.

Ferdman, B. (1990). Literacy and cultural identity. *Harvard Educational Review, 60,* 181–204.

Ferreiro, E. (1978). What is written in a written sentence? A developmental answer. *Journal of Education, 160*(4), 23–39.

Fine, M. (1987). Silencing in public schools. *Language Arts, 64,* 157–174.

Florio, S., & Clark, C. (1982). The functions of writing in an elementary classroom. *Research in the Teaching of English, 16,* 115–129.

Foster, M. (1989). It's cookin' now: A performance analysis of the speech events of a Black teacher in an urban community college. *Language and Society, 18,* 1–29.

Foucault, M. (1977). *Language, counter-memory, practice: Selected essays and interviews.* Ithaca, NY: Cornell University Press.

Franklin, M. B. (1983). Play as the creation of imaginary situations. In S. Wapner & B. Kaplan (Eds.), *Toward a holistic developmental psychology* (pp. 197–220). Hillsdale, NJ: Erlbaum.

Freire, P. (1985). *The politics of education: Culture, power, and liberation.* Hadley, MA: Bergin and Garvey.

Gag, W. (1977). *Millions of cats.* New York: Coward-McCann.

Gardner, H. (1991). *The unschooled mind: How children think and how schools teach.* New York: Basic Books.

Gardner, H., Wolf, S., & Smith, A. (1982). Max and Mollie: Individual differences in early artistic symbolization. In H. Gardner (Ed.), *Art, mind, and brain: A cognitive approach to creativity* (pp. 110–127). New York: Basic Books.

Garvey, C. (1990). *Play* (enl. ed.). Cambridge, MA: Harvard University Press.

Gates, H. L., Jr. (1989). Canon-formation, literary history, and the Afro-American tradition: From the seen to the told. In H. A. Baker, Jr., & P. Redmonds

(Eds.), *Afro-American literary study in the 1990s* (pp. 14–38). Chicago: University of Chicago Press.

Gee, J. (1989). Two styles of narrative construction and their linguistic and educational implications. *Journal of Education, 171*, 97–115.

Geertz, C. (1973). *The interpretation of cultures: Selected essays*. New York: Basic Books.

Geertz, C. (1983). *Local knowledge*. New York: Basic Books.

Genishi, C. (Ed.). (1992). *Ways of assessing children and curriculum: Voices from the classroom*. New York: Teachers College Press.

Genishi, C., & DiPaolo, M. (1982). Learning through argument in a preschool. In L. C. Wilkinson (Ed.), *Communicating in the classroom* (pp. 49–68). New York: Academic Press.

Gilbert, P. (1989). *Writing, schooling, and deconstruction: From voice to text in the classroom*. London: Routledge.

Gilbert, P. (in press). "And they lived happily ever after": Cultural storylines and the construction of gender. In A. H. Dyson & C. Genishi (Eds.), *The need for story: Cultural diversity in classroom and community*. Urbana, IL: National Council of Teachers of English.

Gillmore, P. (1985). "Gimme room": School resistance, attitude and access to literacy. *Journal of Education, 167*, 111–127.

Glesne, C., & Peshkin, A. (1992). *Becoming qualitative researchers: An introduction*. White Plains, NY: Longman.

Goffman, E. (1974). *Frame analysis*. New York: Harper & Row.

Golomb, C. (1992). *The child's creation of a pictorial world*. Berkeley: University of California Press.

Goodlad, J. (1984). *A place called school*. New York: McGraw-Hill.

Goodwin, M. (1990). *He-said-she-said: Talk as social organization among Black children*. Bloomington: Indiana University Press.

Goodwin, M., & Goodwin, C. (1987). Children's arguing. In S. U. Phillips, S. Steele, & C. Tanz (Eds.), *Language, gender and sex in comparative perspective* (pp. 200–248). Cambridge: Cambridge University Press.

Goss, L., & Barnes, M. (Eds.). (1989). *Talk that talk: An anthology of African-American storytelling*. New York: Simon and Schuster.

Graff, H. (1987). *The labyrinths of literacy: Reflections on literacy past and present*. London: Falmer Press.

Graves, D. H. (1975). An examination of the writing processes of seven-year-old children. *Research in the Teaching of English, 9*, 227–241.

Graves, D. H. (1983). *Writing: Teachers and children at work*. Portsmouth, NH: Heinemann.

Gray, B. (1987). How natural is "natural" language teaching: Employing wholistic methodology in the classroom. *Australian Journal of Early Childhood, 12*, 3–19.

Greene, M. (1988). *The dialectic of freedom*. New York: Teachers College Press.

Greenfield, E. (1978). *Honey, I love and other poems*. New York: Harper & Row.

Gumperz, J. (1981). Conversational inference and classroom learning. In J. Green

& C. Wallat (Eds.), *Ethnography and language in educational settings* (pp. 3–24). Norwood, NJ: Ablex.

Gundlach, R. (1982). Children as writers: The beginnings of learning to write. In M. Nystrand (Ed.), *What writers know* (pp. 129–148). Orlando, FL: Academic Press.

Gutierrez, K. (1992). A comparison of instructional contexts in writing: Process classrooms with Latino children. *Education & Urban Society, 24,* 244–252.

Halliday, M. (1977). *Explorations in the functions of language.* New York: Elsevier North-Holland.

Halliday, M., & Hasan, R. (1976). *Cohesion in English.* London: Longman.

Harste, J., Woodward, V., & Burke, C. (1984). *Language stories and literacy lessons.* Exeter, NH: Heinemann.

Heath, S. B. (1978). Teacher talk: Language in the classroom. *Language in Education: Theory and Practice, 1*(9), 1–30.

Heath, S. B. (1981). Towards an ethnohistory of writing in American education. In M. Whiteman (Ed.), *Writing: The nature, development, and teaching of written communication: Vol. 1. Variation in writing: Functional and linguistic-cultural differences* (pp. 25–46). Hillsdale, NJ: Erlbaum.

Heath, S. B. (1983). *Ways with words: Language, life and work in communities and classrooms.* Cambridge: Cambridge University Press.

Heath, S. B., & Mangiola, L. (1991). *Children of promise: Literate activities in linguistically and culturally diverse classrooms.* Washington, DC: National Education Association, Center for the Study of Writing, and American Educational Research Association.

Heller, C. (1992). *The multiple functions of the Tenderloin Women Writers Workshop: Community in the making.* Unpublished doctoral dissertation, University of California, Berkeley.

Holdaway, D. (1979). *The foundations of literacy.* Sydney: Ashton Scholastic.

Holquist, M. (1981). Glossary. In M. Holquist (Ed.), *The dialogic imagination: Four essays by M. M. Bakhtin* (pp. 423–434). Austin: University of Texas Press.

Honig, A. (1988). Research in review: Humor development in children. *Young Children, 43,* 60–73.

Houghton Mifflin Literary Readers. (1989). Boston: Houghton Mifflin.

Hymes, D. (1972). Models of the interaction of language and social life. In J. J. Gumperz & D. Hymes (Eds.), *Directions in sociolinguistics* (pp. 35–71). New York: Holt, Rinehart and Winston.

Hymes, D. (1973). Speech and language: On the origins and foundations of inequality among speakers. *Daedalus, 102,* 59–86.

Hymes, D. (1974). *Foundations in sociolinguistics: The ethnography of communication.* Philadelphia: University of Pennsylvania Press.

Hymes, D. (1975). Breakthrough into performance. In D. Ben Amos & K. Goldstein (Eds.), *Performance and communication* (pp. 11–74). The Hague: Mouton.

Hymes, D. (1980). *Language in education.* Washington, DC: Center for Applied Linguistics.

Jacob, E., & Jordan, C. (1987). Explaining the school performance of minority students [Special issue]. *Anthropology & Education Quarterly, 18*(4).

Jenkins, H. (1988). "Going bonkers!": Children, play, and Pee-wee. *Camera Obscura, 17,* 169–193.

Keats, E. J. (1964). *Whistle for Willie.* New York: Viking Press.

Kochman, T. (Ed.). (1972). *Rappin' and stylin' out: Communication in urban Black America.* Urbana: University of Illinois Press.

Kushkin, K. (1980). The language of children's literature. In L. Michaels & C. Ricks (Eds.), *The state of the language* (pp. 213–225). Berkeley: University of California Press.

Labov, W. (1972). *Language in the inner city.* Philadelphia: University of Pennsylvania Press.

Labov, W. (1982). Competing value systems in inner-city schools. In P. Gilmore & A. A. Glatthorn (Eds.), *Children in and out of school* (pp. 148–171). Seattle: University of Washington Press.

Labov, W. (1987). The community as educator. In J. Langer (Ed.), *Language, literacy and culture: Issues of society and schooling* (pp. 128–146). Norwood, NJ: Ablex.

Ladson-Billings, G. (1992). Culturally relevant teaching: The key to making multicultural education work. In C. Grant (Ed.), *Research and multicultural education: From the margins to the mainstream* (pp. 106–121). London: Falmer Press.

Langer, S. K. K. (1967). *Mind: An essay on human feeling.* Baltimore, MD: Johns Hopkins Press.

Lemke, J. L. (1990). *Talking science: Language, learning, and values.* Norwood, NJ: Ablex.

Levine, L. (1988). *Highbrow/lowbrow: The emergence of cultural hierarchy in America.* Cambridge, MA: Harvard University Press.

Lightfoot, S. (1978). *Worlds apart: Relationships between families and schools.* New York: Basic Books.

Lobel, A. (1970). *Frog and toad are friends.* New York: Harper & Row.

Malin, M. (1991). Make or break factors in Aboriginal students learning to read in urban classrooms: A sociocultural perspective. In P. Cormack (Ed.), *Literacy: Making it explicit, making it accessible. Proceedings of the 16th Australian Reading Association Conference* (pp. 229–245). Carlton South, Victoria: Australian Reading Association.

Martin, B., Jr. (1982). *Brown Bear, Brown Bear, what do you see?* Toronto: Holt, Rinehart and Winston.

McCaig, R. (1981). A district-wide plan for the evaluation of student writing. In S. Haley-James (Ed.), *Perspectives on writing in grades 1–8* (pp. 73–92). Urbana, IL: National Council of Teachers of English.

McCarty, T. L., Wallace, S., Lynch, R. H., & Benally, A. (1991). Classroom inquiry and Navajo learning styles: A call for reassessment. *Anthropology & Education Quarterly, 22,* 42–59.

McCloskey, R. (1963). *Burt Dow, deep water man.* New York: Viking Press.

McDermott, R. P. (1977). Social relations as contexts for learning in school. *Harvard Educational Review, 47,* 198–213.

McDermott, R. P. (1987). The explanation of minority school failure, again. *Anthropology & Education Quarterly, 18,* 361–364.

McDermott, R. P., & Hood, L. (1982). Institutionalized psychology and the ethnography of schooling. In P. Gilmore & A. Glatthorn (Eds.), *Children in and out of school: Ethnography and education* (pp. 232–249). Washington, DC: Center for Applied Linguistics.

McLane, J., & McNamee, J. (1990). *Early literacy*. Cambridge, MA: Harvard University Press.

Meek, M. (1988). *How texts teach what readers learn*. Lockwood, Gloucestershire: The Thimble Press.

Mehan, H. (1979). "What time is it Denise?": Asking known information questions in classroom discourse. *Theory into Practice, 28,* 285–294.

Michaels, S., & Collins, J. (1984). Oral discourse styles: Classroom interaction and the acquisition of literacy. In D. Tannen (Ed.), *Coherence in spoken and written discourse* (pp. 219–244). Norwood, NJ: Ablex.

Miller, P. J., Potts, R., & Fung, H. (1989, March). *Minority perspectives on narrative development*. Paper presented at the Annual Meeting of the American Educational Research Association, San Francisco.

Mitchell-Kernan, C. (1971). *Language behavior in a Black urban community* (Monograph No. 2). Berkeley: University of California, Language Behavior Research Laboratory.

Moll, L. C. (Ed.). (1990). *Vygotsky and education: Instructional implications and applications of sociohistorical psychology*. Cambridge: Cambridge University Press.

Moll, L. C., & Diaz, S. (1987). Change as the goal of educational research. *Anthropology & Education Quarterly, 18,* 300–311.

Moll, L. C., & Greenberg, J. B. (1990). Creating zones of possibilities: Combining social contexts for instruction. In L. C. Moll (Ed.), *Vygotsky and education: Instructional implications and applications of sociohistorical psychology* (pp. 319–348). Cambridge: Cambridge University Press.

Morrow, L., & Rand, M. (1991). Preparing the classroom environment to promote literacy during play. In J. Christie (Ed.), *Play and early literacy development* (pp. 141–166). Albany: State University of New York Press.

Morson, G. S. (1986). Introduction to extracts from "The problem of speech genres." In G. S. Morson (Ed.), *Bakhtin: Essay and dialogues on his work* (pp. 89–90). Chicago: University of Chicago Press.

Nelson, K. (1978). How young children represent knowledge of their world in and out of language. In R. S. Siegler (Ed.), *Children's thinking: What develops?* (pp. 255–273). Hillsdale, NJ: Erlbaum.

Newkirk, T. (1987). The non-narrative writing of young children. *Research in the Teaching of English, 21,* 121–145.

Newkirk, T., & Atwell, N. (Eds.). (1988). *Understanding writing: Ways of observing, learning, and teaching*. Portsmouth, NH: Heinemann.

Newsweek. (1990, Fall/Winter). How to teach our kids [Special issue].

Nicolopoulou, A., Scales, B., & Weintraub, J. (in press). Gender differences and symbolic imagination in the stories of four-year-olds. In A. H. Dyson & C. Genishi (Eds.), *The need for story: Cultural diversity in classroom and community*. Urbana, IL: National Council of Teachers of English.

Nystrand, M., & Gamoran, A. (1991). Instructional discourse, student engagement, and literature achievement. *Research in the Teaching of English, 25,* 261–290.

Ochs, E. J. (1988). *Culture and language development.* Cambridge: Cambridge University Press.

Ogbu, J. (1987). Variability in minority school performance: A problem in search of an explanation. *Anthropology & Education Quarterly, 18,* 312–341.

Olson, D. (1977). From utterance to text. *Harvard Educational Review, 47,* 247–279.

Opie, I., & Opie, P. (1959). *The lore and language of schoolchildren.* London: Oxford University Press.

Paley, V. (1980). *Wally's stories.* Cambridge, MA: Harvard University Press.

Paley, V. (1986a). On listening to what the children say. *Harvard Educational Review, 56,* 122–131.

Paley, V. (1986b). *Mollie is three: Growing up in school.* Chicago: The University of Chicago Press.

Parker, J. G., & Gottman, J. M. (1989). Social and emotional development in a relational context: Friendship interaction from early childhood to adolescence. In T. J. Berndt & G. W. Ladd (Eds.), *Peer relationships in child development* (pp. 95–131). New York: Wiley.

Philips, S. U. (1972). Participant structures and communicative competence: Warm Springs children in community and classroom. In C. B. Cazden, V. P. John, & D. Hymes (Eds.), *The functions of language in the classroom* (pp. 370–394). New York: Teachers College Press.

Piaget, J., & Inhelder, B. (1969). *The psychology of the child.* New York: Basic Books.

Purcell-Gates, V. (1988). Lexical and syntactic knowledge of written narrative held by well-read-to kindergartners and second graders. *Research in the Teaching of English, 22,* 128–160.

Ramsey, P. (1987). *Teaching and learning in a diverse world: Multicultural education.* New York: Teachers College Press.

Ramsey, P. (1991). *Making friends in school: Promoting peer relationships in early childhood.* New York: Teachers College Press.

Redd, T. (1992). *"Styling" in Black students' writing for Black audiences.* Paper presented at the meeting of the American Educational Research Association, San Francisco.

Rizzo, T. A. (1989). *Friendship development among children in school.* Norwood, NJ: Ablex.

Rizzo, W., & Corsaro, W. (1991, April). *Social support processes in early childhood friendships.* Paper presented at the biennial meeting of the Society for Research in Child Development, Seattle.

Roberts, J. (1970). *Scene of the battle: Group behavior in urban classrooms.* Garden City, NY: Doubleday.

Rogoff, B. (1990). *Apprenticeship in thinking: Cognitive development in social context.* New York: Oxford University Press.

Rosaldo, R. (1989). *Culture and truth: The remaking of social analysis.* Boston: Beacon Press.

Rosen, C., & Rosen, H. (1973). *The language of primary school children.* Harmondsworth, Middlesex: Penguin.

Sacks, H., Schegloff, E., & Jefferson, G. (1974). A simplest systematics for the organization of turn-taking for conversation. *Language, 50,* 696–735.

Schank, R. C., & Abelson, R. P. (1977). *Scripts, plans, goals, and understanding.* Hillsdale, NJ: Erlbaum.

Schickedanz, J. (1978). "You be the doctor and I'll be sick." *Language Arts, 55,* 713–718.

Scott, J. C. (1990). The silent sounds of language variation in the classroom. In S. Hynds & D. Rubin (Eds.), *Perspectives on talk and learning* (pp. 285–298). Urbana, IL: National Council of Teachers of English.

Scribner, S., & Cole, M. (1981). *The psychology of literacy.* Cambridge, MA: Harvard University Press.

Seeger, P. (1986). *Abiyoyo.* New York: Macmillan.

Sendak, M. (1963). *Where the wild things are.* New York: Harper & Row.

Seuss, Dr. (1957). *The cat in the hat.* New York: Random House.

Silverstein, S. (1974). *Where the sidewalk ends: The poems and drawings of Shel Silverstein.* New York: Harper & Row.

Simons, E. R. (1990). *Students' spontaneous joking in an urban classroom.* Unpublished dissertation, University of California, Berkeley.

Sims, R. (1982). *Shadow and substance: Afro-American experience in contemporary children's fiction.* Urbana, IL: National Council of Teachers of English.

Sinclair, J., & Coulthard, M. (1975). *Towards an analysis of discourse: The English used by teachers and pupils.* London: Oxford University Press.

Slavin, R. (1988). Cooperative learning and student achievement. *Educational Leadership, 45,* 31–33.

Sleeter, C. (Ed.). (1991). *Empowerment through multi-cultural education.* Albany: State University of New York Press.

Sleeter, C., & Grant, C. (1991). Mapping terrains of power: Student cultural knowledge versus classroom knowledge. In C. Sleeter (Ed.), *Empowerment through multi-cultural education* (pp. 49–68). Albany: State University of New York Press.

Slobodkina, E. (1940). *Caps for sale.* New York: Addison.

Smitherman, G. (1986). *Talkin' and testifyin': The language of Black America.* Detroit: Wayne State University Press.

Smitherman, G. (in press). "The blacker the berry, the sweeter the juice": African American student writers and the national assessment of educational progress. In A. H. Dyson & C. Genishi (Eds.), *The need for story: Cultural diversity in classroom and community.* Urbana, IL: National Council of Teachers of English.

Snow, C. (1983). Literacy and language: Relationships during the preschool years. *Harvard Educational Review, 53*(2), 165–189.

Stern, D. (1985). *The interpersonal world of the infant: A view from psychoanalysis and developmental psychology.* New York: Basic Books.

Tannen, D. (1982). The oral/literate continuum in discourse. In D. Tannen (Ed.), *Spoken and written language* (pp. 1–16). Norwood, NJ: Ablex.

Tannen, D. (1984). *Conversational style: Analyzing talk among friends*. Norwood, NJ: Ablex.

Tannen, D. (1988). Hearing voices in conversation, fiction, and mixed genres. In D. Tannen (Ed.), *Linguistics in context: Connecting observation and understanding* (pp. 89–114). Norwood, NJ: Ablex.

Tannen, D. (1989). *Talking voices: Repetition, dialogue, and imagery in conversational discourse*. Cambridge: Cambridge University Press.

Taxel, J. (1990). Notes from the editor. *The New Advocate, 3*, xi–xv.

Teale, W., & Sulzby, E. (Eds.). (1986). *Emergent literacy: Writing and reading*. Norwood, NJ: Ablex.

Thomas, L. (1983). *Late night thoughts on listening to Mahler's Ninth Symphony*. New York: Viking Press.

Tizard, B., & Hughes, M. (1984). *Young children learning*. Cambridge, MA: Harvard University Press.

Trueba, H. (1988). Introduction: The ethnography of schooling. In H. Trueba (Ed.), *Success or failure* (pp. 1–14). Rowley, MA: Newbury House.

Vasquez, O. A. (1991). Reading the world in a multicultural setting: A Mexicano perspective. *The Quarterly Newsletter of the Laboratory of Comparative Human Cognition, 13*, 13–15.

Volosinov, V. N. (1973). *Marxism and the philosophy of language* (L. Matejka & I. R. Titunik, Trans.). New York: Seminar Press.

Vygotsky, L. (1962). *Thought and language*. Cambridge, MA: Harvard University Press.

Vygotsky, L. (1978). *Mind in society*. Cambridge, MA: Harvard University Press.

Wells, G. (1981). *Learning through interaction: The study of language development* (Vol. 1). Cambridge: Cambridge University Press.

Werner, H. (1957). *Comparative psychology of mental development*. New York: International University Press.

Wertsch, J. V. (1985). *Vygotsky and the social formation of mind*. Cambridge, MA: Harvard University Press.

Wertsch, J. V. (1991). *Voices of the mind: A sociocultural approach to mediated action*. Cambridge, MA: Harvard University Press.

Williams, P. J. (1991). *The alchemy of race and rights*. Cambridge, MA: Harvard University Press.

Willis, P. (1990). *Common culture: Symbolic work at play in the everyday cultures of the young*. Boulder, CO: Westview Press.

INDEX

ABOUT THE AUTHOR

Anne Haas Dyson is Professor of Education in Language and Literacy in the Graduate School of Education, University of California–Berkeley. She is a graduate of the University of Wisconsin–Madison and of the University of Texas at Austin. A former teacher of young children, she has published widely about language and literacy learning in the early childhood and elementary school years. Her research has concentrated on young school children in socioculturally diverse settings, and it has emphasized the interplay of children's literacy learning and their social lives. Among her publications are *Multiple Worlds of Child Writers: Friends Learning to Write* (New York: Teachers College Press, 1989) and *Language Assessment in the Early Years* (Norwood, NJ: Ablex, 1984) with Celia Genishi, with whom she has also coedited *The Need for Story: Cultural Diversity in Classroom and Community* (Urbana, IL: NCTE, in press).